Selected Works of Frits Albers
Volume 3

The Foundations of Our Catholic Faith

The Hedge of the Vine

Frits Albers

Edited by Frank Calneggia

En Route Books and Media, LLC
Saint Louis, MO

En Route Books and Media, LLC
5705 Rhodes Avenue
St. Louis, MO 63109

Contact us at contactus@enroutebooksandmedia.com

Cover Credit: Sebastian Mahfood

Copyright 2024 Michael P. Albers

ISBN-13: 979-8-88870-286-4
Library of Congress Control Number: 2024926467

All rights reserved. No part of this book may be reproduced, stored in a retrieval system, or transmitted in any form, or by any means, electronic, mechanical, photocopying, or otherwise, without the prior written permission of the author.

Dedicated to
St. John Fisher (19 October 1469 – 22 June 1535)

In 1504, at the age of 35, St. John Fisher was appointed Bishop of Rochester, the poorest see in England, from which Bishops were expected to rise as their career progressed. He remained there for the remaining thirty-one years of his life, not seeking any promotion even though a most learned theologian. He was Doctor of Theology and Chancellor of the University of Cambridge. Erasmus said of him "He is the one man at this time who is incomparable for uprightness of life, for learning and for greatness of soul".

St. John Fisher was the sole Bishop in England who upheld the doctrine of papal supremacy and refused to accept Henry VIII as the supreme head of The Church of England. For this Henry had him beheaded. He was made a Cardinal while imprisoned in the Tower of London awaiting execution.

Fisher met death with a calm dignified courage which profoundly impressed those present. His body was treated with particular rancour, apparently on Henry's orders, being stripped and left on the scaffold until the evening, when it was taken on pikes and thrown naked into a rough grave in the churchyard of All Hallows' Barking, also known as All Hallows-by-the-Tower. There was no funeral prayer. A fortnight later, his body was laid beside that of Sir Thomas More in the chapel of St Peter ad Vincula within the Tower of London. Fisher's head was stuck upon a pole on London Bridge but its ruddy and lifelike appearance excited so much attention that, after a fortnight, it was thrown into the Thames, its place being taken by that of Sir Thomas More, whose execution, also at Tower Hill, occurred on 6 July.

Fisher was beatified by Pope Leo XIII with Thomas More and 52 other English Martyrs on 29 December 1886. In the Decree of Beatification, the greatest place was given to Fisher.

He was canonised, with Thomas More, on 19 May 1935 by Pope Pius XI, after the presentation of a petition by English Catholics. His feast day, for celebration jointly with St Thomas More, is on 22 June (the date of Fisher's execution). In 1980, despite being an opponent of the English Reformation, Fisher was added to the Church of England's calendar of Saints and Heroes of the Christian Church, jointly with Thomas More, to be commemorated every 6 July (the date of More's execution) as "Thomas More, Scholar, and John Fisher, Bishop of Rochester, Reformation Martyrs, 1535".

(Source: Wikipedia)

St. John Fisher's Prayer for Good and Holy Bishops

"Lord, according to Your promise that the Gospel should be preached throughout the whole world, raise up men fit for such work. The Apostles were but soft and yielding clay till they were baked hard by the fire of the Holy Ghost.

So, good Lord, do now in like manner again with Thy Church militant; change and make the soft and slippery earth into hard stone; set in Thy Church strong and mighty pillars that may suffer and endure great labors, watching, poverty, thirst, hunger, cold and heat; which also shall not fear the threatening of princes, persecution, neither death but always persuade and think with themselves to suffer with a good will, slanders, shame, and all kinds of torments, for the glory and laud of Thy Holy Name. By this manner, good Lord, the truth of Thy Gospel shall be preached throughout all the world.

Therefore, merciful Lord, exercise Thy mercy, show it indeed upon Thy Church."

Quotations

He said to them, "But who do you say that I am?" Simon Peter answered, "You are the Messiah, the Son of the living God." And Jesus answered him, "Blessed are you, Simon son of Jonah! For flesh and blood has not revealed this to you, but my Father in heaven. And I tell you, you are Peter, and on this rock I will build my church, and the gates of Hell will not prevail against it. I will give you the keys of the kingdom of heaven, and whatever you bind on earth will be bound in heaven, and whatever you loose on earth will be loosed in heaven."

(Mt. 16: 15-19)

Everyone then who hears these words of mine and acts on them will be like a wise man who built his house on rock. The rain fell, the floods came, and the winds blew and beat on that house, but it did not fall, because it had been founded on rock. And everyone who hears these words of mine and does not act on them will be like a foolish man who built his house on sand. The rain fell, and the floods came, and the winds blew and beat against that house, and it fell - and great was its fall.

(Mt. 7: 24-27)

I am the true vine, and my Father is the vinedresser. Every branch of mine that bears no fruit, he takes away, and every branch that does bear fruit he prunes, that it may bear more fruit. You are already made clean by the word which I have spoken to you. Abide in me, and I in you. As the branch cannot bear fruit by itself, unless it abides in the vine, neither can you, unless you abide in me. I am the vine, you are the branches. He who abides in me, and I in him, he it is that bears much fruit, for apart from me you can do nothing. If a man does not abide in me, he is cast forth as a branch and withers; and the branches are gathered, thrown into the fire and burned. If you abide in me, and my words abide in you, ask whatever you will, and it shall be done for you. By this my Father is glorified, that you bear much fruit, and so prove to be my disciples. As the Father has loved me, so have I loved you; abide in my love. If you keep my commandments, you will abide in my love, just as I have kept my Father's commandments and abide in his love. These things I have spoken to you, that my joy may be in you, and that your joy may be full.

(John. 15: 1-11)

Do not harness yourself in a team with unbelievers. What partnership is there between righteousness and lawlessness? Or what fellowship is there between light and darkness? What agreement does Christ have with Beliar? Or what does a believer share with an unbeliever? What agreement has the temple of the living God with idols? For we are the temple of the living God; as God said,

"I will live in them and walk among them,
and I will be their God,
and they shall be my people.

Therefore come away from them,
and separate yourself from them, says the Lord,
and touch nothing unclean;
then I will welcome you,
and I will be your father,
and you shall be my sons and daughters,
says the Lord Almighty."

(2 Cor. 6: 14-18)

"Both apostles share the same feast day, for these two were one; and even though they suffered on different days, they were as one. Peter went first, and Paul followed. And so we celebrate this day made holy for us by the apostles' blood. Let us embrace what they believed, their life, their labors, their sufferings, their preaching, and their confession of faith."

St. Augustine of Hippo
Sermon on the Holy Apostles Peter and Paul. AD 395

"One of the chief uses of religion is that it makes us remember our coming from darkness, the simple fact that we are created."

G. K. Chesterton on Religion and Faith
The Boston Sunday Post, Jan. 16, 1921

"There are those who hate Christianity and call their hatred an all-embracing love for all religions."

G. K. Chesterton on Religion and Faith
Illustrated London News, Jan. 13, 1906

"These are the days when the Christian is expected to praise every creed except his own."

G. K. Chesterton on Religion and Faith
Illustrated London News, Aug. 11, 1928

"The Bible tells us to love our neighbors, and also to love our enemies; probably because they are generally the same people."

G. K. Chesterton on Religion and Faith
Illustrated London News, July 16, 1910

"The truth is, of course, that the curtness of the Ten Commandments is an evidence, not of the gloom and narrowness of a religion, but, on the contrary, of its liberality and humanity. It is shorter to state the things forbidden than the things permitted: precisely because most things are permitted, and only a few things are forbidden."

G. K. Chesterton on Religion and Faith
Illustrated London News, Jan. 3, 1920

Table of Contents

Dedicated to St. John Fisher i
St. John Fisher's Prayer for Good and Holy Bishops iii
Quotations iv
Prologue xv

Book I: The Foundations of Our Catholic Faith 1
    Foreword 3
    Introduction to the Series 5

Chapter One: The Nature of Catholic Faith (I) 11
    A Definition 15
    Human Faith is a Way of Knowing 18
    An Everyday Example 18
    The Primacy of the Intellect over all other Human Faculties .. 22
    The Nature of Supernatural Faith 24
    The Nature of Catholic Faith 28
    The Nature of Catholic Faith Better Understood By Contrast 29
    Catholic Faith Defined 30
    The Catholic Church's Teaching on Catholic Faith 31

Chapter Two: The Nature of Catholic Faith (II) 35
    The Modernist Attack on Catholic Faith 35
    How unique? How precious? 35
    Early Warning System 38
    Resume of the Central Question Facing Us 43

St. Thomas Aquinas 49
The Mystery Solved 52

Chapter Three: The Nature of Catholic Philosophy (I) 59
Intellect in Search of Truth 59
Introduction 59
Section I: The Function of the Human Intellect 62
Topic I: A Description of the Mind's Activities 62
The Principle of Contradiction 63
Cause and Effect 65
Reasoning and the Principles of Logic 66
The Human Intellect Guides the Will 68
Topic II: A Short Investigation into how the Human Intellect Works 70
The Human Soul 70
The Human Mind, or Intellect 72
Truth and the Progress in Knowledge 76
Section II: The Human Intellect and Thomism in Support and Defense of Catholic Faith 79

Chapter Four: The Nature of Catholic Philosophy (II) 85
The Will in Search for Good 85
Introduction 85
The Human Will 86
The Ultimate Object of the Human Will 87
The Moral Order 89
Origin and Nature of the Moral Order 90
Natural Law Explained 92

The Content of the Natural Law 93

Chapter Five: The Nature of Catholic Philosophy (III) 97
The Human Unity Between Intellect and Will 97
Introduction 97
An Excursion into Ontology: The Study of the Philosophy of Being 98
The Thomistic First Principle of Created Being Defined 100
The Nature of Human Conscience 103
Ontological Unity Between Intellect and Will 105
A Unity Between Intellect and Will at the Conscious Level: Motivation 109
A Further Unity Between Intellect and Will: Habit Formation 111

Chapter Six: The Nature of Catholic Philosophy (IV) 113
The Corruption of Human Thinking: 113
A 600 Year History 113
Introduction 113
Lucifer 115
Moses 120
William of Occam 123

Chapter Seven: The Nature of Catholic Theology (I) 139
The Human Study of Divinely Revealed Truths 139
Introduction 139
World Conspiracies 141
The Heavenly Strategy 143

The True Fascination ... The True Perspective 144
The New Creation 146
The Power of the New Creation 149
Not Deceived 151
I Have Made Known to You Everything I Have Learned From
My Father 152
The New Adam 154
Conclusions 157

Chapter Eight: The Nature of Catholic Theology (II) 161
God, Man and the Moral Order 161
Introduction 161
God 163
Man 166
The Moral Order 168

Chapter Nine: The Nature of Catholic Theology (III) 177
The Corruption of Catholic Thinking 177
Introduction 177
Section I: The Origins and Manifestations of the Corruption of
Catholic Thinking 182
The Abandonment of a Truly Catholic Philosophy 182
Some Examples of Thinking Seriously Proposed as 'Catholic'
.... 183
Fr. Karl Rahner S.J. 186
George Devine's "Proceedings ..." 189
The Australian Scene 190
The Stages of Catholic Corruption 191

Table of Contents

The First Signs 192
The Second Hurdle 193
Section II: Analysis of Some of the More Important Examples of the Corruption of Catholic Thinking in Contemporary Australia 195
The First National Conference of Catholic Laity, April 1976, Sydney.. 195
Why bring all this up?.. 199
What, then, was at stake in Sydney?....................................... 201
A Second Analysis: The Thinking Surrounding Spurious Catechetics in Australia 202
A Third Analysis: Psycho-babbling 204
Existentialism versus Thomism.. 205

Chapter Ten: The Discipline of the Mind (Pope St. Pius X) 209
Introduction... 209
Section I: "Faith In Search of Understanding" 213
Section II: "Intellect in Search of Faith" 218
Section III: "Fracto Alabastro ..." (Mk. 14:3) 225

Appendix A: Modernism, Modernists; Teilhardism, Teilhardians
.... 229
Modernists... 231
Teilhardism 232
Teilhardians 235

Appendix B: The "Melbourne Guidelines"................................... 237

Book II: The Hedge of the Vine 241

Foreword 243
    The Purpose of this Book 246
Introduction 253

Chapter One: The Vine 257
    Earliest attacks on the Vine 259
    Cainites – World – Modernists 263
    Sethites – Church - Orthodox 265
    Two Universal Corruptions: Two Universal Frustrations 268
    The Mystery of Perseverance 270
    No salvation outside the Ark 274
    Only 'The Vine' makes sense 276

Chapter Two: The Hedge 279
    The New Strategy From Hell 280
    The Deep Significance for us of the 'Tower of Babel' Incident 282
    Confounding: the most significant aftermath of 'Babel' 285
    The Essentials of Confounding 287
    The Hedge 290

Chapter Three: The Snake in the Hedge 295

Chapter Four: I Will Take Away its Hedge 319

Epilogue 327

Prologue

Presented for publication in this third volume of the *Selected Works of Frits Albers* are the following two books.

The Foundations of Our Catholic Faith

The Hedge of the Vine

The first of these, *The Foundations of Our Catholic Faith*, was published in 1981. It presents in order a series of ten lectures the author gave during 1980. These ten lectures, herein presented as ten chapters, are based on the Church's Teaching on Faith, Philosophy and Theology.

The author is most concerned that Catholics should understand exactly what the Church means by "Catholic Faith" and why this Faith is so vital to the world and to the salvation of each human being, and how it differs from any other kind of faith, including "Christian Faith" and ordinary human faith.

He explains the nature of Catholic Faith and its relationship to the human intellect and human will and how this nature and these relationships are under attack in our times from Modernism. Accordingly he highlights the concern shown by the Sovereign Pontiffs that the Philosophy of St. Thomas Aquinas be restored and studied as a matter of supreme importance, not only in defense of the Faith, but also because of its necessity for the Preambles to the Faith.

From the principles of the Philosophia Perennis he gives a cogent explanation of the human unity of intellect and will, and how there two faculties work harmoniously together; both naturally on the level of human nature, and when divinely assisted in the supernatural order of Grace and Faith which heals, perfects and sanctifies these human faculties. His discussion of conscience finds its natural place here.

The author rounds out the chapters of the book on Philosophy with a summary and analysis of the corruption of human thinking having its historical origin in the Nominalism of William of Occam. He then moves to explain the nature of Catholic Theology.

In the ensuing discussion of Catholic Theology the author is most concerned to provide motivation for its study and acquisition by showing the practical worth it has for everyday living, especially in the hostile environments – both secular and 'catholic' - of modern society where we have to work out our salvation and help our brothers and sisters to do the same. He rightly treats of Theology as the human study of the New Creation: of redeemed man, sharing in God's Divine Nature through sanctifying grace; and the Supernatural Faculties of Faith, Hope and Love by which we are elevated to participate in that Nature. Catholic Theology centred on God, Man and the Moral Order is discussed in a practical, inviting and thoroughly orthodox way.

As stated above, a chapter on the corruption of human thinking is included in the section of the book devoted to Philosophy. Likewise, and to further develop that discussion and to show just where it is ultimately leading, he includes a chapter on the corruption of Catholic thinking in the section devoted to Theology.

Finally I will 'ask' the author to introduce the crowning chapter of *The Foundations of Our Catholic* in his own words: "We have come a long way to the commanding position of this final lecture: the synthesis between Reason and Faith, found in the true Wisdom of 'The Discipline of the Mind'."

It is this discipline of the mind which Pope St. Pius X was so insistent upon: that formidable unity and interplay between supernatural insights in the Light of Catholic Faith and natural understanding according to right reason or the Philosophy of St. Thomas Aquinas, which Philosophy is truly the hedge and fence protecting the supernatural vine of Catholic Faith.

On that note it is appropriate to move seamlessly to the second book published in the present volume, *The Hedge of the Vine*.

This book has been described as "a gem" by some who read and studied it when first published in 1991. The golden thread running through *The Hedge and the Vine* is the everlasting enmity pronounced by God against Satan after the temptation and fall of our first parents. "I will make you enemies of each other, you and the Woman, your seed and her seed. She shall crush your head and you will strike at her heel". (Gen. 3: 15)

From the central perspective of the everlasting enmity and from the time of its primeval pronunciation against the devil, the author takes us through its historical development in the Old Testament. He highlights and focuses upon (i) the temptation and fall of our first parents, particularly of Eve; (ii) Cain's murder of Abel; (iii) the Ark and the Flood; (iv) the Tower of Babel.

At each of these four junctures the author discusses and analyses in depth the everlasting enmity from the perspective of each of its two sides: from the perspective of the side of the Woman of Genesis (Our Lady) and her seed; and from the perspective of the side of the devil and his seed. At each of these instances he shows what actions God took to preserve the Promise of Redemption and Faith in the Promise, the vine; and what action the devil took to thwart and oppose the Promise by corrupting human thinking, the hedge protecting the vine.

From this historical analysis and what it teaches about the vine of Faith and salvation, and the hedge of clear thinking and right reason or Thomistic Philosophy surrounding and protecting the vine, the author is ultimately concerned that Catholics should know and understand the principles of each; for these principles are permanent and stand outside time no matter how advanced is the state of moral corruption and unified evil around us. These principles are the principles of sanctity, salvation and sanity; and it is only to people who firmly possess them that the future and safety of the Church and the world can be entrusted.

This sufficiently explains why *The Foundations of Our Catholic Faith* and *The Hedge of the Vine* have been included in this third volume of the works of Frits Albers.

Book I

The Foundations of Our Catholic Faith

A Course of 10 Lectures
on
The Catholic Church's Teachings
on
Faith, Philosophy, Theology

Frits Albers, Ph.B.

Originally Published
1981

Foreword

Since the beginning of the Church, the forces of evil have been trying to bring about Her downfall. This of course will not happen; we have God's Word for that. Nevertheless, Satan does try, and each day redoubles his efforts. After the publication of Pope Pius XII's encyclical *Humani Generis* in 1950, an ex-Dominican friend of Teilhard de Chardin who had left the Priesthood and the Church, invited Teilhard (now that the Pope had publicly rejected the principal theses of 'teilhardism') to do likewise, that they might together destroy our Holy Catholic Church. Teilhard replied that he would remain within the visible confines of the Church – therein he could work more effectively to bring about Her demise. We have the testimony of Pope Saint Pius X, that satanic Modernism would strike at the very root of our Holy Catholic Faith (*Pascendi*), and again that of Pope Paul VI, that Her enemies are all the more dangerous when they remain within Her fold.

'Understanding' is the Second Gift of the Holy Spirit. In order to understand as the Holy Church wants us to, it is necessary to know the very foundations of our Catholic Faith. Hence this very necessary and timely book by Frits Albers. The attempts 'Teilhardism' has made to undermine the Philosophy of that great Doctor of the Church, St. Thomas Aquinas, are clearly shown and answered. It is an honour to have been asked to write the Foreword to *The Foundations of our Catholic Faith*, which comprises the texts of 10 lectures delivered in Sydney during the second half of 1980.

The faithful can see numerous 'changes'. Many of these changes offend, and the oft-quoted words 'since Vatican II' by the modernists leave many speechless. Mr. Albers, might we call him a modern day Thomas More, will leave his readers consoled with the joy of being a Catholic, and a child of Our Lady of Fatima, as he leaves no doubt at all in the reader's mind, that not everything that has happened within the Church since the Council, can be validly claimed as having emanated from the council. And certainly not the innumerable deviations from true Philosophy, Theology and Catechetics.

We recommend this book for every Catholic home, school, university and other places of learning.

Jim and Margaret Gresser
Call For Mary Publications

Introduction to the Series

For a very down-to-earth, common sense reason, and if viewed from a practical angle, I consider the Second Glorious Mystery of the Holy Rosary: 'The Ascension of Our Lord into Heaven' the more important one in a whole series of extraordinary Mysteries. In all the ones that went before it, we see the Son of God work out His own program. We watch Him choose His Mother, embrace poverty, practice obedience. And after an all too short teaching career, we contemplate with mounting awe, how He willingly accepts for us the ending of it all, dictated to Him by His Love. We are still there, with the other uncomprehending disciples, when we await further developments, and He appears to us after His Resurrection. But then, just as we could go on quite happily seeing Him take charge and command, by a sudden twist of the Divina Comedia, He thrusts the steering wheel into our hands with the simplicity of One who does not expect any reaction: 'Here, now you do it. Go and teach all the nations …'. And with that, He leaves us for good, not to return until the end of time, and suddenly we find ourselves confronted by the stark reality, that we are supposed to finish what He barely had started. That we have to do this with our talents, in our way, as best we can. It is of course a great honour to be trusted to that extent, but where does one start?

And time and time again, the Holy Pontiffs God has placed in charge over us have shown us that they, too, not only have felt a sudden renewed repetition of the first dawning of that awesome Reality, at the time of their election; but also that, to a man, they have all answered that first question, still hanging even over our own century: 'Where does one start?' With the monotonous routine that can only come from having reached rock bottom: 'By proclaiming the Truth!'

Is there any difference, really, between the beginning of Leo XIII's encyclical *Aeterni Patris* (1879), on the restoration of Catholic Philosophy, and Pope St. Pius X's encyclical *Pascendi* (1907), against Modernism, or his encyclical *Acerbo Nimis* (1905) on sound catechetics, or Pope Pius XII's great encyclical *Humani Generis* (1950), concerning Modern Errors?

"The only-begotten Son of the Eternal Father, who came on earth to bring salvation and the light of Divine Wisdom to men, conferred a great and wonderful blessing on the world, when, about to ascend into Heaven, He commanded the Apostles to go and teach all the nations, and left the Church He had founded to be the common and supreme teacher of the peoples. For men, *whom the truth had set free*, where to be preserved *by the truth* … And the Church built upon the promises of its own divine Author, whose charity it imitated, so faithfully followed out His commands, that its constant aim and chief wish was this: to teach true religion, and contend forever against errors." (1879)

Note that teaching the Truth is here equated with supreme Love: imitating the Love of Christ.

"One of the primary obligations assigned by Christ to the office divinely committed to Us of feeding the Lord's flock, is that of guarding with the greatest vigilance the Deposit of Faith delivered to the Saints, rejecting the profane novelties of words and the gainsaying of knowledge falsely so called." (1907).

"... Those who still are zealous for the glory of God are seeking the causes and reasons for this decline in religion ... But it seems to Us, that we are forced to agree with those who hold that the chief cause of the present indifference, and, as it were, infirmity of soul, and the serious evils that result from it, is to be found above all in Ignorance of things divine ... It is a common complaint, unfortunately too well founded (bishops of Australia, please take heed!) that there are large numbers of Christians in our time who are entirely ignorant of those truths necessary for salvation ... It is hard to describe with words how profound is the darkness in which they are engulfed, and, what is most deplorable of all, how tranquilly they repose there ... And so Our predecessor, *Benedict XIV*, had just cause to write: 'We declare that a great number of those who are condemned to eternal punishment suffer that everlasting calamity because of ignorance of those Mysteries of Faith which must be known and believed in order to be numbered among the elect'. (*Instit. 27:18.*)" (1905).

This abundantly bears out why *Pope Leo XIII* linked teaching true religion and contending forever against errors with imitating the charity of Christ.

"It has ever been a cause of deep and heart-felt sorrow to honest folk, and above all to good loyal sons of the Church, that the judgements of mankind in the sphere of religion and morals should be so variable *and so apt to stray from the truth*". (1950).

And what did the Pontiff write who convened the Second Vatican Council? Is he of a different mind than the ones before him? This is what we read in the beginning of his very first encyclical:

"The source and root of *all* the evils which affect individuals, peoples and nations with a kind of poison, and confuse the minds of many, is this: *Ignorance of the truth*; and not only ignorance, but at times a contempt for, and a deliberate turning away from it." (1959).

This last, we recognise, is done by the authors of the *Melbourne Guidelines for Religious Education (1972 – 1981). Pope John XIII* never veered away from these convictions, nor from the way he kept referring to the Catholic Church in all his writings, quoting *1 Tim. 3:15*, as "the pillar and ground of truth". These same sentiments are not only preserved, but openly proclaimed by the Second Vatican Council itself. In the very first chapter of its very first document, we read in the opening lines the following reference to *1 Tim. 2:4:* "God who wills that all men be saved and come to the knowledge of the Truth".

After that, the unbroken lines of the paramount importance of the Truth in the minds of the Holy Fathers, is maintained by the post-conciliar Pontiffs: Pope Paul VI's *Credo of the people of God*; and Pope John Paul II's encyclical *Redemptor Hominis*, which is expressly based on "a key Truth of Faith" and "the first fundamental Truth of the Incarnation".

So there is the constant and unvaried answer given by the Church to out first question, when we find ourselves entrusted with continuing and completing the task initiated by Our Lord: 'Where do we start?' We start by proclaiming the Truth, and by contending forever against error.

And once profoundly aware of the magnitude of the task entrusted to our weakness, in the Second Glorious Mystery, we look around, with Pope John Paul II in his first encyclical *Redemptor Hominis*, and with him we arrive at the Third Glorious Mystery, with these words:

"... letting myself be guided by unlimited trust in and obedience to the Spirit that Christ promised and sent to His Church. On the night before He suffered He said to His Apostles: 'It is to your advantage that I go away, for if I do not go away, the Counsellor will not come ... that *spirit of Truth*, Who proceeds from the Father ... When the *Spirit of Truth* comes, He will guide you into all the truth (*John 16:13*)."

It is significant that no Modernist, nor any priest tainted with Modernism, calls the Holy Spirit by the name given to Him by Christ Himself and quoted here by the Holy Father: 'The Spirit of Truth'. They only want him to be known as the Spirit of love, breaking the bond laid by the Magisterium: that proclaiming the truth and contending forever against error is imitating Christ's charity. These, then, are the foundations on which I will build this series. And this is the mandate of the Church. I have to proceed with it.

Chapter One

The Nature of Catholic Faith (I)

The spectacle of an orthodox Catholic in our modern society is truly a sorry one. No one resembles the suffering Christ more than he. No one is closer to Our Lady of Sorrows than she. From the four corners of the globe we hear the same reports: how misunderstood and mistrusted they are by their own bishops and priests, shunned and ignored by fellow catholics who have followed 'the winds of change' and no longer share their beliefs; how they are treated with impatience and contempt by the catechists, who go through the motions of pretending to teach their children the catechism, and how disobeyed they are by their teenage sons and daughters: the products of this teaching.

Redress by their bishops is denied them; the road to the parish priest is blocked; they are unable to get a hearing in the 'catholic' press; sister and curate are altogether on another wavelength, and the few words they manage to utter at parents meetings are drowned in a torrent of modern jargon spiced with derision and intolerance.

To add to their daily agony, what do they see? They see a renewal which has been cleverly hijacked and twisted into some unrecognisable shape, which bears no resemblance to what was originally intended. They see bishops silent in the face of a monstrous perversion of Catholic doctrine 'in name of renewal'. They see the seminaries empty 'in the name of renewal'. They see their Priests and Nuns leave the Church and leave Catholic education 'in the name of renewal'. They see teenagers refuse to attend Mass on Sundays, and adopt practices contrary to Catholic teaching, 'in name of renewal'. They see apostates and atheists appointed to Catholic schools as teachers 'in name of renewal and ecumenism'. They see their children come out of 'catholic schools' with hardly any knowledge of their Faith and with barely the rudiments of morality, again in the name of some 'renewal'. To say nothing of what they read in their 'catholic' papers, or hear from the pulpit, or in the never ending seminars and gatherings; where it is all explained to them that this 'renewal' comes from Vatican II, and must be seen as the work of the Holy Spirit, who is preparing us for some united, ecumenical, 'renewed' church of the future …

And then it is finally brought home to them that the only thing that stands in the way of this 'renewal' is they themselves. They are the obstinate obstacles, the cross of the bishops, the bone of contention in parish life: the splitters, the wreckers, the cause of divisions. They have constantly to show cause for their existence, for their Faith: all the others have it made. Their opposition to Modernism is suspected: the intolerance of Modernism to them is claimed to come from the Spirit and is taken for granted.

It is obvious to friend and foe alike, that this situation cannot go on indefinitely. Sooner or later one camp will prevail over the other. One camp will show itself to have Supernatural Faith, Hope and Love on its side; the Communion of Saints; the Catholic Church. That camp will first suffer apparent defeat and rejection, like Christ had to go through. And to sustain that camp through the agony of defeat and rejection, before it can take heart in the final victory, God has given to His camp one thing and one thing only that the opposite camp can never claim and will never possess, and that is Truth. Finally, when all is said and done, when it no longer matters who had the ear of the bishops; who had the numbers; who monopolised the 'catholic' press; who could lay hands on unlimited sums of money for their propaganda; the deciding factor is: who is in the company of the same Jesus who divinely revealed before Pilate that He had come into this world to testify to the Truth, and that all who are of the Truth would hear His voice. For Truth and Christ are synonymous, are one and the same, as He himself told us: "I am the Truth".

And so this very first lecture in this whole series, this foundation lecture, must deal with the Light in which Jesus' Truth is seen and recognised; and with the faculty in the human being that contains this Light, recognises the Truth, and makes it its own.

That Faculty is none other than Catholic Faith.

For well over one hundred years our Holy Mother the Catholic Church has been warning us that the Enemy has been concentrating his attack on the Catholic Faith. This attack has become very refined, subtle and brutal.

Everywhere in the world our good Catholics are being put under an almost unbearable pressure to hand over their Catholic Faith in exchange for a teilhardian, modernist persuasion, which is being proclaimed as the new catholicism ensuing from Vatican II in line with modern evolutionary trends. It is the purpose of these first two lectures to put a stop to this, by showing every Catholic reader or listener what it is they are asked so insistently and relentlessly to surrender.

As will be fully explained in the course of these first two lectures, Catholic Faith is, in a real sense, undoubtedly the most precious gift of Almighty God to finite little man here on earth. For, although nothing could surpass in greatness the Gift of Himself in the Blessed Eucharist, where on this earth is this Gift accepted and appreciated other than by a lively Catholic Faith? And the same goes for all the other Holy Realities revealed by God and given to us: Our Lady, the Sacraments, the Catholic Church itself: all only seen and appreciated in the Supernatural Light of Catholic Faith.

Yet, how many today are there who would not know what this exceptional Gift is, and are unable to tell the difference between It and any other faith, including so-called 'christian' faith? This startling fact alone is sufficient to bring home to us how very successful the ferocious attacks on Catholic Faith have become, and that a discussion of these matters has become imperative. For, if there are many Catholics - teenagers especially - who no longer can recognise Catholic Faith, and are no longer able to see how it is different from any other faith; then they are no longer in a position to know if they have lost their Catholic Faith, and have gone over to another persuasion.

Christ's promise that He will be with His Church till the end of time, and His assurance that His Elect – in final analysis – will not be deceived are synonymous, and together mean that Catholic Faith will not disappear altogether from this earth, no matter how reduced the number of His Elect at one time. For Catholic Faith to exist, the Catholic Church is essential: no other faith will do, no other church will do. And so, modernism and teilhardism are doomed. They may succeed in gathering millions of catholics:

Chapter One: The Nature of Catholic Faith (I)

bishops, priests, nuns, lay folk into their modernist ecumenical church of darkness; but they will never deceive the Elect who in the Supernatural Light of their Infused, Divine, Catholic Faith will always be able to unerringly tell the difference and so preserve the Catholic Church, and with it the salvation of mankind. And that is what it is all about.

A Definition

Even the Jerusalem Bible will concede in a footnote, that *Hebr. XI: 1* has been adopted as a theological definition of faith. Here follow the various translations of this text:

Vulgate (Douay): Now faith is the substance of things to be hoped for, the evidence of things that appear not.

Knox: Faith is that which gives substance to our hopes; which convinces us of things we cannot see.

Jerusalem: Only faith can guarantee the blessings that we hope for, or prove the existence of the realities that at present remain unseen.

RSV: Now faith is the assurance of things hoped for, the conviction of things not seen.

Two things stand out immediately from this definition, inspired by the Holy Spirit:

(i) Faith is the foundation of Hope;

(ii) Faith is first and foremost an intellectual activity, which is born out by the various words used: Evidence, Convinces, Prove, Conviction.

From now on, right from the very start of these lectures, and right through till the end, the two things Holy Scripture and the Catholic Church teach us about Catholic Faith must be clearly brought out and understood, must never be confused, and yet must also be brought into perfect unity and harmony with one another:

that the act of Catholic Faith is a Supernatural Act, wholly above and beyond human nature at the same time that it is an act of the human intellect, a human act, and so very meritorious in the Eyes of God.

The classic example of this duality, this dual aspect of the one act of Faith, is Peter's famous Profession of Faith in Caesarea Philippi, immortalised in *St. Matthew's Gospel, chapter XVI, v. 16*, and Our Lord's confirmation in the very next verse, *v. 17*.

v. 16: "Simon Peter answered and said: 'Thou art the Christ, the Son of the living God'."

v. 17: "And Jesus answering said to him: 'Blessed art thou, Simon Barjonah, because flesh and blood hath not revealed it to thee, but My Father Who is in heaven'."

Peter attested here to something, which, according to the words of the Creator of the human intellect, he could not possibly have arrived at by his own natural powers; but was revealed to him from above. Yet, it was Peter's profession; and just as Our Lady had been called 'blessed' for grasping and believing what had come to Her from above by the message of an Angel, and just as Christ called Peter 'blessed' for believing and professing what had been revealed to him, for his very own meritorious Act of Faith, so others will, in the end, be held personally responsible for not believing: for not performing a supernatural act …

Chapter One: The Nature of Catholic Faith (I)

"But he that believeth not shall be condemned." *(Mk. XVI: 16.)*

We do well, therefore, never to separate again Mt. 16:16 from Mk 16:16.

This leads us directly to an initial appreciation: that just as we have a natural life, a human nature, with natural, human powers and faculties to properly live that life: a human intellect to know the truth and guide all our actions; a human will to perform our actions, and human freedom of choice to lift us above the deterministic necessity of physical equations and chemical reactions to a created likeness of God, so we must also have a participation in a Supernatural Life, the Divine Nature, with its own supernatural powers and faculties to live that Life: a participation in the Divine Intellect, to see the way God sees Reality, and to appreciate the way God thinks about things; a participation in the Divine Will 'to be perfect as our Heavenly Father is perfect' and to love what Christ embraced in love, with the freedom of the children of God.

And if, by Analogy, we can come to a better understanding and deeper appreciation of the way God sees and does things and the way we share in that Divine Life and its Faculties, from the way we possess and operate our human faculties of Intellect and Will, we do well, therefore, to subject to a more thorough examination the gifts of intellect and free will the Creator has endowed us with. As a first approximation to the appreciation of the inestimable Gift of Catholic Faith, we must first analyse in more detail the nature and activity of ordinary, human faith. The foundation to such a research is the surety that the supernatural does not destroy, but perfects, the natural.

Human Faith is a Way of Knowing

All faith: ordinary human faith we use in everyday life; scientific faith; supernatural Faith, is the discovery of a reality hidden or veiled by a symbol or sign. In faith we are in contact with that unseen reality. An Act of Faith gives the consent to this contact, i.e. to the reality itself on the conviction that

(i) a truth relation has been set up by means of the symbol between the mind of the believer and the reality so discovered, and

(ii) that it is good for us to possess this truth. This means the will allows this consent to be given. The act of faith becomes a truly human act and no longer an act of the intellect. The will of man, always in search for some good, gives the believer the go-ahead after the intellect has convinced the believer that, on the strength of the available evidence, the truth will be known and is worthy of assent. It mainly hinges on what the intellect assess to be suitable evidence. If the intellect is satisfied that so far the evidence can be trusted, and is prepared to remain open for further evidence, then faith is a common way of Knowing.

An Everyday Example

A modern substitute for 'symbol' or 'sign' is 'instrument'. Faith in an instrument. An aircraft flying by night or in dense cloud is only absolutely safe from a collision, if it flies higher than the high-

Chapter One: The Nature of Catholic Faith (I)

est obstacle in its path. The height of the plane is then the only reality that counts. No pilot has a direct, intuitive knowledge of the actual height of the plane so he transfers the acquiring of this knowledge to faith in a symbol: an instrument called altimeter. Through this instrument he comes in contact with the actual height of his craft: the reality that matters. But this reality remains hidden from him: he still cannot see the actual height of the plane. It all hinges on the evidence available to him with regard to the reliability of his instrument in recording faithfully the true reality, which is a great good for him and his passengers. No sane pilot will refuse to believe all his symbols: his whole instrument panel, and start flying by guesswork, on a purely theoretical possibility that his instruments may not be 100% accurate, but only 99.9%. He will only resort to this when there is ample evidence (evidence again!) that there is a complete breakdown in power or in his electronic equipment. It is good to keep this in mind when we see the erratic behaviour of theologians and some bishops with regard to Papal teaching and Tradition.

Authority is another universally accepted symbol which – especially in teaching – will guide the subjects' faith in it to come into contact with, and to the knowledge of, many other unseen realities. Misuse of authority by means of so-called 'experts' therefore leads directly to a change in faith and so to false knowledge. We have seen ample evidence of this over the last 12 years or so in Australia in the vital matter of Catechesis. By the same token: abdication of (episcopal) authority, or the direct break-down of authority through violence (democracies) eventually lead to chaos: a climate where truth and the good it brings can no longer flourish. (It is already good to remember here that by far the greatest authority in the Catholic Church is the authority to teach: to teach the truth. The name given to this authority is Magisterium, which, by Divine injunction, demands faith in it. That this teaching authority is, at present time, mainly upheld by the Holy Father in almost total isolation, does remind one of what the great Card. Newman so aptly described as a 'suspense in the function of the teaching Church' during the sixty year period of the Arian heresy.)

By far the greatest use of faith as a way to knowledge in everyday life, is made by means of 'symbols' or 'signs' called Words. '*Fides Ex Auditu*' says St. Paul in *Rom. 10:17*, which means: 'Faith comes from hearing, from listening to the spoken word'. St. Thomas Aquinas tells us the same some 1200 years later in his beautiful hymn to the Blessed Sacrament, *Adoro te Devote*: 'Sed auditu solo tuto creditur', which translates as 'We only believe safely through listening'. Listening to the Word of God, in Sacred Scripture and the Dogmas of the Catholic Church. By listening to a testimony. Why should this be so?

Restricting ourselves here to the purely human condition, but – as we will later see – by no means excluding the Supernatural condition of redeemed man, we can say that all teaching plays its role in that no-man's land between the enquiring mind and the symbol behind which an unseen truth is veiled. And there, the teaching fulfils a triple purpose:

(i) it creates a situation where mind and symbol can meet;

Chapter One: The Nature of Catholic Faith (I)

(ii) it gathers evidence for the enquiring mind to induce it to give its consent in order to reach the truth, and the good that goes with it;

(iii) it incorporates the already mentioned 'symbol of authority' to facilitate the transition from 'enquiring' to 'assent'.

(Here we can already gather up the glaring deficiencies of the Modernists as 'teachers': they refuse to create the situation mentioned in (i), preferring to work by stealth and by deception; they refuse to bring out evidence for their gravely erroneous doctrines, preferring coercion; they constantly try to stifle opposition by browbeating ordinary folk into accepting the 'fact' that the long strings of 'degrees' their so-called 'experts' have behind their names are a substitute for authority.)

Faculty	Symbol/Sign	Unseen Reality
Mind	Teacher	"Existence of America"
Mind	Authority	"Killing is wrong"
Mind	Word	"We promise freedom"
Mind	Instrument	"It is 30° C"

Illustration, showing how ordinary human faith is a way of knowing

If the Symbol [the teacher, the authority, the words, the instrument] is accepted [believed], the mind comes in contact with the Unseen Reality. If the Symbol is rejected, the mind does not come in contact with the Unseen Reality.

Believing the Symbol is coming to the knowledge of the Unseen Reality.

Not believing the Symbol is rejecting the knowledge of the Unseen Reality.

If there is a Truth-Relationship between the Symbol and the Unseen Reality, the mind's knowledge of the Unseen Reality is True, if the Symbol is believed. The mind is in Error if the Symbol is not believed. (In this case Ignorance of the Unseen Reality cannot be claimed.) If there is a relationship of Error between the 'symbol' and the unseen reality it veils, the mind is in error if the 'symbol' is believed. The mind is guarded from Error (but not necessarily in the possession of the truth) if in this case the 'symbol' is rejected.

The Primacy of the Intellect over all other Human Faculties

One final question is to be settled, before we can launch into a study of the Catholic Faith, leading us to a deeper understanding of the inestimable Gift: the role of the intellect and its acquired knowledge, including knowledge acquired by faith.

The role of the intellect is to guide the will; and so it is found at the foundation of all well-ordered human actions. It acts as a light to the human being in its quest for happiness and fulfilment.

"For since it is in the very nature of man to follow the guide of reason in his actions, if his intellect sins at all, his will soon follows; and thus it happens that looseness of intellectual opinion influ-

Chapter One: The Nature of Catholic Faith (I)

ences human actions and perverts them. Whereas, on the other hand, if men be of sound mind and take their stand on true and solid principles, there will result a vast amount of benefits for the public and private good."

With these words in *Aeterni Patris*, His Holiness Pope Leo XIII comprises one of the strongest and most persistent teachings of the Catholic Church; prevailing even today over every modernistic effort of making 'feelings' synonymous with the 'prompting of the Holy Spirit', to be followed, so they claim, even in the glaring presence of contradictions and error. The Church bases Her teaching on the revelation by Christ, that love, like any other thing under the sun, is subject to Truth. Love must be true love; but Truth is not subject to anything, and is not a truth only if it is a 'loving truth', as the modernists try to make out. Modernists hate the Truth and do everything in their power to smother it under 'luv': that sickening non-entity they tar and feather everything with to make it look the same …

They deny the intellect its primary role and primacy of place, precisely because their Number One target: Catholic Faith, has such a lot to do with Intellect and Truth. [More about this in the Second Lecture.]

Another way of putting the fundamental truth that the Intellect is the guide of human actions, is by saying *Ideas Have Consequences*; the title of a brilliant book by the late Prof. Richard Weaver of Chicago, in which he connects the decay of Western Civilisation to the corruption of human thought. [More about this in Lecture No. 6.] Ideas are inevitably translated into actions: the heretical ideas of the modern theologians as much as the woolly ideas of many a modern bishop, as much as the glorious ideas of the modern martyrs, as much as the erroneous ideas of the modern dissidents from Papal Teaching.

We are now ready to tackle the task God will require an account of from every Catholic at the end of his or her life: the task of doing everything in one's power to understand and appreciate the priceless possession of one's Catholic Faith. May the innumerable Holy Martyrs who died for the difference between Catholic and Protestant faith help us and inspire us in this delightful undertaking.

The Nature of Supernatural Faith

We started our investigations into ordinary human faith from the teachings of the Catholic Church and Holy Scripture, basing ourselves on a definition of faith found in *Hebr. 11:1*. But since this definition – as we saw – is accepted as a Theological Definition of Faith, we do not have to start our investigations into Supernatural Faith from another definition in the full knowledge that the Holy Spirit and the Word of God are primarily interested in teaching us the principles of salvation and the Faith that leads to it. In other words: the same definition that set us off into a study of human faith, is even more apt for starting us off into an investigation into Supernatural Faith, the Faith that leads to salvation.

Chapter One: The Nature of Catholic Faith (I)

1. Just as ordinary human faith covers two distinct things:

(i) the Act of Faith, by which we believe a message given in words, or believe an instrument, or an authority guaranteeing the truth of the message or testimony, and

(ii) the faculty which enables us to perform this act of faith: the human intellect capable of assessing the value of the evidence supplied, the light supplied to and needed by the will to allow the human being to give its consent in the guidance of its actions towards a human goal, so Supernatural Faith also distinguishes itself into these two components:

(I) a Supernatural Act believing a Supernatural, Revealed Truth, clothed in Words guaranteed by Christ and by the authority of His Church to bring us directly in contact with the Saving Realities veiled by these symbols (words); in other words, guaranteed by God's Authority and that of His Church to bring us in contact with the truth that sets us free, and

(II) a Supernatural Faculty, or Power that enables us to perform this act of Faith, meritorious in God's Eyes as our own Act ('Blessed are you, Peter' and 'He who does not believe, will be condemned'.) This share into the Intellect of God is ours by virtue of our share in His Divine Life through Baptism. This faculty which enables us to see things the way the Blessed Trinity sees things, natural and Supernatural. This Supernatural, Infused, Divine and Free Gift from Almighty God, is called by its proper name the Supernatural Virtue of Faith. A virtue is not only a faculty or power to perform acts: it is a Habit to make us perform those acts more readily and more easily.

This Virtue of Faith and its acts of believing must be further extended and translated into Christian Living to escape the stigma of being a dead Faith. And here is where Commitment, or Witness, comes in. Commitment must not be confused with Faith, as the Modernists love to do because they hate the Church's teaching on Faith; preferring Existentialism and its totally irrational act as the foundation of their heresies. Commitment to Christian living shows Faith, alive and lively; but even commitment, if not guided by the Divine Light of Supernatural Faith, can be blind, and can be used in pursuit of wrong causes and principles, inspired by erroneous doctrines.

2. Just as the faculty which enables us to perform the ordinary Human acts of faith in our natural daily life is not given indiscriminately to the human body, but is vested in the human intellect, a prime faculty of the human soul; so this Supernatural faculty which enables us to believe in God's Revelation and to see the things of God, is also not given randomly to the human being, but is also infused with the Divine Life into the human soul, and so manifests itself through the human intellect: not to destroy this human intellect, or to take over its role, but as an Added Light in order to perfect it. In God's creative vision, then, there is no

discord or opposition between what is to be perfected: the human intellect, and its perfection: Supernatural Faith. Or between Science and Faith. If there is, it does not come from God or the Supernatural. Its root causes must be found in human weakness, in undirected passions and sins, and in the work of the Devil.

3. Just as ordinary faith is the meeting of the enquiring mind with a truth hidden behind the veil of signs and symbols (usually words), which truth, once accepted, then becomes a knowledge for the mind [I believe that America exists then becomes, on overwhelming evidence and numerous authorities: I know that America exists, even if I have never been there and have never seen it]; so Supernatural Faith, on the evidence supplied by God and on the authority of God, becomes a sure way of Knowing for the human mind. This knowledge is vital for the direction of human acts and actions to their supernatural, eternal end and destiny. [Believing that artificial means of contraception are always intrinsically evil, then becomes full knowledge, in the Supernatural Light of God, that this teaching is true.]

4. Finally, just as all teaching enters into that no-man's land between the enquiring mind and a truth hidden and to be discovered behind the veil of words, and with its authority facilitates the human assent to this truth; so the Catholic Church too enters into this no-man's land between the believer and a Supernatural Truth to be discovered and embraced in an Article of Faith (very appropriately called Symbolum Apostolorum!) in Her role as Teaching

Church, or Magisterium, but with a difference so unique, that it necessitates a separate heading in our investigations.

The Nature of Catholic Faith

As I will fully substantiate in a moment, it is an established Dogma of the Catholic Church that Christ made it a prerequisite for the Redemptive Power of Faith, that His Authority would always be present in that no-man's land and that this authority would be vested in the Papacy. In other words: the Teaching Authority of the Catholic Church has the right and the duty to be present between the believer and the Article of Faith to be believed, and this Teaching Authority is vested in the Papacy. And only through the Papacy is it also vested in the College of Bishops united by Catholic Faith with the Pope.

All legitimate authority to teach religion thus receives its mandate ultimately from the Holy Father. This means that Catholic Parents, and teachers, and catechists, and theologians, and Bishops, must instruct their entrusted charges NOT according to what they may think 'is in the mind of Christ'; but according to what the Holy Father teaches 'is in the mind of Christ'. But once in complete union with the Holy Father, they share in the teaching authority of the Catholic Church, each according to its God-given mandate, and so share in the right to be present in that no-man's land between the believer and the Truth to be believed, proclaimed by the Catholic Church. This is a very serious matter, and many, many modern catechists and theologians must be denied access to this delicate territory (and many bishops have forfeited the right to be

Chapter One: The Nature of Catholic Faith (I)

present) since they no longer teach in union with the Pope, but only expound what they think ought to be in the Mind of Christ ...

The Nature of Catholic Faith Better Understood By Contrast

It is precisely here that we touch on the fundamental difference between Protestantism and Catholicism; between Protestant faith and Catholic Faith. Protestantism claiming that Christ did not put any mediator between Himself and the believer willing to give his assent in faith, whilst the Catholic Church maintains that She received Authority from Christ Himself to teach

(i) to what symbols assent must be given in Catholic Faith in order to reach Supernatural Reality: Truth, Life in God, Salvation, and

(ii) from what symbols assent should be withheld as not reaching Supernatural Reality and Truth, and so no life in God and Salvation.

And it is also precisely in this area that the true Catholic Children of the Catholic Church will maintain their fierce and absolute opposition to Teilhardism and Modernism, and their hostility to the three 'Agreed Statements' in England which all require the abandonment of the Catholic position with their claims that Catholic Faith has shifted ground and has substantially changed since Vatican II. According to bishop Alan Clark, it is essential to the modern ecumenism to see Catholic Faith and Protestant Faith as one, with the same Apostolic continuity, his reason being that the Catholic Church cannot validly claim any longer to be the one true Church founded by Christ, and must come to an (as yet non-existing) unity found in the so-called 'universal (ecumenical) church'. (See in view of these claims Bishop Bernard D. Stewart's Pastoral of Feb. 29, 1976.)

Catholic Faith Defined

What, then, is Catholic Faith? Catholic Faith is all that has been stated so far about Supernatural Faith: a Supernatural, that is Divinely given, Infused Virtue, (habit or faculty) whereby a mere human being becomes capable, in the Light of God's Intelligence to believe what God has revealed and through the Catholic Church proposes to us to believe. It is the Act of Catholic Faith, i.e. the Act of believing what the Catholic Church proposes to us to believe as having been revealed by God, which makes the Act of Faith of a Catholic essentially different from any other act of faith. A Catholic believes in the existence of God, because the Catholic Church tells him that God exists. He believes in the Divinity of Christ, because the Catholic Church tells him that Christ is Divine.

Since the Reformation and the dogmatic teaching of the Council of Trent, there is an essential difference between 'believing in the Divinity of Christ' (Protestant or 'christian' faith) and 'believing in the Divinity of Christ because the Catholic Church teaches me to believe in Her teaching on the Divinity of Christ' (Catholic Faith). Before this great Council's teaching it could be assumed that 'Christian Faith' and 'Catholic Faith' were the same. After Trent, when the Popes use the word 'Christian Faith', it is always

Chapter One: The Nature of Catholic Faith (I)

understood to mean 'Catholic Faith, and that part of non-Catholic faith that is in conformity with it'. The same cannot be said when modernists use the term 'christian faith' ...

The Catholic Church's Teaching on Catholic Faith

And so we have finally found our way into the presence of 'the pearl of great beauty, for which the merchant-in-the-know sacrificed everything'. The Doctors of the Church, the great writers and Saints, have all extolled this magnificent Gift of Almighty God to finite little man: "Faith, without which it is impossible to please God" (Hebr. 11:6.) says the holy author of the Letter to the Hebrews, before launching into the most magnificent exultation of Faith, World Literature has ever known, since it was inspired by God Himself. Where, then, do we begin our final analysis? We begin where Christ Himself began. Calling sinners to a personal salvation through repentance, forgiveness and holiness of life in obedience to the teachings of the Church He founded, is still the central core of Jesus' Mission and Message, no matter how much Teilhard de Chardin and his modernistic followers deride this as a perversion of the original 'inspiration' (*The Human Sense*, 1929.) It is still the central message from Heaven. "*Stop Sinning*" was the very first injunction from Our Blessed Lady at Fatima, 1917 to the whole world. (*Cf. also Phil. 2:12; 1 Cor. 9: 27; Peter. 1: 17-18; etc.*)

According to the Will of Our Saviour, and according to the solemn teaching of the Church He founded, this personal salvation has a distinct beginning. Its Initium: 'beginning', Radix: 'root' and Fundamentum: 'foundation' is the Act of Supernatural, Infused,

Divine, Catholic Faith. The Catholic Church's teaching on this is quite clear and specific. In its 5th Session, the *Council of Trent* has laid down as Catholic Doctrine how the text of *Hebr. 11:6* is to be understood for all times. Referring to the text directly, it states:

"It is our Catholic Faith without which it is impossible to please God." (*Denz Schm. 1510.*)

And again in its 6th Session, elaborating on this most important doctrine, the Council continued:

"When the Apostle tells us that man is justified by Faith, and freely so, then these words must be understood in the sense that the Catholic Church has held and expressed this with perpetual unanimity, namely that we are said to be justified by Faith, because Faith is the beginning of the salvation of man, the foundation and root of all justification, and without which it is impossible to please God", referring and quoting once again the same quote from *Hebr. 11:6*. Referring us once again to this quotation from the Letter to the Hebrews, and having previously authoritatively taught us that this text is to be understood as Catholic Faith, the Council herself now gives herewith the explanation of her own teaching contained in the words: ... "these words must be understood in the sense that the Catholic Church has held and expressed this with perpetual unanimity namely that we are said to be justified by Catholic Faith, because Catholic Faith is the beginning of the salvation of man, the foundation and root of all justification, and without which it is impossible to please God".

The *First Vatican Council* took over the same teaching, the same quotes and confirmed that the same interpretation must be given to Catholic Faith in her Dogmatic Constitution '*Dei Filius*'

Chapter One: The Nature of Catholic Faith (I)

De Fide Catholica: On the Catholic Faith. It then took the matter further.

What does this mean?

1. It does not mean that only people who profess the Catholic Faith will be saved. But it does mean that the Catholic Faith, the Faith professed in humility and obedience to the Catholic Church's teaching is so precious and pleasing to God, that without that Faith, no other Faith on Earth will be pleasing to God; be it Buddhist Faith, Mohammedan faith, or the imperfect 'christian faith' of the Protestants, which, on their own, will not save the believer. But, if they save, it is only because of the saving power extended from the Catholic Faith found within the Catholic Church. If it is true that Catholic Faith is the beginning, the root and foundation of <u>all</u> justification, then Catholic Faith and the Catholic Church are absolutely necessary on earth for the salvation of everybody, even if they do not profess the Catholic Faith.
2. By God's saving Will and Institution, only one Faith is now meritorious in its own right: the Catholic Faith. Only one Thing can be the beginning, the root and the foundation of justification, sanctification, the inhabitation of God in souls. Trent and Vatican I have taught us with supreme authority that it is Catholic Faith: not any other faith, nor love. Since the Acts of Faith which are to be the beginning, root and foundation of all justification are to be freely per-

formed to be meritorious for all, only the acts of Catholic Faith are therefore to be understood to be meritorious in their own right. For other people to be saved by their 'faiths', the graces are to be merited and distributed by the Catholic Church, and the Faith it professes.

Chapter Two

The Nature of Catholic Faith (II)

The Modernist Attack on Catholic Faith

It is the purpose of this 2nd Lecture to shed ever more light on the nature, the uniqueness, the inestimable value and the power of the Catholic Faith, by studying the ways and means by which the Modernists attack it in order to destroy it. In order to do this in a systematic way, and from the teachings of the Church, it is necessary to pick up once again the final points made in the previous Lecture.

How unique? How precious?

If it is Catholic Dogma that only Divine and Catholic Faith, the '*Fides Divina et Catholica*' as defined by the Councils of Trent and Vatican I, has been proclaimed by the Catholic Church as being the beginning, root and foundation of all justification, sanctification and God's inhabitation in souls, then it must be synonymous to say that only Catholic Faith is Life-Giving in its own right and only Catholic Faith is Meritorious in its own right. For with these three words: beginning, root and foundation, the Church could not have been more specific. And so, any other faith: Protestant Faith, so-called 'christian faith', the modern 'faith of commitment', faith in the soul of evolution, etc., cannot be the beginning, the root or the foundation of salvation, since they are not Catholic Faith, and since only one thing can be a beginning, a root and a foundation. This clearly means that no other faith can be life-giving, or meritorious, in its own right; but if it saves, it can only do so because of a tenuous connection with the Una Sancta Catholica et Apostolica Ecclesia. And with the Catholic faith within it. A good, strong and vigorous Catholic Faith is necessary, to help others to come to a life-giving faith as well: belief in God, as a rewarder of good and punisher of evil; and a to a life according to that belief. Just as any good act done by non-catholics is accepted by God as meritorious and life-giving only through its unseen connection with the Catholic Church, so a defective, but well-intended faith of a non-catholic will also be accepted by God as meritorious and justifying through its unseen connection with a strong and healthy Catholic Faith, which make the Catholic Church and its Catholic faith absolutely necessary for Salvation: Anyone's Salvation … And by that Decree of God, by which His Son instituted the Catholic Church.

No one can go to Heaven unless through Christ, but that does not mean that everyone has to be a Christian. He affects everybody who ever lived. Since He instituted His Catholic Church on Peter the Rock, giving him the Keys of the Kingdom, no one can go to Heaven unless assisted by the Church over which Peter is the Head; but again, that does not mean that everybody has to be a Catholic.

What it does mean is, that everybody who received from God the gift of Catholic Faith is through it made responsible for the salvation of all others who did not (yet) receive this Faith.

We may now start to understand the fury of hell against Catholic Faith. For, if Catholic Faith was to disappear from this earth, no

Chapter One: The Nature of Catholic Faith (I)

other faith would be pleasing to God, since no other faith would be life-giving or meritorious in its own right.

Wipe out the Catholic Church, and you would have destroyed the one instrumentality which is life giving in its own right and on which all other life-giving depends: the salvation of the whole world.

Since by God's Decree and Promise, such a total wipe-out is impossible, Catholic Faith will never disappear from this earth; but could quite well disappear from the lives of many Catholics, now, as it did in the past. We must never forget that the Anglicans at the time of Henry VIII, and the Lutherans at the time of Luther, were all Catholics who exchanged their Catholic Faith, Life-Giving in its own right, for another faith, maybe an 'easier' one; but no longer either meritorious, or pleasing to God, or Life–Giving. After their exchange, these unfortunate catholics depended for their salvation on the graces dispensed by the Catholic Church; earned by the faithful Catholics, especially the Holy Martyrs, who preferred to remain in the Una Sancta with their Catholic Faith wholly intact.

This is a very serious matter. The teaching of Sacred Scripture and of the Catholic Church is quite clear. The 'beginning, foundation and root' of Justification and Sanctification will only be given once. Any other lapse or sin can be forgiven because in the Light of Faith we can see the enormity of Sin, and, in the same Light, seeing the supernatural Reality of God's Mercy, we can ask for forgiveness. But what if that Light is extinguished after it was given, and Catholic Faith is killed, aborted? Not just kept dormant and inoperative by a life of sin and debauchery, as is so often the case; but given up, exchanged? We do well to read what Holy Scripture has to say on this in various passages, but especially in *Hebr. 10: 26-31*.

With the Gift of Catholic Faith, God has given to the recipients a priceless possession. If the repercussions in abandoning it are devastating for the human race, so must the consequences of living according to that Faith be enormous ...

Not only is the matter serious: the matter is also most urgent. After studying and learning for 2000 years, the Prince of Darkness and Enemy of Human Nature (as St. Ignatius of Loyola keeps on referring to the Devil) has finally devised a scheme and mode of attack so diabolically clever, that the unprecedented paralysis in the face of it is a sure sign of its global success. May we, through the study of this attack, become even more appreciative of the fantastic Gift of Almighty God to finite little man, for with this strategy Hell surely must have exhausted its resources ...

Early Warning System

Almost 70 years ago, a Saint had a clear idea of what lay ahead. He wrote about it and told us about it. Many Catholics, the ones for whom it was written most, did not understand him. This Saint also happened to be a Pope, and so he told us about it urgently, with God's Authority, Infallibly. He should have been understood in the Light of Supernatural, Infused, Divine, Catholic Faith. That he was not, shows the necessity of what he stated: that Catholic Faith was under attack, and that it was diminishing. Whoever did not believe him can only lay the blame for his undoing to himself.

For the Church believed him. The vision remained preserved, gaining in clarity as time went on.

In *Our Apostolic Mandate*, his letter to the French Bishops of 1910, about the dangerous aberrations of a movement of well-meaning, social catholics in France and possibly elsewhere, Pope St. Pius X revealed for the first time to the world, that he foresaw in the future the establishment of a one-world 'Church'; which according to the characteristics and scope he attached to it, would not be the Catholic Church. One of the marks, by which this *'church of darkness'* can be recognised according to his description, is the absence of the Discipline of the Mind. And with this formulation, the Saint went to the heart of the Modern trouble.

Three years earlier, in 1907, this same Pope and Saint had given us a clear indication that he knew what the enemy was about, when he wrote in his world-famous Encyclical *Pascendi*:

"Moreover, these enemies, thoroughly imbued with the poisonous doctrines taught by the Modernists, lay the axe not to the branches and shoots, but to the very root, that is to the faith itself and its deepest fibres. And once having struck at this root of immortality, they proceed to diffuse poison through the whole tree, so that there is no part of Catholic Truth which they leave untouched, none that they do not strive to corrupt."

So, we have only ourselves to blame if we do not know what the fight is all about. The final assault on our most priceless possession was being conceived and set in motion some 100 years ago. The Popes have left us in no doubt whatsoever that they knew what it was all about; yet they have been doing something that, at first glance, could be considered as most unusual: they have been stressing and promoting a Philosophical System. In the 1960's and 1970's, the attacks on Catholic Faith had become so open, so strong and so all-embracing ('no part of Catholic Truth was left untouched', as predicted) that not a single person in the whole world remained immune from them. Consequently, 100 years ago, God started His preparation through His Church, and through the Popes appointed over Her, and in the Light of what we can see now, this 'most unusual stressing of a philosophical system' as part of this preparation, proved to be deadly accurate! Amazing? No, not really. Not to anyone, that is, who kept his Supernatural, Divine, Catholic Faith, and the fantastic Light it gives, and in that Light can see how Divine the Catholic Church really is. Nothing, absolutely nothing escapes Her. She will always cater for every soul, Catholic and non-Catholic alike, who is entrusted to Her care. She will never abandon: She can only be abandoned.

Now all these Holy Fathers, appointed by God to prepare us for this all-embracing assault on our Catholic Faith, knew Scripture. And what do we read there? In *Rom. 8: 39 St. Paul* has this to say:

"I am convinced that neither death nor life, no Angel, no Prince, nothing that exists, nothing still to come, not any power, or height or depth, nor any created thing can ever come between us and the Love of God made visible in Christ Jesus Our Lord."

meaning of course, that no Catholic can be robbed outright of his Catholic Faith. And so these Popes knew that the attack would come from an entirely different quarter. They viewed with alarm the decline in sound Catholic Philosophy, and in drawing our attention to that disturbing trend, they set in motion what they con-

Chapter One: The Nature of Catholic Faith (I)

sidered, in the Light of the Holy Spirit, as the most effective counter-offensive against the onslaught of Modernism.

Let us then, in this second Lecture, subject to a thorough investigation this seemingly amazing fact: that for well over the last 100 years the Holy Fathers, (in the full knowledge that the modernist attack would be on Catholic Faith, a Supernatural Reality, the Beginning, Root and Foundation of all Justification), in the defence of that Faith unanimously stressed the overriding importance of the Philosophy of St. Thomas Aquinas. In this very late hour, the Holy Fathers are not worrying us with trivialities, or with things they know are good and worth a try: they are determined to give us the best defence, the most effective offense. They owe it to us to give us faithfully what the Holy Spirit considers the rout of the Enemy ... and with their strategy, they revealed to us most clearly where the Enemy of Human Nature had concentrated his forces for the final and all-embracing assault.

> *Aeterni Patris*, Leo XIII, Aug. 1, 1879, *Encyclical*,
> *Doctoris Angelici*, St. Pius X, June 29, 1914, *Motu Proprio*,
> *Quod De Fovenda*, Benedict XV, Mar. 19, 1917, *Letter to Jesuits*,
> *Studiorum Ducem*, Pius XI, June 29, 1923, *Encyclical*,

are four major Papal works entirely devoted to St. Thomas, and the study of his works. Furthermore, there is the clear

> *'Directive'* of the Sacred Congregation of Studies, Mar, 7, 1916,

and further extensive directives laid down, in fact whole sections entirely devoted to this whole serious question in another two Papal Encyclicals:

Pascendi Dominici Gregis, St. Pius X, Sept. 8, 1907, and *Humani Generis*, Pius XII, Aug. 12, 1950.

This surely is an impressive list, which was not abandoned or discontinued by Vatican II; but reinforced and supported by every Holy Father implementing the Decrees and the Spirit of that great Council [*Allocutio to the 6th International Thomistic Congress of Sept. 10, 1965*. Paul VI, AAS 57 (1965), pp 788 – 792], etc.

This consistent body of teaching by the Church ought to have been accepted by Catholics with the customary humility and obedience we owe to the highest teaching authority given by God to men. But humility and obedience are precisely the two virtues in which a lot of intellectuals are lacking for their own ruin. For, when all is said and done, is the Church's insistence on humility and obedience and trust and Faith really all that bad as it looks? Are not we asked to be humble before, and obedient to, the greatest Light God has communicated to mankind on earth; the brilliance of which can only be appreciated and grasped by anyone who is privileged enough to share in it through a life of Catholic Faith? Because it was in that Light, that the Popes started to get the educators in the Church interested once again in the Philosophical thoughts and system of St. Thomas Aquinas. And only now can we start to see for ourselves the remarkable accuracy that this move had. If only Catholic educators, of times gone by, and even now, had shown more trust in the Holy Spirit; and in the Light and guidance He communicates to the Magisterium of the Catholic Church. A Light, so strong and so sure, that it is impossible for the Catholic Church to err or to go wrong; to deceive or be deceived.

Chapter One: The Nature of Catholic Faith (I)

Resume of the Central Question Facing Us

And so, if Catholics cannot be robbed outright of their Faith, and the Popes knew that the Enemy of Human Nature knew that too, and if their Catholic Faith is so all-embracing, that even the salvation of non-Catholics depends on the preservation and full strength of that Faith, then something had to be devised and put into operation to induce Catholics to abandon their Faith in exchange for something that would not be the beginning, the root and foundation of salvation and immortality. And that is now at the heart of the modern problem. For 100 years, Catholic educators have by and large found great difficulty in accepting and heeding Papal directives for the preservation of Catholic Faith and sound Catholic Philosophy; and now, because of this lack of humility and obedience, their problem has now become the problem of us all.

I am sure that you will agree with me that, if we can isolate and bring to the surface that 'something' that was devised and put into operation, (and which escaped altogether the attention of the educators because of the blindness of these educators caused by their lack of humility and obedience) then we stand a good chance, even at this very late hour, to save the Catholic Faith of all the ones entrusted to our care and love.

[How accurate the Papal vision has been, how beneficial compliance with that Vision is for the Church, and how acute the problems become when compliance with that Vision is abandoned for whatever reason or motive, can be gauged from the local (i.e., Sydney) scene since it is verifiable by local history. One of the Papal directives, laid down as early as 1879, 100 years ago, by Pope Leo XIII in *Aeterni Patris*, one of the Encyclicals, as we saw, entirely devoted to Thomism was:

"Let the Academies already founded or to be founded by you (the Bishops) illustrate and defend this doctrine and use it for the refutation of prevailing errors ... Be careful to guard the minds of youth from those (fountains) which are said to flow from St. Thomas, but in reality are gathered from strange and unwholesome streams."

In the vision of the late great Doctor Woodbury, totally coinciding with this Vision and consequent directive of the Holy Father, the Aquinas Academy founded by him was meant to contradict the false doctrine and pseudo-intellectual climate of Sydney University, and to refute the errors prevailing at the time, openly and unashamedly. Can the same be said with truth of the present Academy? Are not we waiting in vain for a studious and thorough refutation of teilhardism and modernism, and of the Melbourne Guidelines from this Academy, precisely because, far from contradicting the prevailing errors, it is vying with Sydney University to be considered equal? To share a place in the 'intellectual sun' of evolution and broad-mindedness? Think of the great service Dr. Woodbury's Academy would have rendered the Church in Australia by its systematic demolition of Modernism and Teilhardism, not only from the authentic sources of St. Thomas, but also because of its original inspiration to serve the Truth and to guard the minds of Youth against the corrupting influence of error passed on as pseudo-truth and pseudo-science, exactly as the Holy Father saw it in his Vision. Having become silent and timid in the face of monstrous perversions of Catholicism everywhere being passed on as the new and exciting 'catholic insights', the Aquinas Academy has fallen away from its original inspiration, its raison d'etre, and the Papal Vision of Academies being used to refute the prevailing errors as was done by the late great Dr. Woodbury.]

And so, in the absence of any help and inspiration from the seminaries as well as academies such as the Aquinas Academy in Sydney, we have to battle on as best we can ourselves in the firm conviction that this study and research and public refutation of the prevailing errors is the unanimous wish and command of every Holy Father that ever lived … And if this means setting up a rival academy, more attuned to the great need of the Church at present time, more in love with the minds and the Catholic Faith of youth than with worldly honours and recognition: so be it. Siding with and basking in the 'glory' of the Angelicum in Rome is no recommendation, as there is prima facie evidence that the Angelicum contradicts *Humane Vitae* in public and teaches teilhardism to its students, not to be outdone by the Gregoriana. This means that the Angelicum will not issue degrees on dissertations critical of Teilhard.

There are two roads open to us that we could take from now on:

1. We could proceed with an analysis of modernism, lay bare its essential evil, and so come face to face with its evil intentions. From this we could hope to acquire a better understanding of the Catholic Church's counter-offensive.

This is an inferior method, and although it may seem plausible, its logic is only apparent. The Devil does not dictate God's timetable, nor does error force Truth to walk a certain path. Teilhard de Chardin did not foul up Genesis, so that now we would be forced to look elsewhere for the defence of Holy Scripture. On the contrary: the Holy Spirit wrote Genesis to foul up Teilhard. Genesis was written thousands of years ago with Teilhard in mind; and everything else that Modernism or any other heresy could throw up at it.

The same is true for the Catholic Church's doctrine expressed in Her marvellous Encyclicals. They are written for the good of souls when future trends that were hidden from the flock were already understood by none better than the occupant of the See of Peter at that time. Time and time again even scholars have expressed their surprise about the way Encyclicals dealt with matter which had barely surfaced at the time of writing, in the same manner that future scholars expressed their amazement about the accuracy with which past Encyclicals dealt with trends and developments fully visible in their lifetime.

Had these Encyclicals been received with the same brilliance of Light of Faith in which they were written, and their Truths and Precepts received and adhered to (even if ill-understood at the time of writing) with the humility and obedience required of Catholic Faith, the Evil that was to come and which was foreseen in those Encyclicals, would have been thwarted and nullified.

2. Therefore, since the *Melbourne Guidelines* do not dictate our timetable either, and since we will not tolerate to let the darkness of Modernism guide our footsteps, we will walk the superior road of the Catholic Church; and with the brilliant Light of the Truth and Goodness in Her doctrine, flood the dark workshops of Modernism, thereby inevitably showing up not only its evil nature, but also the evil intentions it has about the destruction of Catholic Faith.

In this we will follow the footsteps of the present Pontiff, His Holiness Pope John Paul II. The modernists will have us believe that he is travelling so extensively to learn, so that he will change his mind and his teachings: evil once again portrayed as guiding the footsteps of Truth and Goodness. This perversion could not be further from the Truth. Pope John Paul is sowing seeds: not so much the seeds of learning how to overcome Modernism: that has been done quite adequately as we already know, and will better understand later on, by previous Holy Fathers. No, like all other Pontiffs, this one too is ahead of his time for the glory and consolation of us all. Pope John Paul is scattering the seeds of hope and exhilaration in the victory over evil: a Hope and Consolation so necessary for the Church of our own times, as She enters the darkest hour of Her existence on the road: the Royal Road to Her own Calvary. Let the 'church of darkness', the one-world church of communism and modernism, deck herself out as the champion for the 'theology of liberation', masquerading for the true Bride of the Lamb of God. The Catholic Church knows that She is about 'things eternal': about a Faith in, and a theology of, Liberation from sin and hell; and in that Faith and in that Light she will castigate the oppressors of the poor as much as the misguided people who claim that armed revolutions are the answer to the world's problems. And if no one is prepared to live by that Truth, or even show belief in it, then the Catholic Church is prepared to die for it. And that is the Mystery of the Church. That is Her Mystical Life in Christ, and that is the Mystery and Mystique in which Vatican II shared so liberally, to pass it on to all who understood this great Council in the Light of their own Catholic Faith.

And so, rather than look into modernism in the hope of finding some explanation for the behaviour of the Catholic Church; we will let ourselves be guided by the Mystique and the Truth of the Catholic Church, to discover in passing also the evil designs of Modernism. In the mind of the Church, teilhardism and modernism and communism are dead: Her past teaching destroyed them. And even if they try, in desperation, to form their own, break-away 'church of darkness', the Catholic Church is pre-occupied with the glorious time ahead to strengthen the faithful in Her own crucifixion. And so, if Her own past teaching is brought out faithfully now, the faithful will find ample reasons not to fall for the siren songs of the 'church of darkness'; but to stick with the Church already starting to glow, in Her own Good Friday, with the Eternal Light of Her delivery from the present evils.

Chapter One: The Nature of Catholic Faith (I)

St. Thomas Aquinas

It is the Will of God that the most priceless Gift of Catholic Faith is to be appreciated, is to be valued, cherished, nurtured and allowed to come to perfection by human acts which, in order to be human, have to be free. This process of providing a sound human mind as the prepared soil for a mature Catholic Faith is a human endeavour and both an Art and a Science. Under the direct influence of the Holy Spirit, this Art and this Science has always flourished in the Catholic Church; and its rules and principles have been studied and completely mastered by the great Scholars of Catholic Philosophy.

"Among the Scholastic Doctors, the chief and master of all towers Thomas Aquinas, because, as Cajetan observes, he so venerated the Ancient Doctors of the Church, that, in a certain way, he seems to have inherited the intellect of all. The doctrines of those illustrious men, like the scattered members of a body, Thomas collected together, enlarged them, put them in methodical order, and made such copious additions to them that he may be rightly and deservedly regarded as the glory and matchless defender of the Catholic Faith."

With these words, taken from his 1879 encyclical *Aeterni Patris*, 'On the Restoration of Catholic Philosophy', His Holiness Pope Leo XIII has set the tone and the pace for all future generations and for all the Holy Pontiffs after him, where exactly the foundations for the safeguarding of Catholic Faith have to be found, in order that a suitable citadel could be constructed. As we will see, we are not lacking in examples to see what dazzling heights future Pontiffs have elevated the teachings of the Church in this matter from the foundations laid down in this extraordinary encyclical from the one who was referred to by all as *'Lumen De Caelo'*: 'Light from Heaven'.

Where else, but in this foundation encyclical, do we read sentences like this one:

"… reason, borne, on the wings of Thomas to its human height, can scarcely rise higher, while Faith could scarcely expect more stronger aids from reason than those she has already obtained through Thomas."

And this one:

"His teachings are such, that those who hold to it are never found swerving from the path of truth, and those who dare assail it will always be suspected of error."

a testimony which Pope Leo XIII took over from Pope Innocent VI, and whose powerful reverberations still proclaim the same Truth for today's modernistic theologians and seminary professors.

With this encyclical the Holy Spirit taught the whole Church infallibly from what quarter to expect the onslaught on Catholic Faith: the subject-matter of this second Lecture. For in this Encyclical the Holy Father quotes the testimony of two opponents, Bucer and Theodore Beza:

"If the teaching of Thomas Aquinas were only taken away, they could easily battle with all Catholic teachers, gain the victory, and abolish the Church."

"a vain hope indeed", continues the Holy Father, "but no vain testimony".

Chapter One: The Nature of Catholic Faith (I)

To any intelligent person it must be obvious that, if there exists such a thing as 'the defence of the Catholic Faith', the most important thing on earth, such an enterprise must be built on the most solid foundations available. The Holy Fathers have not left us in any doubt, by their choice of words and the strong language they use, that they found the natural and supernatural bonding of this foundation in the Philosophy of St. Thomas Aquinas.

"the invincible bulwark of Faith,"

as Pope Leo XIII so succinctly put it in *Aeterni Patris*. The Papacy, built on the Rock of Peter, did not hesitate to extend the strength of that foundation to Thomism.

His successor, Pope St. Pius X, continued the same line of thought and the same sacred teaching in the same strong language in his own Moto Proprio of 1914 *Doctoris Angelici*:

"If Catholic Doctrine is once deprived of this strong bulwark, it is useless to seek the slightest assistance for its defence in a philosophy whose principles are either common to the errors of materialism, monism, pantheism, socialism and modernism, or certainly not opposed to such systems. The reason is that the capital theses in the Philosophy of St. Thomas are not to be placed in the category of opinions capable of being debated one way or the other; but are to be considered as the foundation upon which the whole science of natural and divine things is based. If such principles are once removed or in any way impaired, it must necessarily follow that students of the sacred sciences will ultimately fail to perceive so much as the meaning of the words in which the Dogmas of Divine Revelation are proposed by the Magisterium of the Church."

Are these words written for the 1970's and 1980's, or are they not? Do these words accurately describe the situation of 'theology' and the 'seminaries' of today, or not? Have we been forewarned from what quarter the final global assault on Catholic Faith was to come, or were we not? In my first article on the wholesale, shabby sell-out to Teilhardism, I referred to this sacred use of Thomistic science as Hallowed Thomism: the use of St. Thomas' teaching in the formulation of Dogmas. Tamper with Thomism, and you tamper with Dogma. Tamper with Dogma, and you destroy the Faith. No wonder the praises heaped upon the person, the mind and the teachings of the Angelic Doctor by the Supreme Magisterium of the Church ever since his death have been unanimous. No wonder the satanic assault on this sacred teaching has been as determined as it was desperate.

Now that we have been made aware of the general mode of attack on Catholic Faith, let us now further examine, in the Light of subsequent Papal teaching on these matters, how the Holy Fathers saw and analysed for us the details of the strategy, employed by the underworld of modernism, and how it could be possible that, given the attack on Thomism would be successful, the loss of Catholic Faith would become inevitable.

The Mystery Solved

In order to even begin to understand the enormity and complexity of the problem at hand, and to be guided in our efforts to come to grips with its solution, we can, once again, only listen to

Chapter One: The Nature of Catholic Faith (I)

the ones appointed by God, to teach us with authority in these matters.

In *Humani Generis*, Aug. 12, 1950, Pope Pius XII had this to say:

"the same Divine Truth, they tell us, may be expressed on the human side in two different ways, nay, in two ways which in a sense contradict one another, and yet really mean the same thing."

Here the Holy Father puts his finger unerringly on the fundamental bond between natural insight and supernatural knowledge: the fact that no true intelligence or knowledge can be contradictory. This is the first and great service the natural human mind can give to the safe-guarding of Faith and all Supernatural insights: to detect and root out any admission of a true contradiction. No wonder the Holy Father further on has to elaborate on the true use and function of human reason:

"And so, if reason is to perform this office adequately and without fear of error, it must be trained on the right principles. It must be steeped in that sound philosophy which we have long possessed as a heirloom, handed down to us by former ages of Christendom. These principles on which it is based have been made by the teaching Authority of the Church into the touch-stone of Divine Revelation."

Strong words: making a philosophical system the touch-stone of Divine Revelation. But before the Holy Father uses even stronger words about the all-embracing importance of Thomism, echoing as we have seen, the words and sentiments of all the Popes before him, he will give us first a clear indication why he considers the principles of Thomism about the relationship between 'the mind of man' and Revealed Truth of such overriding importance.

"The mind of man when it is engaged in a sincere search for truths, will never light on one which contradicts the truths already ascertained. The christian will weigh carefully the latest fantasy, making sure that he does not lose hold of the Truth already in his possession, or contaminate it in any way with great danger and perhaps great loss to the Faith itself."

If a system contradicts a Catholic Truth, even if not a revealed or dogmatic Truth, then the system is false and should be discarded. Proper thinking demands that, and here the Holy Father supports reason in its duty to safeguard the discipline of the mind.

The Holy Father is now well on the way, unravelling for us the perplexing problem of 'modern man'. If a man can be persuaded to abandon what the Holy Father so far has called 'the right principles of reason' and 'the sound philosophy', he will – for reasons still to be explained – run the greatest danger of losing his Catholic Faith altogether. Furthermore, the Holy Father also confirms for us what we were already told by his predecessors: that the assault of the Enemy has been directed 'on proper thinking'. Seminary professors were supposed to teach the future parish priests and curates *The Proper Discipline of the Mind*, and once 'steeped in that sound philosophy', these Pastors of souls would help preserve in the body of the faithful the sound principles of reason, which would guarantee a well-prepared receptacle for the reception of the Grace of Catholic Faith.

We are now ready to face the last and most fundamental question of them all, the burning question: 'what is the precise relation

Chapter One: The Nature of Catholic Faith (I)   55

between 'proper thinking' on the human level, and Catholic Faith on the supernatural level, so that, if an attack on the former is successful, there is the greatest danger for the loss of the latter? Which will lead us inevitably to ask another equally important question: What is this 'sound philosophy', this 'system of proper thinking', this 'Philosophy of St. Thomas', this 'Discipline of the Mind'?; so that we can recognise it and make it our own, in order that we may receive the immense benefits the teaching of the Holy Church has attached to its acquisition.

And once again, by the Grace of Almighty God, we do not have to look far for total enlightenment and satisfaction. After having quoted the profound words of the Holy Father, stating ' ... that sound philosophy ... made by the teaching authority of the Church into the touch-stone of Divine Revelation', I remarked that the Pope was going to use even stronger words about the all-embracing importance of Thomism. It is here the proper place and moment to quote these supremely important words, enshrining a most profound and consoling doctrine:

"In view of this it is not surprising that the Church will have Her future Priests brought up on a Philosophy which derives its methods, its system and its basic principles from the Angelic Doctor. (Can. 1366, 2.) One thing is clearly established by the long experience of the ages: his teaching appears to chime in, by a kind of pre-established harmony, with Divine Revelation. No surer way to safeguard the First Principles of the Faith."

For one carillon of pealing bells to be in perfect harmony with itself, is already a feast for the ears and an achievement of no mean merit. But here the Holy Catholic Church is not talking about a whole Philosophy, a complete system of Truths, being wholly consistent and in perfect harmony with itself; but of a System of Harmonious Truths being totally consistent and in complete harmony with a Divine System of Eternal Truths: a whole carillon of earthly bells, pealing and chiming in, by a pre-established harmony, with the heavenly carillon of Eternal Truths; Father, Son and Holy Spirit. This is an accolade of such formidable genius that it can only be given to *one* Philosophy, to one philosophical system, as the Crown and Glory of all attempts at human greatness: the Philosophy of St. Thomas Aquinas.

And now we know the whole truth. Now the Church has held nothing back. Now we know the evil nature of modernism, and we are able to see laid bare before our eyes the diabolical designs it has on us and our children. For now we know that its determination to unseat Thomism is not for the sake of Thomism itself; but to suppress, by its strident discords, the heavenly music of Eternal Truths. To deprive the Church, and all creation for that matter, of the one and only carillon with which the Heavenly one is in perfect harmony. And to replace it with 'doctrines' with which Revelation is no longer in accord. And in order to present some semblance of 'harmony' to the world with the cacophony of the 'new philosophy', Revelation itself will have to be changed so drastically, that it would silence forever the powerful Word of God which comes to us through the teachings of the Catholic Church He founded. And once effectively silenced, the receptacle for that Voice: the priceless gift of Supernatural, Infused, Divine and Catholic Faith would be rendered inoperative for the millions of catholics prepared to ac-

Chapter One: The Nature of Catholic Faith (I)

cept the strident discord as the final sound and the 'revelations from Hell' as the new 'carillon from heaven' in tune with it ...

This is really the absolute minimum that ordinary, faithful Catholics around the world should know about this all-important matter: the Church's precise teaching on sound Philosophy and proper thinking with which Catholic Faith in Revealed Truths is in perfect harmony. But even this minimum they are being denied, and so they remain ignorant of the clear reason and the powerful thrust of that teaching: not to abandon this sound philosophy nor their Catholic Faith in Her past and present teaching. For together these two make "that powerful, two-edged sword, separating the evil thoughts of the modernists from the thoughts of the Catholic Church". (Hebr. 4: 12-13.)

But it is of course possible to penetrate much more deeply into the nature of Thomism and from that gain a much more concise knowledge of the nature of its opponent: Modernism. And that is the purpose of the remaining 8 lectures in this series on the Foundations of Catholic Faith. Now that we better understand the overriding importance the Holy Catholic Church attaches to an intelligent knowledge of these things, both the nature of Thomism and its bitter opponent, Modernism, we must be close to the Church's Mind and Heart if in subsequent lectures we probe deeper into what is so dear to Her Motherly concern: the safeguarding and defense – and if necessary, the restoration – of Catholic Faith. The one reality on earth, which is the Foundation, the Root and the Beginning of all justification in Grace. For this it is necessary that the precise relationship between the Earthly Carillon and the Supernatural One is better understood, so that we will feel more confident to meet modernism head-on, strengthened and protected by the armament of God.

Chapter Three

The Nature of Catholic Philosophy (I)

Intellect in Search of Truth

Introduction

This whole series of 10 lectures is based on the Catholic Church's teaching. This means that it is not my intention to put before you my own private opinions about Catholic Faith and Thomism, but all that which the Catholic Church teaches us in those matters. This does not prevent us, in fact we are encouraged to do so, to collect and evaluate evidence that exists in support of Church teaching, and the skill needed to do this properly is left to our own individual resourcefulness and ingenuity, once we have taken to heart the basic teaching from the Church's Magisterium.

Consistent with this, my original intention, I have so far outlined what the Church teaches us about the nature of Catholic Faith and about its overriding and all-embracing importance. I have shown further that it is the consensus of the Holy Fathers that this Supernatural Gift is based on 'proper thinking' and that the Church recognises only one system of 'proper thinking' as 'chiming in with Revelation by a pre-established harmony': the Philosophy of St. Thomas Aquinas. Finally, I have made it my business to put before you, that for well over 100 years now, the Holy Fathers have warned us that the deadliest of all attacks on Catholic Faith by the enemy of human nature would come through a ferocious and sustained assault on its base: the destruction of Thomism.

It is obvious, that all this lends itself to further investigations and developments, leading us to some very interesting and needy discoveries. If we love the Church, and we would want to make Her defence of Catholic Faith our own, we would certainly like to know how the Catholic Church sees this intimate relationship between Faith and Thomistic Philosophy; and how the 'proper thinking' of the system of St. Thomas supports and defends Catholic Faith.

This, then, will be the subject-matter of this third Lecture. We will explore what the Church has to say to further our understanding on the acquisition of Truth, and what evidence we have to support Her teaching.

Once again, I want to emphasise that we go into these matters on the Church's insistence, and with Catholic Faith constantly before us as the final goal. We are not passing the time of day in pursuit of some abstract philosophical knowledge for its own sake. We have been told by the Popes that we are dealing with matters of life and death: life and death of Catholic Faith in countless innocent children. We are dealing with matters of which one Holy Father summed up the mind of them all:

"The capital theses in the Philosophy of St. Thomas are not to be placed in the category of opinions capable of being debated one way or the other, but are to be considered as the foundations upon which the whole science of natural and Divine things is based." (Pope St. Pius X, *Doctoris Angelici*, 1914.)

Catholic Faith is beleaguered and viciously under attack right here in Australia as everywhere else. In Catholic Schools, in semi-

Chapter Three: The Nature of Catholic Philosophy (I)

nars, in the seminaries and the churches; because Thomism has been placed, by the modernists, in the category of opinions capable of being debated right out of existence ... and what the Holy Pope foresaw would follow from this disaster, that which he wrote down immediately after his above-quoted words, that we now know did happen:

"If such principles are once removed or in any way impaired, it must necessarily follow that students of the sacred sciences will ultimately fail to perceive so much as the meaning of the words in which the Dogmas of Divine Revelation are proposed by the Magisterium of the Church."

These principles have been removed: they are no longer to be found in places where once they were readily available to us. And crooked thinking, on which no Supernatural Edifice of Faith, Hope and Love can be built to the Glory of God, has taken its place. Thomism has weapons which possess such deadly accuracy against heresies, that the modernists and teilhardians, in sheer self-defense, were forced to pursue a policy of total and universal disarmament. And through the long period of disuse, these deadly weapons have become unfamiliar, and Catholics have fallen silent in the face and the presence of the enemy.

And so it is with Catholic Faith uppermost in our minds, and for the sake of the life-and-death struggle it has with Satan, that we embark on this crash-course in human thinking in order to come to the aid of Faith.

May the Virgin Mother of God, our Glorious and Blessed Lady, the only one who was never deceived, help us to understand its enormous importance, and always keep us close to Her, so that we too may never more be deceived.

Section I: The Function of the Human Intellect

Broadly speaking, this first section will have two distinct topics for us to consider: a description of what actually the human mind does, followed by a more penetrating analysis of how the intellect works, and does what it does. On the first topic, the Church is very vocal and there is much rich material to be gathered from Her teaching. On the second topic, the Church Herself is mainly silent; but since she urges us to study St. Thomas for our enlightenment, this is one important area, where we will let ourselves be guided by him to the full truth. Only when we have a good understanding of these two topics, can we have a deep appreciation of the way the Creator of the human mind allowed the creature to be the humble but adequate recipient of the priceless possession of Catholic Faith. For only that Faith is the pivot of Salvation. Everybody's Salvation depends on it.

Topic I: A Description of the Mind's Activities

The mind is a faculty of a living soul. Just as a living body has organs to enable it to perform the various activities appropriate to its nature, so a living soul has faculties for the same purpose. The relationship between body and soul is complex, and does not immediately concern us here. For the time being it is sufficient to accept, that a spirit needs awareness, knowledge, understanding, and

Chapter Three: The Nature of Catholic Philosophy (I) 63

if it is a created spirit, that it stands in need of a faculty that allows this awareness, this acquisition of knowledge and understanding to be achieved. The human mind, or intellect, is the prime faculty. The organ through which the human spirit works its mind-activities is the human brain. [Since the human mind, as we will see in Topic II, is both active and passive, the human brain is not a one-way street, through which the brain controls the body; but a two-way street, by which the body also affects the mind. This, of course, is very important in the area of Faith.]

The Principle of Contradiction

"Contrary 'truths' cannot exist. (Pope John XIII in his first encyclical, *Ad Petri Cathedram*, 1959.)

In the quest for knowledge, understanding, awareness and truth, the human mind by its very nature has built into it by its Creator some principles which are there to prevent it from acting contrary to its nature. One such fundamental principle is the principle of contradiction; which holds that a truth and its contrary, its denial, cannot be both true in the same sense or meaning. If it is true that a thing exists, then it cannot be equally true that it does not exist, if 'existing' is taken with the same meaning, in the same sense.

Thus, if all the modernists (there is no exception) on the inspiration of Teilhard de Chardin and others, give equal 'truth-value' to the denial of a Dogma in their 'explanations' of the dogma, then this can only be brought about by forcing their evil wills over their intellects. The human intellect will not accept the violation of the principle of contradiction, and very soon the advocates of the 'philosophy of sameness': that the denial of a Catholic Truth is the same as being a believing Catholic, will let go of the Catholic Truth and will start to proclaim that the denial of a Catholic Truth and the acceptance of its contrary is 'The New Catholicism, the one we always should have had' ... the 'authentic christianity'. But contrary truths cannot exist anywhere: not in the Catholic Church, not in Christianity, not in Protestantism, in business, in universities: nowhere, never ...

Needless to say, this will be a very powerful aid the humble human mind can give to Supernatural Faith. The abandonment of this principle brings chaos to any thinking, and to undermine Catholic Faith, the principle of contradiction has been done away with, and the 'philosophy of sameness', the 'principle of identity' has taken its place, as I have outlined in many of my articles. Now we may start to understand the concern of so many Holy Fathers when they became aware that the attack on Catholic Faith would not be frontal, but was directed at the human mind and its true philosophy.

"The mind of man, when it is engaged in a sincere search for truths, will never light on one which contradicts the truths it has already ascertained. God is Truth itself; He it is who has created, and who directs the human intellect." (Pope Pius XII in *Humani Generis*, 1950.)

Same doctrine, same concern and the same remedy: Thomistic Philosophy.

Cause and Effect

Another innate power by which the human mind rises above the mere determination of matter to the likeness of the Divine Intellect, is the recognition of the intimate relationship between cause and effect. So powerful is this ability of the mind, that the Holy Fathers do not hesitate to proclaim it another fundamental aid that reason can give to Faith, basing themselves on the very teaching of St. Paul (Rom. 1: 19-21, 28.)

So, it is natural for the human mind to recognise the watchmaker when it comes across a watch. But the Law of Recognition of Cause and Effect goes beyond this primary function of linking an effect to its appropriate cause after the effect has been caused.

(i) The human mind is capable of foreseeing a certain effect as a result of some action causing it. This has given rise to the qualification of Homo Sapiens the Toolmaker. Tools are made and invented to bring forth the most appropriate cause for a desired effect. This we recognise as innate and natural to the human mind.

(ii) The human mind is capable of seeing evidence as evidence. Seeing beyond a fact to its natural link with a cause and even an intention. It is one thing to see in the Effect of flowers in a vase the Cause of human hands who put them there; it is quite another thing to see in these flowers the evidence of loving hands. This again will be a powerful aid the human mind can give to Faith. The absence of sound doctrine in the *Melbourne Guidelines,* and the accumulation of distortions, heresies, falsehoods and sophistry in them, become clear evidence of something that is going on in the minds of their compilers. The absence of serious discussions on catechetics in every Episcopal Conference in Australia in the Seventies, and the refusal to support Bishop Stewart in his manly efforts at sound catechetics, could be nothing more than just effects caused by some causes. But the human mind would not be what it is, if it did not see beyond these effects to evidence pointing to a way of thinking in the majority of Bishops in Australia …

Reasoning and the Principles of Logic

One of the most powerful thrusts of the human mind is the discovery of the Laws of its own reasoning. And it is to the glory of the *Philosophia Perennis*, the Everlasting Philosophy of St. Thomas Aquinas, that these Laws and Principles not only have been fully developed and preserved, but made use of. Logics alone would warrant a complete treatise on its own to show the passionate hatred for Thomism and the determination for its total and utter destruction as the 'invincible bulwark of the Faith' (*Aeterni Patris*). Logical Reasoning, that Royal Road to Truth and Certainty, simply had to be obliterated, discredited and by-passed by false road signs and guides, if the attack on Catholic Faith would pride itself with any hope of success. [More about this in Lecture 6.] The reasonings of the Modernists and Teilhardians are so infantile, puerile and sick, that they simply have to hide them beyond detection (so they fancy) under arrogance, contemptuous silence, coercion and above all: Existentialism, the most telling admission of their own bankruptcy. Many, many letters-in-reply we nowadays get from 'catholic instances', be they letters from bishops, secretaries or the vast, anonymous bureaucracy, carry prima facie evidence of the tortuous roads their authors are aimlessly walking, far removed from Thomism and the Love of Truth and Logic... Deep in the waterless wilderness of existentialism and socialism.

All agree that progress in thinking is mainly done by reasoning. The detection of valid conclusions from legitimate premises is called inference. Inference is the birth of the conclusion in reasoning, pregnant is the premises. True inference is the light of reasoning by which progress in thinking is effected. It all depends upon what one understands by 'progress' ... So great is the 'darkness over the earth' (an encyclical by Pope Pius XII), that it is now quite acceptable to force the human mind to believe as true even what is being deliberately proposed as false: so great is the arrogance displayed towards human beings by Satan and his emissaries. For just as the Communists have a Department of Supply to create scarcity, and a Department of Religious Affairs to suppress Religion, and the Humanist have Human Development courses to destroy development and procreation by enslavement to impurity; so the modernists and teilhardians have catechetical guidelines to destroy Catholicism and Catholic Faith. The *Melbourne Guidelines* so clearly, openly and unashamedly proclaim a non-catholic 'faith-course' as the best and most profitable 'model' on p. 7 of their *Overview*, advocating the doubting of Faith as a means to progress in faith, that only a complete imbecile can see this to be in the best interest of Catholic Children and catechists. What sort of 'reasoning' lies at the bottom of this sort of 'progress'? The complete anti-thesis of the magnificent faculty of reasoning the Creator of the Human Mind has so powerfully and liberally endowed His creature with.

With this we are coming close to the subject matter of Topic II: an investigation into how the human mind works. But before embarking on this enlightening phase in our endeavours to support and defend Catholic Faith, it is necessary to look at one more activity of the human mind, which (must we repeat it once again?) has been totally obscured, negated and even inversed by the enemies of Catholic Faith.

The Human Intellect Guides the Will

It is the true nature of existentialism to allow the isolated Existential Act to forcibly (i.e. with violence to everything human) replace the Thomistic Act preceded by a proper investigation into its Nature, its final Object and its Morality by the human intellect. The Existential Act not only excludes the human intellect and its proper functioning: it forces its will over the intellect, forcing the poor intellect to accept it as 'reasonable'. As said before: pages could be written on this sort of 'reasoning' in a treatise on true Logic.

In true Catholic Tradition, the faithful still ask their pastors, for the guidance of their will and actions:

> 'What is the Nature of modern catechetics?'
> 'Please, tell us the Truth about modern 'theology'?'
> 'What is the True interpretation of *Humanae Vitae*?'
> 'What is the Nature of Pentecostalism?'
> 'What is the Truth about ecumenism, and where can we find the True ecumenism, so we can direct our actions?'

Chapter Three: The Nature of Catholic Philosophy (I)

Are not all the answers (if we ever get answers!) something like this:

'Look, Act as human beings. Act as Christians. Your actions and the world have been sanctified by the Incarnation, so you thus trust in God and act in the modern world. Don't you see? The Holy Father receives communists and pentecostalists in audience. That's good enough for you and me. I follow his actions and join them in work and prayer. You follow my actions: go and do likewise. I will not tell you if pentecostalism and communism are good or bad, true or false. I just go along. They are people, aren't they? You have to be ecumenical these days. That is the will of the Church and the inspiration of the Holy Spirit. Only people who doubt the Holy Spirit doubt the modern ecumenism. I will not bore you with an analysis of whether the modern ecumenism is good or bad, true of false. Just run along. Don't ask for its nature, or if it is true.'

'Is the pill forbidden?' you ask me. 'I will not tell you. One doesn't ask those questions any longer. Are you doubting my actions in allowing the *Melbourne Guidelines*? Or the good and sincere intentions of all those hard-working catechists? I will tell you nothing about your objections to the *Melbourne Guidelines* or the new sex courses.

Trust my actions. They are now my teachings …'

Showing the abject capitulation to the modernistic, evolutionary 'philosophy' of the Existential Act, killing Thomism, and so the living substratum, the only one, on which the Supernatural Order of God can be built and maintained. The existential act. The truly 'irrational act', the act without the proper guidance of the human intellect; and so, eventually, without the proper guidance of Catholic Faith. The rudderless will, left roaming hither and tither as the winds of whim, imagination and passion direct it.

Topic II: A Short Investigation into how the Human Intellect Works

We are now standing before the door which leads to the quintessence of Thomism. It is through this door, that we may get a glimpse of the Mind of the Creator of the human mind. It is the door through which we will have to go, if we ever hope to understand what animated and inspired a Pope to write that Thomism 'chimes in with Revelation by a pre-established harmony'. For this door will reveal to us how the gift of God: believing in Revealed Truths, is at the same time a human act, supported by Divine Assistance. But it is also through this door, that humanity had a last glance at the truth of its own true existence. For, shortly after the Angelic Doctor, this door was slammed shut; and it is the Miracle of the Catholic Church's Divine Existence in Her human appearance, that she kept the vision of what lies behind this door alive, and before the conscience of us all. For after this door was closed once again, it was, that humanity's long slide into present-day barbarism began. And that the Catholic Church accepted Her Divinely appointed role of defending humanity against it.

The Human Soul

Since the mind is a faculty of the soul, it is necessary to understand what St. Thomas teaches us about the human soul. All visible

Chapter Three: The Nature of Catholic Philosophy (I)

things consist of matter and an outward, characteristic appearance or shape, called 'form'. The complex appearance form of a motor car differs from that of a house, or a tree. The soul is first and foremost that which gives form to the human being: the form of a body. ('Forma corporis'.) On reflection, already carried out in Antiquity, it was discovered that the soul of a human being differs from that of an animal. Since it is capable of rising above matter, performing immaterial acts and grasping immaterial things, the human soul is shown also to be immaterial, called spiritual. Unlike some other Scholastics, St. Thomas did not believe that the spirituality of the human soul is a Revealed Truth, only to be accepted in Faith. He knew it and proved it to be a truth which the human being can ascertan by its own created powers, even if it is a difficult thing to understand, how the form of a material thing, the body, can also have a spiritual existence independent of the body, whilst depending on the body for its existence. God creates a soul, when the material conditions of conception have been fulfilled. The parents, although not producing the soul of their offspring, nevertheless provide God with the substratum which determines the 'type' of soul so to speak.

The normal way of a pure spirit to know is by intuition. The human soul, being a spirit, has intuition; but because the soul is foremost the form of a body, this intuition is implicit, and cannot manifest itself explicitly. This means that the human spirit has its very own way of knowing: it must go outside itself, through the body and its senses, in order to be able to return to itself in reflection. Its intuition comes into this, but it is 'blocked' by matter, not completely, [like an animal which cannot know its own existence, lacking reflection] but only capable of dissociating itself from sense-perception, or withdrawing or abstracting itself from sense-perception only after sense-perception has taken place. With this complex process of knowing, we have landed at the faculty by which the human being performs his actions of knowing, understanding and learning.

The Human Mind, or Intellect

How can we give adequate glory to God for inventing the human mind; capable of knowing Him, giving Him glory, and by which we enter into the likeness of the Creator. To what dazzling heights of understanding is it capable! To what depths of absurdity can it sink, and is sinking today ... Let us probe a little into its mystery: into the mystery of how it knows, and learns and understands and gets hold of the Truth. In itself an exercise that should lead us to profound adoration and thanksgiving; but carried out here for the benefit of greater good: in obedience to Papal directives for the support and the defence of Catholic Faith.

When the human soul is created, its faculty of knowing like a spirit is there: the intuition, but inoperative, since, for its operation, it needs to be 'triggered' by sense-perceptions. This means that the human being, in coming into this world, enters life with a mind which at the same time is active (as a faculty of a human spirit) and passive (as the form of a body, waiting for stimuli produced by the senses). This means at once several things.

(i) The human mind cannot operate without 'Images'. We mean this to be stimuli produced by any of the 5 senses, but the

Chapter Three: The Nature of Catholic Philosophy (I)

name is borrowed from the most powerful stimulus: that of the sense of seeing. Once the brain has received the corporal image (or stimulus), the mind of man can now start to operate, and from the corporal image (which is unique and singular: 'I see this dog, that house, etc.') the mind abstracts a mental image: the universal 'house', or the universal 'dog', by which it recognises that what is being seen, is a house or a dog. The universal, mental image lives in the active mind, so that, when a house or a dog is seen, or otherwise perceived, it is immediately recognised as a particular case of this universal image. Imagine the chaos in the human mind, if this was not so. If every single object was not recognised by its universal characteristics. It would be totally new to the poor brain which would have to go to the trouble of 'getting to know' every motor car if it came across one, if it did not recognise it as a motor car.

I think it is safe to say that Thomism is unique in maintaining that Universals actually exist in the human mind. Other philosophers would admit to universals, but would not attribute to them existence.

This question is of the utmost importance, and, as already stated, with it we have landed on the corner-stone of Thomism and on the corner-stone of the Church's teaching of the overriding importance of Thomism. Unlike Plato, St. Thomas does not teach that the mental images have an existence outside of the mind. Unlike Plato, therefore, St. Thomas does not teach that the Idea or Ideal of 'house' or 'dog' exists somewhere in heaven; in which Idea (or Ideal) all houses and dogs share in an imperfect way. But according to St. Thomas, the mental images DO live. They live in the Intellectus agens, in the active mind, and through associations and combinations, progress in thinking can be made; even if external stimuli are at a minimum (here on earth never non-existent). How important the maintaining of Existing Universals is, we will take up a bit further on. But first:

(ii) This whole complicated process of acquiring knowledge is, in human beings, not a One-Way street; but a Two-Way affair. If the human baby comes into this world not possessing preconceived, innate ideas and images, but depends on its environment for the formation of them, then learning (and consequently teaching) becomes an exceedingly important matter. For, not only is the human mind affected by the stimuli it receives, but, reversely, the mind gives orders to the will for the guidance of actions according to the knowledge it has acquired. And here we can see a glimpse of the explanation of how it is possible, that the One seed of Supernatural Faith, produced by the One Baptism instituted by Christ, can produce, and grow into, either a perfect Catholic Faith as meant by the Redeemer, or into a defective Protestant faith, very much in need of a Catholic Faith for its perfection and viability. The fault lies not with Baptism, but with concept formation.

(iii) In the acquisition and formation of millions of concepts, or mental images, the human mind will come across some, which exceed all the others in importance. The human mind is capable of reflecting on its own existence, but in doing so it discovers concepts which defy limitation. They seem to point beyond human existence, even necessitating an existence upon which the very existence of the human being depends. They are beyond effect, beyond change, beyond time, beyond error, beyond imperfections and evil. Yes, the human mind **acknowledges them as Absolutes.**

Chapter Three: The Nature of Catholic Philosophy (I)

This is the quintessence of Thomism. It is here that God, and the Human mind, and St. Thomas, and the Church and us and Catholic Faith meet and come together. And now, at last, we can fully understand why the door on Thomism had to be slammed shut. For, if existence must be given to Universals inside the human mind, then existence must be given to Absolutes outside the human mind. For absolutes are concepts, alive in the human mind first as Universals. If they live there, and point by necessity to a transcending existence, then transcending existence must be given to them. Concepts such as First Cause, Motor Immobilis, Total Perfection, Absolute Truth, Eternal Being: God, are concepts in the human mind. If they are Real, and alive and existing in the human mind, existence beyond the senses is assured, and absolute existence becomes perfectly logical. But if these concepts are denied existence as Universals in the human mind, existence beyond the senses becomes problematic and not only the idea of God, but also God itself can only be given the assurance of a supposition or hypothesis. We can then at most postulate the existence of God, or absolute truth as a function of the human mind. And man remains the measure of all things ...

And with that, the collapse of Catholic Faith is assured. No Supernatural, Infused, Divine Catholic Faith can be given to, and built on a substratum which denies the existence of Absolutes. Therefore, the corner-stone of Thomism is and remains the question of the real existence of Universals in the human mind; and through the consistent and unanimous recommendation of Thomism by the highest teaching authority on earth: the Magisterium of the Catholic Church, the truth of the corner-stone of Thomism is certain and beyond doubt. Universals do have a real existence in the human mind, but not beyond; and Absolutes not only acquire existence within the human mind as Universals, but also have an existence outside the human mind in God. In Lecture 6 we will further develop how the corruption of human thinking after St. Thomas began with the denial of universals by William of Occam.

Truth and the Progress in Knowledge

Before we depart from this rich field, the study of how the human mind works, it is necessary to see how the mind comes in contact with the Truth, and how true progress in knowledge is made. We have already seen that, because of the fact that the human soul is primarily 'forma corporis', the 'form' or life-giving principle of the body, the soul is forced to go 'outside itself' so to speak, and first acquire sense-perceptions before it can return to itself, and from these sense-perceptions gather the necessary information for further mental activities. Since, unlike an animal, the human soul is aware of this process, and is aware that she is aware, and through the out-going process discovers itself on reflection: the discovery of 'I', Ego phenomenale and Ego noumenale, the soul is proven to be spiritual as well as the form of a material body. A first Approximation of Truth is made, when it is discovered that the human mind is in agreement, in conformity, with the object outside the mind; in other words that through proper sense-perceptions, proper mental images of the object have been formed. If, according to St. Thomas, my knowledge of a thing matches the thing itself, then I call the relation Truth, and my knowledge of it truthful.

Chapter Three: The Nature of Catholic Philosophy (I)

But, to the same St. Thomas, this is not enough. It will help as a first approximation, but even primarily, Truth, according to St. Thomas, lies somewhere else. Truth lies primarily in the judgement the human mind makes about its mental image. I may have a true perception of Peter as white, but truth is primarily found in the judgement: Peter is white. A linking of the mental image of Peter with the mental image of 'white' through the copula 'is'. If this totally mental activity, the linking of a Subject with a Predicate by means of the copula 'is', is true, the knowledge I have of Peter is true knowledge.

The word 'judge', 'judgement' has frightened many people off, because of Christ's demand: 'Judge not ...'. This is unfortunate [and believe you me, the modernists are making millions out of this confusion, or double meaning], because the same Christ is the Creator of the human mind, and the human mind simply cannot operate without making judgements: thousands and perhaps even millions of times a day. We are incessantly linking subjects and predicates all day long, even involuntarily. 'This is my car.' 'I must go shopping'. 'Put the key in the ignition.' 'Turn the key.' 'Turn left.' 'Slow down.' 'The road is clear.' 'I can just pass him.' ... etc. By the will of Christ, these judgements must also extend to cover people. 'Be circumspect like a snake ...'. 'Beware of false prophets ...'. 'By their fruits you will know them.' We must judge people's sayings, teachings, actions. St. Paul sums it up quite succinctly and quite bluntly when he commanded: 'Judge Everything, hold on to what is good.' (*Omnia probate, quod bonum est tenete.*) (1 Thess. 5: 21.) And he means what he says: 'Of those who are inside, you can surely be judges'. (1 Cor. 5: 12.) 'It follows that we can judge matters of everyday life.' (1 Cor. 6: 3.) He even tells his Churches to judge him: 'Judge for yourselves what I am saying.' (1 Cor. 10: 16.) We must even judge the spirits: 'If the world is to be judged by you, how can you be unfit to judge trifling cases? Since we are also to judge angels, it follows that we can judge matters of everyday life.' (1 Cor. 6: 2-3.) And: 'It is not every spirit, my dear people, that you can trust; test them to see if they come from God'. (1 John, 4: 1.) Finally, the Discernment of the Spirits is a Gift from the Holy Ghost. (1 Cor. 12: 10.)

Discernment is done by judging, by judgement, by testing. 'Judge everything!' Judge the 'Imprimatur' attached to the *Melbourne Guidelines*. Judge the spirit that motivates anonymous compilers to produce guidelines which guide teachers to teach children to doubt their Catholic Faith; to believe that Christ is present in the bread. Judge the actions of a Cardinal to allow the spread of such guidelines in his own archdiocese. Test, probe, find out, collect evidence. And if they are bad, **call them bad, as Christ taught us to do**. Only refrain from doing one thing: to pass judgement on others. Do not sit in judgement over the Cardinal, the Archbishop, the Compilers. Leave their motives, their inner intentions and their final worth to God; and to the Church which alone has powers of excommunication. But to confuse the judgement of the actions of people with sitting in judgement over them is manifestly false, and produces the type of paralysis and inactivity the modernists need so badly to consolidate their bridge-head within the confines of the City of God. Proclaiming the Truth, **which by Divine Injunction we must**, carries with it the condemnation of the falsehoods of others, but not necessarily the condemnation of

Chapter Three: The Nature of Catholic Philosophy (I)

others; and in that way, we show great charity for sinners, if we show up in our defence of the Catholic Church, and of the Catholic Faith, the evil which necessitates this defence.

And with this, we have arrived at the final Section of this lecture.

Section II: The Human Intellect and Thomism in Support and Defense of Catholic Faith

Here we can be brief, as we have only to gather together what went before, supported by quotations from Papal Teaching. The guiding principle here is that, what is brought against the Catholic Church and against Catholic Teaching, does not have to be contested and refuted in the Supernatural Light of Catholic Faith, since it was not conceived in that Light, nor produced by it. Heresy and error are on the human level alone, since heresy and error cannot be produced in God's Light. Denying, e.g., the Divinity of Christ, or the Dogma of Papal Infallibility, is not only a 'Sin against the Light': it is also, as we will hear the Popes declare, an Irrational Act. The same as believing in the Divinity of Christ is not only a Supernatural Act of Catholic Faith, but also a perfectly Rational Act. The human intellect cannot produce the Light of Faith, but once endowed with it, it can make good use of it to strengthen its own natural light and insights. (The Discipline of the Mind, as we will fully investigate in the final lecture.)

1. The Human Mind detects contradictions in the sayings and the writings of the detractors of Catholic Faith. If that is so,

then these sayings and writings could never be proposed to be believed by Supernatural Faith.

2. The Human Mind detects faulty reasoning, spurious argumentation, defective logic and fallacies in the utterances of the Modernists. Conclusions drawn from this type of sophistry could never be seriously considered to be substitute material to be believed with Catholic Faith.

3. Since the essence of Modernism, as we saw, is the destruction of Thomism with the ultimate goal the destruction of Catholic Faith as a prerequisite for entry into the man-made 'church of darkness', the Human Mind will detect the absence of Thomistic Philosophy in the writings and reasoning of the modernists, and unearth the 'philosophy of error' as the foundation of Modernism. Chief hallmark of this error is the denial of Absolute Truth because of the acceptance of 'relativism' as a foundation principle.

4. Finally, the Human Mind can pave the way towards Faith by gathering evidence conducive to the reception of the Grace of Catholic Faith. The mind is capable of advancing arguments in favour of Faith and of the position of the Catholic Church. (Arguments from history and Tradition.) All of this is reflected in the writings of the Holy Pontiffs in support and defence of Thomistic Philosophy.

To avoid unnecessary repetition, the readers of these notes will recognise some of the texts already quoted earlier as applying equally in this Section, which relieves me of quoting them again. Here then are a few more telling quotations taken from Papal doc-

Chapter Three: The Nature of Catholic Philosophy (I)

uments mentioned earlier. I leave it to the intelligence of the recipients of these notes to decide if they are in support of any of the 4 paragraphs numbered immediately above.

"Therefore Divine Providence itself requires that in calling back the peoples to the paths of Faith and Salvation, advantage should be taken of human science also, an approved and wise practice which, history testifies, was observed by the most illustrious Fathers of the Church. They indeed were wont neither to belittle nor under value the part that reason had to play, as is summed up by the great Augustine, when he attributes to this science 'that by which the most wholesome Faith is begotten, ... is nourished, defended and made strong'.

In the first place, philosophy, if rightly made use of by the wise, tends to smooth and fortify the road to true faith ... In the first place, then, this great and noble fruit is gathered from human reason, that it demonstrates that God is ... It shows God to excel ... In like manner reason declares that the doctrine of the Gospel has even from its very beginning been made manifest by certain wonderful signs, the established proofs of unshaken truth; and that all, therefore, who set Faith in the Gospel do not believe rashly, but by a most reasonable consent subject their intelligence and judgement to an Authority which is Divine. And of no less importance is it that reason most clearly sets forth that the Church instituted by Christ ... is in itself a great and perpetual motive for belief.

Lastly, the duty of religiously defending the Truths Divinely delivered, and of resisting those who dare oppose them, pertains to philosophic pursuits. Wherefore it is the Glory of Philosophy to be esteemed as the bulwark of Faith and the strong defence of religion. As Clement of Alexandria testifies: the doctrine of the Saviour is indeed perfect in itself and wants naught, since it is the power and wisdom of God. And the assistance of Greek philosophy makes not the Truth more powerful. But in as much as it weakens the contrary arguments of the sophists and repels the veiled attacks against the Truth, it has fitly been called the hedge and fence of the vine ... So the defenders of sacred science draw many arguments from the store of philosophy which may serve to uphold Revealed Dogmas ... Moreover, the Church Herself not only urges, but commands, Christian teachers to seek help from Philosophy. For the 5th Council of the Lateran, after it had decided that 'every assertion contrary to the Truth of Revealed Faith is altogether false ...' advises teachers of Philosophy to pay close attention to fallacious arguments, since as Augustine testifies 'if reason is turned against the Authority of Sacred Scripture, no matter how specious it may seem, it errs in the likeness of truth, for true it cannot be' ... But since it is established ... that those things which war against Faith war equally against right reason, the catholic philosopher will know that he violates at once Faith and the laws of reason, if he accepts any conclusion which he understands to be opposed to revealed Doctrine.

Moreover, the angelic doctor pushed his philosophic conclusions into the reasons and principles of things in a manner so comprehensive, that they contain in their bosom so to say the seeds of almost infinite truths, to be unfolded in good time by later masters and with a goodly yield. And as he also used this philosophic method in the refutation of error, he won this title of distinction for himself: that he single-handed combated victoriously the errors

Chapter Three: The Nature of Catholic Philosophy (I)

of former times and supplied invincible arms to put to rout those which might in after times spring up ... so much so that reason borne on the wings of Thomas to its human height, can scarcely rise higher, while Faith could scarcely expect more stronger aids from reason than those which she has already obtained through Thomas ... Those who hold to it are never found swerving from the path of Truth, and he who dare assail it will always be suspected of error."

These quotes give a powerful resume of the 1879 Encyclical of Pope Leo XIII, *Aeterni Patris*, and may give the reader some idea, why this magnificent Pontiff considered this encyclical the most important one of all the 80 or so he wrote, amongst them 13 on the Holy Rosary, in a Pontificate of 25 years. This extract clearly sets forth that, what I have endeavoured to explain in these lectures, is drawn from official Catholic teaching, and is supported by that teaching. Human Reason does not give Faith, but can and must defend and keep intact the receptacle into which this Holy Gift is to be received and nurtured. Similar quotes can be gathered from the other Papal documents mentioned in the beginning of these lectures. Some I have already quoted, notably in the second lecture.

Chapter Four

The Nature of Catholic Philosophy (II)

The Will in Search for Good

Introduction

"It not those who say to Me 'Lord, Lord', who will enter into the Kingdom of Heaven, but the person who does the Will of My Father in Heaven." (*Mt. 7: 21.*)

With these words, Our Lord acknowledges the existence of Faith and knowledge in man as primary functions; but, as the Creator of the Human Being, and not only of the Human Intellect, He clearly establishes without argument that the primary function of believing is not the same as obtaining one's final end: entering into the Kingdom of Heaven.

We are here on earth to Do! To Do God's Will. Our understanding and our Faith are given to us, not for their own pursuit and excellence, but as a guide for our actions; that is, for the direction of our will.

There is only one Philosophy, which does full justice to the intellectual order in conformity with the requirements of Catholic Faith. We must now extend this same Philosophy to the study of human acts and the will, i.e., to do justice to the moral order, again, to the complete satisfaction of Catholic Faith. Since all the Holy Fathers know that people have to go to Heaven, their enthusiasm for Thomism can hardly be explained only, because Thomism is such a brilliant light for the intellect; but more importantly, because it is such a brilliant light for the dragging footsteps of the human race on its road to its ultimate goal: the vision and possession of God. This not only provides us with a reason for further study and investigations into the minds of the Popes recommending Thomism so earnestly to us: it provides us with a motive and stimulus to go on. If, without Thomism, the human mind is working at below-level capacity, then what will become of the will, if the light for its direction is so dim? If a strong Faith is necessary for a strong moral life, then the extension of Thomism to the moral teaching of the Church follows from its earlier study as a foundation of Faith.

The Human Will

Since Thomism proves the human soul to be a created spirit, it follows that it will develop a metaphysics which allows for the fullest realisation of the soul's potentialities. If the human mind is the faculty for coming in contact with the Truth, the human will is the faculty that strives after its own proper object: Good. But mind and will operate differently. The proper object of the mind is the Nature of a particular object, presented to it by one of the five senses in sense-perception. This nature is – as we saw – abstracted by the mind from the particular, and known as universal. The will, on the other hand, realises its specific object, good, in individual acts. The will is the faculty by which human acts are performed. In saying that the will has a reason for dictating a particular action or series of actions is tantamount to saying that the will has a goal, an intermediate good, understood by the mind. From this it is not difficult to see, or even conclude by reasoning, that ultimately, the will is after a final good, or ultimate end. Conscious, intermediate steps being taken towards a broader, but still intermediate goal, is a well-known human phenomenon.

And so, the starting point of St. Thomas in the philosophy of the will is the concept that in every human act the will is directed to an end, apprehended by the intellect. Each end must be a good for man, and so the ultimate or final end must be the ultimate good for man: it must be his perfection. It must be an object that completely satisfies his will and all his desires. And the possession of this object must perfect man in the highest and most complete way. For, if not, the will of man will continue to strive for this ultimate until it rests in its possession.

[Needless to say, all this presupposes (a) that such an object exists, and (b) that the fulfilment is possible.]

All this goes to show that Thomism, as far as the will is concerned, is distinctly Goal Orientated. This is called Teleology, which contains the Greek word for 'goal' or 'end'.

The Ultimate Object of the Human Will

As we already know, man is not born into this world with innate concepts or explicit intuition. So, he has not got an innate concept or intuition of his final end in the concrete situations of his everyday actions. So there must be some means, satisfactory to unbiased persons, to come to grips with a growing awareness of the human situation and its solution. Every human being strives for the 'actualisation' or 'realisation' of its own potentialities. If the objection is raised that no two people agree on what constitutes for individuals 'their own potentialities', then Thomism will answer that, in the concrete situations of daily living this could well be the case; but nevertheless, it will continue, there is such a thing as Human Nature, and all 'natures' strive after their own good by the will of the Creator. That means that it is quite legitimate to consider what is the ultimate good of Human Nature, and then to see the striving after This Good underlying all human actions.

'Since we bear the stamp of our origin.'

Although man lacks an innate concept of his ultimate end or goal, he nevertheless has an innate tendency to perfection; but not an innate knowledge of what constitutes this perfection. He will strive after the fullest development of his potentialities as a rational being. All the goals attainable in this life lack something of the complete satisfaction and the highest completeness possible, and so no human goal in this life qualifies for the final end of man. Not even great sanctity. The true goal of human happiness and fulfilment, even philosophically speaking, i.e., without the Light of Faith, lies beyond the grave in the Beatitudo: the vision of God and the happiness that brings with it. True Thomism maintains that God as such is not the ultimate goal of man, because God is external to man's actions and outside the faculty producing the actions. It is the *possession of God* which constitutes the lasting happiness of man, as the fullest realisation of all his potentialities.

From this it is already obvious that such a philosophy shows a great affinity with the tenets of Catholic Faith about the supernatural destiny of man.

Chapter Four: The Nature of Catholic Philosophy (II)

The Moral Order

St. Thomas has a great number of predecessors and followers all declaring with him that 'moral' is the attribute of every human act in relation to its Final End. A human act is Morally Good if it is directed towards the realisation of the final end of man; and is morally bad, if it prevents man from reaching his supernatural destiny. From this it follows immediately that every human act is either morally good or morally bad.

There are many acts which either remain totally unseen within man, without any external manifestation (as his plan to steal some money which got thwarted) or else are so seemingly aimlessly done that they only appear on the outside – seemingly lacking any interior motivation or drive, like getting up for a stroll in the garden. Both categories of acts become morally good or evil because of Intentions.

In the study of Intentions we discover a first way of interplay between intellect and will. Intentions are formed in the mind for the sake of the will. But here one makes a very interesting discovery: not every good intention makes a human act morally good. 'Intentions do not justify the means.' But, on the other hand, a bad intention always vitiates the whole act and renders it morally bad. For a human act to be morally bad, the absence of one single requisite factor is sufficient. But for a human act to be good without qualification, the presence of one single requisite factor – like a good intention – is not sufficient.

If this means anything, it means that there are factors outside human control which have a say in the morality of a human act. If the human contribution: the intention, does not necessarily make any human act a good human act, then it is obvious that there exists something outside the human situation, exercising a definite authority within the human situation – to such an extent that it can even override good intentions. An authority that can declare a moral act a morally bad act in spite of good intentions of the will.

Such an authority has all the qualifications of a Law: the Moral Law.

Origin and Nature of the Moral Order

So far we have considered an outline of St. Thomas' idea of man as drawn by an innate impulse of the will towards the good. Mention was made of 'right reason': reason considered as giving direction to man's acts for the attainment of the true objective good, or final end. This seems to be an ideal set-up: the will drawn towards good, the mind of man deciding what is a true goal to be pursued, and the will giving the man the strength to perform the act. But this is not all there is to it. Not only do we not live in the ideal state, but even if we did, there is more to it than a closed-circuit, self-contained system which starts with 'man' and finishes with 'man'. We seem to know, many would call it 'feel', that even if good intentions were involved, some acts are forbidden, as if we live under some Law. A law coming from outside us, but involving us all, supposedly, as the law claims, for our protection on the road to our final end. And for most people morality has a lot more to do with Do's and Don'ts, than with abstract talk of our ultimate goal or final end.

Chapter Four: The Nature of Catholic Philosophy (II)

But St. Thomas is right: he has studied man's nature accurately, and Catholic Faith supports him and depends on his findings. The moral law is not the prime objective of man's nature and striving to perfection. The Moral Law is part of man's nature, hence the name Natural Law; not as its prime objective, but as its safeguard. In the broad context of the Natural Law, man has to find his perfection; the perfection of his nature: right intellect, properly ordered will and passions and motives and intentions. A life of true love for God, his final end, and his neighbours; and a proper use of creation to help him find his true fulfilment. In such a set-up purity is not pursued, because impurity is forbidden. 'The new creation in Christ' about which St. Paul writes so eloquently and invitingly, lives above the law.

Nevertheless, the law, and its obligations, are there, but; as with all laws, in the background. And it would be a great help if they could stay in the background, and people knew a lot more about the true order St. Thomas teaches us for their own benefit with regard to proper use of intellect and will, as well as for their own Catholic Faith, which depends on the Thomistic vision if only to enlarge it into a truly supernatural life in God already here on earth.

So, once again, we are not dealing here with an abstract system of thought; but with something so alive and warm and vibrating that its great good for humanity can only come forth because it chimes in with eternity. And it is precisely there, in Eternity, that St. Thomas discovers the origin of the Natural Law: the Eternal Law of God. Divine Law.

Natural Law Explained

The positive part of God is, that he lives according to His Nature: God is His Nature. His Nature is to be God. When God creates, He leaves an imprint of Himself in every creature: to exist, and even live, according to its nature. That is the positive part St. Thomas discovered in the moral order, as we saw. Man must live according to his rational and spiritual nature.

The negative part of God is that which must be denied of God. He is the Sinless One: no sin, no imperfections, no evil. And this imprint of Himself, this aspect of the Divine Law, is implanted in human nature as the part of the Natural Law that says: Forbidden. Do Not Transgress. Since that is not the object in the Divine Being: not to do wrong, it is not the object in the nature he gave the human being either; but this aspect of the Eternal Law is there. And for the majority of people, it seems, that this part of human nature and of the natural law, seems to be the only part they know and understand. No wonder the Holy Fathers wanted Thomism studied and understood, so that its hidden treasures, not only in the intellectual order, but maybe even more so in the moral order would be better understood for the immense benefit on earthly living. Because the Natural Law, positive and negative aspects, are the human participation in the Eternal Law, the Divine Law. And once again: the Concept of the Natural Law is a Universal, but its existence transcends the human situation, which makes it an Absolute. Ultimately, the Natural Law is a radiation from the Eternal Law in God.

Chapter Four: The Nature of Catholic Philosophy (II)

To sum up: God wants us to look for our human perfection within our human nature; which perfection ultimately is the possession of Himself. He wants us to do that as a positive good, which radiates out of the positive part of His Own Divine Law. But He also wants us to seek this perfection within the ambit of the negative aspects of the Natural law: not to commit the acts which are forbidden; which never lead to our true happiness and eternal salvation. Since this order of things, this moral order, chimes in with what He revealed of Himself in Jesus Christ, it is the foundation of the order seen in the Supernatural Light of Catholic Faith; and advocated and perfected by it. It is the great treasure the Popes wanted us to enjoy again in all its fullness.

The Content of the Natural Law

Man does not receive the Natural Law as an imposition from above. The positive aspects blend with his own nature, the negative aspects protect him against doing damage to his nature. Since reason is the primary faculty in man, on which will and actions depend, it is Thomistic philosophy that man with his intellect, can recognise and abstract the Natural Law from his very nature and promulgate it to himself, since it is natural for man to live according to his nature. This, as we saw, he shares with his Creator.

The primary aspect of every law, according to St. Thomas, is, that good must be done and pursued and evil avoided. Since every human being would like to know what 'good' and 'evil' mean in the concrete situations of their everyday living, it is the genius of St. Thomas to give Content to the general notions of 'moral good' and 'moral evil' by examining the fundamental natural tendencies and inclinations of man. The order of the precepts of the law of nature follows the order of natural inclinations. From this principle St. Thomas enunciates the various By-Laws contained in the General Law of Nature.

1. The Law of Conservation of his nature: conservation of life, avoidance of death.
2. The inclination to propagate the shared aspects of his nature: the law of the conservation of the species.
3. The inclination of man towards his good as a rational being: the inclination to the possession of the Truth and of the knowledge of God, and of the society in which he lives.

Reason, reflecting on these inclinations and their consequent formulation into Natural Law, promulgates the precept (1) that life must be preserved; (2) that the species must be preserved and children begotten and educated; and (3) that man should seek the truth and avoid ignorance, especially about those things which are necessary for the right ordering of his life, and that he should live in society, accepting the consequent restrictions and limitations (positive law) necessary for the good of the community.

It is obvious that in this way the rational and natural foundation of every precept of the Ten Commandments can be detailed.

To Catholics who value their Catholic faith, knowing that the salvation of everybody depends on the preservation of that Faith in all its integrity, the foregoing should be ample to see why the Holy Fathers put such a great store on the revitalisation of Thomistic thought. With him we are not in airy-fairy land, but come to grips with the fundamentals of man's existence here on earth.

Alas, there are only too many who will find St. Thomas' approach excessive, rationalistic, or even unreal. Objections have been raised against an immutable, unalterable moral law, when we see empirically that relativism is held high and the existence of absolutes denied.

One of the main factors in human moral activity is the question of passions and emotions. The whole moral life is bound up with the will's movement towards good, and particular emotions can greatly help or hinder moral choice. In this area of 'help' the good habits, called virtues, play a significant part. According to St. Thomas, it is not possible to have the moral virtues without the intellectual virtue of Prudence, or to have prudence without the moral virtues. An investigation of the high place allotted to Prudence and of its role in the moral life of man and the immediate consequence: the impossibility of dissociating the moral virtues from the intellectual ones would make rich material to investigate. Such an investigation into the central question of Prudence could quite well prepare one for the next lecture on the unity between Intellect and Will.

Chapter Five

The Nature of Catholic Philosophy (III)

The Human Unity Between Intellect and Will

Introduction

By now we should be fully convinced, first of all of the fact that the Holy Fathers have gone out of their way to extol Thomism and recommend it to us; and secondly, that they appeared to have had good reasons to do so. But down-to-earth Holy Fathers, who know what the flock of Christ consists of: that it is made up of ordinary, hard-working people who need things of importance spelled out to them, are also fully aware that, unless the Practicality of Thomism is brought home, they have wasted their time recommending its study and understanding to us. This vital adaptability of Thomism to every day life must be clearly brought out, and must measure up to the glowing attributes the Holy Fathers have attached to it to encourage the spread of it. In other words: if Thomism in the Mind of the Church (which has the Mind of Christ) is of overriding importance, it must be of overriding practical importance. It must lend itself to being expressed in terms that everybody can understand.

So far we have seen that Thomism lies close to our human thinking, and has such a lot to do with clear thinking, proper action and the guidance of our will: all necessary for a sound foundation of our Catholic Faith, that at least we are willing to concede to all these Holy Fathers our conviction that it must be possible to discover the practicality of Thomism, and to express it in terms we can understand. And furthermore, we are prepared to concede that we will do all we can to follow their strong lead in whatever still needs to be elucidated in order to make us happy with Thomism as they apparently want us to be.

In this lecture I hope to go a long way to showing that our trust in the Holy Fathers is not misplaced, that it is not hard to show the practicality of Thomism for our everyday life and that we are not wasting our time listening to the Popes as, what they have to tell us, is of great practical value. It is one more example that God's Truth, which cannot be exhausted in all eternity, nevertheless can be made crystal clear to children on a very down-to-earth, practical level. For children have the Holy Spirit to help them understand. It is with confidence in Him that we continue our story.

An Excursion into Ontology: The Study of the Philosophy of Being

We already know that the creature receives from the Creator the Stamp of its origin. In practice, this mark is mainly manifested in the Law, the Natural Law by which every creature participates in the Divine Law: To Act according to its Nature. All creatures at least share with God 'existence'; each exists according to its given nature.

On the Divine level of existence, the Divine Law is identical with God's existence, and manifests itself in this, that God by necessity is His own existence. God's Nature is: to exist. The Divine

Chapter Five: The Nature of Catholic Philosophy (III)

Essence is to be His own free and uncreated, eternal and necessary existence. God's Existence is to Act, God's Act is to Exist.

This divine Essence cannot be communicated in all its fullness to anybody outside God. No creature shares with God this absolute fullness of necessary existence; this total, unlimited, eternal and free perfection: this possession of one's self and one's own existence, by necessity and by nature.

In the study of 'being', therefore, the first deep split we discover down the line in any creature is the division between Existing, or being, and What the creature is: its created essence, or nature. This division is absent in God. God's essence is to exist. Clear thinking demands that of God. It equally denies it of the creature. No creature IS his own existence. We say that our nature exists. It is not our nature to exist.

Behind every creature's existence, behind his limited 'is', lies the unlimited, infinite and eternal chasm of what he is NOT. In practice this means that no creature can ever become God (the philosophical death-knell to the teilhardian nonsense of evolution's omega-point). This reality alone has very great, practical value for us in our everyday life. God is not only Infinite: He is Infinite Perfection allround. Even if the creature had an eternity to do it: it would never cross the infinite gulf between it and God. Both the Church and Thomism want us to be always in awe of God's Majesty and Holiness, no matter how sorely we are tried and vexed. Not so much for the sake of God as for our own sake and Good. We must become perfect Creatures, and the first step to that is the acknowledgment of what God is and what we are. There is a lot of what we are NOT behind us. There is a lot of "growing" to be done by us; there is plenty of room and scope for "becoming" what we are not yet, and we only have our earthly life-span to do it in. But try as we may, we will never become God: the first and fundamental split in our existence as creature between what we are and what we are not will remain forever, even if, like the Most Blessed Virgin, we achieve the fullness of perfection as creature. (See next lecture what God thinks of all this!)

The Thomistic First Principle of Created Being Defined

It is of the utmost importance for what follows, that at this stage we fully understand the Two Names St. Thomas gives to these two first and fundamental aspects of every created existence.

1. The created existence, St. Thomas calls *Actus Primus*, the First or Primary Act, which, as we saw, is by necessity limited; a limited existence or a limited participation in God's existence.
2. The principle of limitation, that what the creature is not, or not yet, St. Thomas wisely calls Potentia; which in English is usually (and unhelpfully) translated as 'potency', but would be better understood as 'potential': possible existence according to the nature allotted to the creature by the Creator. By necessity, each creature therefore exists of Actus and Potentia: a first act, by which God gives it existence, limited existence; and potential, by which it is capable of becoming more, and hopefully more perfect, according to its given nature. As no created 'first act' can exist like God's exist-

ence: unencumbered by non-existence, 'first act' and 'potential' are therefore not two separate existing things, each again with its own nature and split, because then we would have to go on ad infinitum. They are the two sides of the one 'coin': two principles of the one existing created Nature or thing, being.

This is a most fortuitous explanation of the first two and fundamental principles of created existence. For, in whatever direction we look from this vantage point, we see Truth.

1. If we look in the Divine direction, we see the total absence of potentia, 'potential' as a limiting factor, or possible existence, and we admit that the actus primus, the primary act of created existence, disappears in God, and becomes what St. Thomas calls the Actus Purus in God: Pure Existence. No beginnings: no first act, as with created existence. Just pure existing, actus purus.
2. If we look in the created direction, we not only see 'existence': actus primus, or primary act, we not only see impotentia: the impossibility of ever becoming God, or even becoming like God, but we also see much scope for progress and growing in the potentia, the potential, allotted by the Creator, and recognised by St. Thomas, to each creature.
3. Furthermore, this most fortuitous terminology allows for a very practical and understandable terminology of how this growing, this gradual perfection of one's given nature can take place. If the actus primus, as we saw, is the existing na-

ture allotted by the Creator to each creature, then it is natural to assume that the perfection of that nature, of that primary act, is done by Actus Secundi, or Secondary Acts each creature can perform according to the very nature (actus primus) allotted to him.

A stone is 'in potentia' of becoming a sculpture; seeds are potential flowers, or trees; human beings are not only 'in potential' of becoming engineers, teachers, housewives, saints, but also children of God, according to the very nature received by the actus primus: even a share in the Divine Nature by Baptism. And no one can claim, that this aspect of Thomism has not got tremendous practical application and value. All the secondary acts are there to realise, i.e. to make real, to bring into existence, the Potentia, the Potential, that the Nature of the Creature, the Human Being Here, is capable of. That is: to bring the 'actus primus' of its existence, the first primary act, to perfection.

If we limit ourselves to the human being from now on, and concentrate ourselves on its actus primus: its existing nature and its potential: what an almost limitless panorama unfolds itself before us. Richly endowed in its 'first act': the creation of its human nature, with spiritual gifts of intellect and will, feelings, freedom of choice, memory, inclinations and aspirations, and with the beautiful attributes that belong to his corporal and material make-up: the five senses, his physical strength and great endurance, his avidity to learn and master his surroundings, and his powers of recuperation: all contributing to an almost endless variety of choices of secondary acts leading up to the perfection of the primary act, the act by

Chapter Five: The Nature of Catholic Philosophy (III)

which he came forth from the loving hands of the Creator. Even with the flaw of Original Sin, his weakened nature is still capable of great perfection in every direction. Our history books are full of what human nature is capable of. Civilisations abound with testimonies to the greatness, the genius, of what human nature is capable of: in art and literature, in science and inventions, in techniques, discoveries and mastery.

So great is the glory of human nature, that the Psalmist could truthfully exclaim under God's direct and truthful inspiration:

"You have made him little less than a god;
You have crowned him with glory and splendour,
Made him lord over the work of your hands,
Set all things under his feet." (Psalm 8. v.5)

The Nature of Human Conscience

If the foregoing has already quite acceptable aspects of practicality, the doctrine of Thomism on Human Existence assumes aspects of overriding practical importance, if we study, and make our own, the Thomistic Doctrine on the human Conscience. If only this doctrine had been as widely understood and accepted as the Popes had wished for, the total and almost absolute confusion on conscience, rampant today, would never have been on the scale that it now is. In fact, it is becoming crystal clear that the architects of the 'church of darkness', the modernists and teilhardians, wanted to discredit Sacred Thomism in order that people, accepting their totally erroneous doctrines on freedom of conscience, would freely accept their caricature of the 'new catholic church' for the Bride of the Lamb of God. The compilers of the *Melbourne Guidelines* have depicted a caricature of Catholic Doctrine in order that Catholic children, whose beautiful natures came from the loving hands and Mind of God, would lose their Catholic Faith: that powerful Light by which any harlot 'church' can be distinguished from the true Bride of the Lamb of God; and would use their faked freedom of conscience to enter the great new one-world 'church' at their eternal peril. That great new exciting 'church' where you can believe what you like, do what you like, and where 'general absolution' is readily available in case the faked freedom of conscience allowed you to do things against which your true conscience is in protest.

Divine Law demands that Secondary Acts are performed according to the nature of the Primary Act, and lead to its perfection, i.e. make real or bring into existence its potential. God lives according to His Nature, and as we saw, this stamp or mark is left on every creature that comes from His hands; and is practically or in practice expressed as the Natural Law. Acts performed in accordance with this Law therefore are the first indication of some Unity between intellect and will. The secondary act itself is not the unity between intellect and will, but shows that there is some unity. Diversity can never be the foundation of unity, although it could show a remarkable underlying unity. As already stated, secondary acts show an almost unlimited variety of choices, but the principle of unity between intellect and will cannot lie in the human acts themselves. Furthermore, the human act is performed after intel-

Chapter Five: The Nature of Catholic Philosophy (III)

lect and will have concurred, and so cannot be the principle (or origin) of that unity.

Intellect and will are not the same, and so their unity is not an identity. And so we can at least discover two 'unities' between these two great faculties of the human soul: (i) an organic unity, i.e., a unity in origin, and (ii) a unity of purpose; both 'unities' allowing for diversity of components or partners. With these two established, there is a way of looking at a third unity between these partners: (iii) a working unity.

Ontological Unity Between Intellect and Will

Let us first, by way of example, endeavour to bring out where exactly St. Thomas places the existence and activity of the human faculty of conscience.

Imagine a magnificent Rolls Royce coming off the assembly line in all its majestic beauty and gleaming royal dignity. A veritable Actus Primus, called into existence by human ingenuity. What potential has this first act, this 'first appearance' got? What is it capable of, according to the genius of its maker? Maybe it can reach a top speed of 200km/hr. Maybe it can accelerate to 100km/hr in 6 seconds. Maybe it is capable of pulling 10 times its own weight. Or go round corners at 60km/hr. It will be able to carry five people and their luggage in undisturbed comfort and luxury. It probably ... It will ... It can ... The possibilities seem to extend as far as the dreams of the young enthusiasts. But even allowing for a comparatively versatile nature, there are certain things it cannot do, and so it would be unrealistic to expect these from the creature. It is not in its nature to fly, or to travel under water, or even to repair itself, impressive as the list of its performance may be.

Who will grace the Driver's Seat? Who will be in charge of the Secondary Acts that this machine is capable of performing? A butler? A chauffeur? A man who studied the manual and was prepared to listen attentively to the instructions supplied by the makers? Someone who has a working knowledge of this wonderful mechanism at his command? Or a lout, a punk, who just won $100,000 in the soccer pools?

Out of the ranks of admiring bystanders and photographers, a diminutive figure dislodges herself: the proverbial 'little old lady who has never done anything else but drive herself to church on Sundays'. She hands over the cheque, receives the keys and proceeds to install herself behind the wheel. Mistakenly assuming that she has put her car in 'drive', when in reality she just put it into first gear, she lurches out of the showroom and even from the fair distance along the road to the nearest highway, the company executives and mechanics, the newspaper boys and admirers are closing their ears to the subdued but even for a Rolls painful whine, imploring the driver to put the car in second gear … To be driven to 60 and 70km/hr in first gear is too much, even for a machine as noble as a Rolls. It is not according to its nature, and involuntarily the punished primary act will protest.

That noise is an exact picture of the voice of conscience. Conscience lies in the border region between the primary and the secondary act, and is roused to protest when the human being performs, or even contemplates, a secondary act that is not in conformity with human nature, the primary act. It is a safety device for

Chapter Five: The Nature of Catholic Philosophy (III)

human nature, an alarm that rings when the natural law, that participation in the Divine Law that says that everything that exists must live according to its nature and according to the perfection of that nature, the actus primus, is being violated.

And there lies also the first and organic unity between Intellect and Will. Conscience arrests both intellect and will. Conscience is neither Intellect nor Will, but in sounding a warning surrounding the performance of a certain act, it tries to stop dead in their tracks for reconsideration, both intellect and will: the will which had implored the intellect to give its consent to this particular 'good' it had perceived; and the intellect to ascertain if the good proposed by the will is a True good.

Conscience can be overruled by intellect and will. One can try to silence the voice, like the little old lady can turn up the car's radio to drown the 'voice' with noise. But until the total breakdown in hell, where the ruin of human nature is 'fixed' forever, will this friction between the actus primus and the wrong actus secundus remain: as a guide for both intellect and will.

Conscience is not directly the 'voice of God' speaking within us. It was not the company directors who were protesting to the little old lady in the Rolls: it was the car itself which made its protest heard. By the same token, it is human nature itself which raises the alarm against a proposed violation of its natural law.

Once conscience penetrates into the conscious level its message may be misinterpreted. Just as the little old lady in the Rolls may think that the persistent whine is a sure sign that the brakes have jammed, because she cannot get the car past a certain speed; so it is possible that for various reasons of environment, upbringing and the like, the voice of conscience is perceived by the human being at the conscious level with uncertainty. This is particularly true, not so much in the warning against performing certain secondary acts, but in interpreting correctly the 'dictates of conscience' when the primary act makes known to us what specific actions, out of a myriad of choices, will lead to the greater good and perfection of human nature in which the individual human being participates. The protest against revenge e.g., or against the detraction of the good name of a neighbour, may be strong in a Western Christian, but almost non-existing in the dark forests of Africa, or the media-jungle of the degenerate West. And so the duty to acquire an *informed conscience* is itself a dictate of conscience. The whine of the Rolls Royce will not stop, if the lady persists in driving the way she did, but only has the brakes adjusted. Even if its voice has been dulled, a persistent uneasiness about a certain way of life is conscience's way of asking for an investigation and consequent further information. It is more common, in the fickle, wilful and self-opinionated human being, to mistake wishful thinking for the dictates of his conscience and to leave it at that. Especially if he can find an 'expert' to agree with him. And although we will return to this later on, in Lecture 7, it is already possible at this stage from what has been said so far, to appreciate the fact that, whilst conscience is a natural quality of the soul, capable of fallacious interpretations because it finds its way from the sub-conscious to the conscious, Catholic Faith is a Supernatural Gift to the soul. And consequently, if any correction is necessary to make the human conscience an Informed conscience, the correction is to be made with the aid of the Superior Light of Catholic Faith. Therefore, for a

Chapter Five: The Nature of Catholic Philosophy (III)

Catholic it is almost impossible to be in invincible ignorance with regard to an erroneous conscience, precisely because of the superior Light of Catholic faith, and because of the known teaching of the Church. It is Catholic Faith, which is superior to the human conscience in deciding what will truly lead to the perfection of the primary act: Redeemed human nature, which is needed to make any conscience an informed conscience, and not the other way round, as all the modernists teach us ad nauseam.

A Unity Between Intellect and Will at the Conscious Level: Motivation

Maybe it would be better to talk here about Harmony between the human intellect and the will. But since harmony is not a forced unity, but a freely obtained one, it is a further expression of an original unity found in conscience. At least it is a good description, in keeping with human dignity.

There appears to be a widespread mistaken assumption amongst some educators that repeated acts of the will make a strong will. I think psychologists will bear me out here that this is a fallacy. Training of the will appears to be painful and laborious, without much hope of success, if it only consists in certain repetitive acts of the will without due regard for the original unity between intellect and will. The story goes that in the convent in which the Little Flower, St. Therese of Lisieux, found her way to Heaven and her little road to perfection, there also lived a good Sister who, to train herself to overcome any temptation for eating outside specified hours, persisted in having on her little night table by her bed, all sorts of delicious fruits. It became a great source of temptation against charity for the poor Nun that the Little Flower could make such great progress in perfection, not sharing the Sister's training of the will. It is certainly not uncommon to hear stories of children who show no great interest in learning at school, and who seem to be devoid of all willpower to get them going towards what adults may think is vitally important for their future, but who later on appear to be capable of great endurance and perseverance when it comes to the realisation of a previously unrecognised ambition. It is not a secret training of the will that has taken place: it is a suddenly discovered motive for enduring the hardships that has triggered the will. And motive has a lot to do with the intellect. In a good motive, intellect and will come together initially, and the harmony persists, as the child has suddenly found a great interest in wanting to know more about the project that has captured his fancy.

In 'training' the child for heaven, it is equally necessary to trigger his will by a strong motivation, which in the Light of True Faith and in the Lives of the Saints, is not hard to come by. Scolding and nagging only affect the will, leaving the intellect out. Arguing affects the intellect. The true solution is found in providing him with a strong motive for wanting what, in the Light of Faith, should be his final end ...

By the same token, evil, even great evil, is being done for a strong enough motive. If a tendency is discovered towards the wrong way of life in young adults, do not immediately suspect a weak will, or the bad influence of television. Even bad company and bad example are secondary to the prime mover: A Bad Motive.

All the other circumstances are excuses, or bad occasions of sin, and are strong, but outside the child. In final analysis, a human being will have a motive for acting the way he does, and it is the motive which will have to be changed.

A Further Unity Between Intellect and Will: Habit Formation

Thomism is very strong on this. Even the best intentions and the highest motives eventually will lose some of their glamour and appeal, and consequently much of their 'pull'. Or at times sudden strong reasons for the opposite behaviour present themselves with sudden and unexpected force. It is then that sheer habit will help the weak human will over the crisis, when the intellect has no time to properly assess the new set of circumstances, but remains with the will in the previously found 'harmony' that the behaviour that formed the good habit was a true good.

Again, by the same token, if bad habits have been allowed to take root, then there is not much chance that a sudden and unexpected demand on a good action will be met with the desired result, causing further shame and even despair.

Much will still have to be said about the Supernatural influences on human actions as seen by Thomism. But since they will never be at the expense of human nature, and very seldom with a short-term violence to it, as was the case with the conversion of St. Paul, the bridge for grace is a good and practical understanding, as so eminently supplied by St. Thomas, of the complex entity: Man. It is for the practical, day-to-day perfection of the human being, that the Holy Fathers have been so anxious to see Thomism understood, and have been so alarmed at the decline of this understanding.

As the story unfolds more and more in these lectures, we will become more and more convinced of the Truth: that Thomistic Philosophy chimes in, by a pre-established harmony, with Divine Revelation. No surer way for the safeguarding of the First Principles of Faith.

And if it is true, that reason, borne on the wings of St. Thomas, could scarcely rise higher, then this understanding of where exactly human conscience lies and how it acts, and a thomistic working knowledge of motivation and habit formation, will not only help us to see right through the fallacies thrown up against us by the modernists; but to counteract them, and to undo much of the damage done to our children in 'modern' education. It is meant not only to give us confidence in what good was done in the past, but to give us unlimited confidence in our age-old Catholic Faith: built so solidly and persistently on the rock-like extension the Papacy gave to Thomism from the Rock of St. Peter.

Chapter Six

The Nature of Catholic Philosophy (IV)

The Corruption of Human Thinking:
A 600 Year History

Introduction

We seem to have reached a critical stage in our efforts to plumb the depth of human thinking. Initially, 'critical' did not have the bad connotation it has acquired in the press, meaning 'fatal' or 'final', or the combination: 'with fatal finality'. 'hopeless'. Initially, 'critical' meant: 'with discernment', with such intellectual mastery as to be able to see both points of view. To be in the possession of such evidence as to be able to give a critique, a verdict, one way or the other.

In context, this requires from us not only an understanding of 'thinking chiming in with Revelation', but also of thinking that goes in the opposite direction. There are weighty arguments in favour of this practice. God, according to St. Ignatius, knows human nature so well, that He did not only reveal to us His Love and His Truth, but also Hell. In his Spiritual Exercises, the Saint gives us an explanation for this. At the beginning of the 5th Exercise of the 1st Week: the meditation on Hell, St. Ignatius lets the one who does the Retreat "implore God to give him an intimate sense of the punishment suffered by the damned, so that, in the event that the love of God be forgotten, at least the fear of the punishments would help him to avoid sin". The thought of Hell used as a deterrent ...

We may have the best intentions now of letting our thinking be guided by St. Thomas and by the doctrines of the Church. But there are other forms of thinking which have proven themselves to be delectable and persuasive to the eager human mind. According to God, and to His servant St. Ignatius, it is useful to be acquainted with the direction of this thinking, and with the damage it has caused over the long centuries of human existence ... The corruption of human thinking, acting as a deterrent, when the truth of Thomistic thinking loses some of its power and appeal.

In this lecture we will come face to face with what St. Paul in 2 Thess. 2:7 has called by its proper name: *'Mysterium Iniquitatis'*, or 'the Mystery of Evil'. It is with the study of this Mystery, that the understanding of human thinking will be made complete. When the essence of this mystery is understood, when its significance is grasped, when the ramifications, down to the finest consequences, are clearly seen: only then will we be in the critical position to understand both sides, to give a verdict one way or the other; to have reached intellectual mastery. For, from the vantage point of this position, we will see that there is no longer any excuse for us, if we close the eyes of our minds to these profound insights in a desire to back away from the ultimate consequences Thomistic thinking will demand of us. For, like with Lucifer, this knowledge brings with it, that we no longer sin out of weakness, but out of pride, as our sin would be a deliberate sin against the light: the light of reason ...

But the Mystery of Evil would not be a true Mystery, shrouded in incomprehension, were it not for the fact that human beings, more often than not, have taken this second road; have closed the eyes of their minds to the clear light of reason, have refused to chime in with Revelation and so have darkened the Supernatural Light of Faith in which we come to the knowledge of the ways of God's Thinking. And with that, have given to the word 'critical' its popular, sinister meaning of 'fatal finality'. A state of affairs in such an advanced stage of deterioration, so 'critically wounded and ill' that nothing short of a miracle will be necessary to prevent fatal finality.

Lucifer

In order to better understand what 'fatal finality' has overtaken the Human Race in the 14th Century, i.e. just after 'reason could scarcely have risen higher, borne on the wings of St. Thomas', we will have to go back to the dawn of history, to the deep roots of God's Salvation history: but even that, as it turns out, will not be far enough …

In what is to follow we must bear in mind that, although History is mainly about actions and deeds, we are for once only interested in a History of Thought, and crooked Thinking had its origin beyond human history, in a realm of which we have no written records. But, since the effects of that thinking have affected us all, it is subject to a penetrating analysis, since in God's saving Will it is to act as a deterrent for a fallen Human Race, prone to give in to a temptation even Lucifer in all his created glory could not withstand …

"I shall put enmity between you and the Woman, and between Her seed and yours; and She shall crush your head ..."

With these words God reveals here the existence of Absolutes: Absolute Good, eternally, totally and irrevocably opposed to Evil, but not Absolute Evil. There is no such thing as absolute evil, for Good will overcome it: the Woman will crush it.

Notice here that God did not say: 'I will put enmity between you and Me', as Satan dearly would have loved him to say, to force God to be his opponent. But as already observed elsewhere: evil cannot force Good and Truth to walk a certain path. No, the opposition to, and the final victory over, Created Evil will come from a Woman and Her children. Created Intelligence, created thinking then, will be allowed by God to oppose the evil genius of the Devil. But, created thinking Chiming in with Revelation. Mary's created intelligence in support of Her Supernatural Faith in God. Mary's free consent, Mary's 'Fiat' not only produced in the Incarnation the One Seed necessary for the total victory over evil, but also made possible the Catholic Church; Her other children, in which Her Thinking and Her Faith would be perpetuated in the struggle to overcome the evil of the 'knot of Eve' at any given time.

The quality of clear thinking and the quality of Faith it supports are so clearly geared to the acceptance of Absolutes: Absolutes existing in the existence of God; and this acceptance appears not only central to the Creative will of God, but also to the Saving will of God, as witnessed by this first profound quotation from Genesis, that it must give us a clue to the thinking that led to the downfall and subsequent 'destruction' of Lucifer.

Chapter Six: The Nature of Catholic Philosophy (IV)

What did happen in eons past, long before the dawn of our created Universe in time? What sorrow was inflicted on the great and loyal Spirit, St. Michael, when it started to dawn on him what direction the thinking of his great friend Lucifer was taking? Would he not put up a fight to battle valiantly for the salvation of the greatest mind God had ever given the light of intelligence to? Michael coming to grips with the 'mysterium iniquitatis', the mystery of evil. Prepared to do everything possible for the safety of his friend and all the other Angels Lucifer was leading to ruin in the period of their probation. And when he failed, what agonies prepared him for his eternal glory, and made him determined, in the Light of God's presence, to support, from then on, every effort that was made to prevent a repetition of that fatal finality ... 'Blessed Michael Archangel, defend us in the hour of conflict'.

From what we can gather now we can form a clearer picture, if not of the actual thoughts then at least of the Type of Thinking that Lucifer must have pursued. Theoretically, there were two roads that Lucifer could have walked to his self-destruction. One was the admittance of Absolutes, which belief could subsequently be nullified by his desire to turn himself into one, i.e., to make himself equal to it, equal to a Divine Being. The other road was to deny the existence of Absolutes, to admit only his own individual existence, and if God existed, to allow him at most an existence equal to his own.

How far did Lucifer penetrate with his created intelligence into the Mystery of God, without actually being in the presence of God? Did his superior intelligence perceive the possibility of other spirits which would at the same time be the forms of bodies? And did God want him to let this true perception 'chime in with Revelation', the Revelation of the Incarnation? God's Love for those tiny matter-spirits? For even angelic thought, in order to be meritorious for Eternal Life, must chime in with Revelation. As we said, we may never know here below what the actual thoughts of Lucifer were; but from weighty evidence available to us, both from God's Revelation and from the recorded words of the Devil himself, we do know that Lucifer took the Second road: he denied the existence of Absolutes, making God equal to himself.

Let us briefly examine the first road. If Lucifer had taken that road, he would have given initial glory to God by acknowledging His absolute existence, which would have put him in a state of adoration. His next step, to make himself equal to an Absolute Being, would be totally illogical and altogether out of place. By his angelic intuition he knew that he was not the cause of his own existence. But if that had to be denied of himself: to be the cause of his own existence, so he could also deny that of God, making out that God was perhaps a bit more powerful spirit, but not essentially different from himself. That thinking landed him on the second road.

Does e.g., Teilhard de Chardin, one of those seeds of the Serpent, invite us first to adore the Absolute, God, and in the process also invite us to adore him, Teilhard, because he is equal to God? No, Teilhard denies God the power to create ex-nihilo, from nothing: he denies God the power to perform miracles. He makes God the soul of evolution, allotting to God a place in his self-perpetuating system; allowing Him to evolve with it until omega-point. Teilhard clearly also took the second road, denying Absolutes; and placing Man on the altar as being equal to a non-absolute 'god', or by making a non-absolute 'god' equal to himself.

Did Lucifer himself, in the Third-Temptation of Christ, invite Christ to acknowledge with him first an Absolute Being, and in the process also invite Him to adore him, Satan, as being equal to an Absolute: God? No, again, the recognition of the existence of an Absolute Being was totally ignored, and Satan made out that his individual existence was the only existence that mattered and was therefore worthy of adoration.

Acknowledging the existence of an Absolute Being, and then proceeding to make oneself equal to it, is not the same as denying the Absolute Being any absolute existence and then allowing him at most an existence equal to oneself. But the end-product is the same: God is at the creature's level, and the creature is at God's level.

We know from Sacred Scripture that it was Pride that made Lucifer walk this second road which ended up in his self-destruction as Satan. But the Mystery of Evil shrouds from us in its secrecy the understanding of WHY he allowed himself to walk that road. It is the Holiness of God that must demand from the creature the recognition of the Absolute Existence of God and His glorious Attributes. But it is at the same time the Eternal Goodness and Love of the Almighty which secures that this demand for recognition is at the same time in the greatest interest of the creature … When all is said and done, it was this saving Love of God that was not reciprocated by Lucifer. And it was left to the lesser light, Michael, to understand that it was God's Love for Lucifer, which demanded from Lucifer the recognition of his Absolute Existence.

And with this, the stage was set for the greatest Drama in History: the Battle for the Mind of Man …

Moses

"I shall put enmity between you and the Woman, and between Her seed and yours; and She shall crush your head …"

With these words, as already mentioned, God, in His Saving Will, shows His concern for the preservation of the belief in Absolutes in the fallen human race. For He knew that the stricken Lucifer would try to perpetuate the denial of Absolutes in the thinking of the equally stricken human race, so that corrupted Human Thinking would cease to chime in with Revelation, and so with Supernatural Redemption.

But, in quoting these words again, I have a second motive. For, if it is true to say of these words: 'So spoke God when addressing the Serpent', so it is equally true to say: 'So wrote Moses in the 3rd chapter of the Book of Genesis'. Moses, an instrument of God, specially chosen and prepared by Him.

Brought up in Pharaoh's court, not without a special design by God Who has a hand in human affairs, Moses came into contact with the thinking that destroyed Lucifer; but which, as Satan, he was now at pains to pass on to his seed as the Secret Knowledge by which one day his adherents would Rule The World. Destruction passed on as the road to victory. Deception passed on as the Truth. Slavery in Hell passed on as the power to rule the earth. Annihilation passed on as 'equality with God'. It will always be the same: the road to Hell depicted as the road to paradise …

Chapter Six: The Nature of Catholic Philosophy (IV)

But just as Abraham some centuries earlier had turned his back on this 'secret knowledge of Babylon' in preference to the submission to the Supernatural Light of Revelation and of the True Faith in the one true God, thereby becoming the 'blessing of the Old Testament'; so here Moses, by killing the Egyptian and taking up the case of the Jew, showed that he too had turned his back on the mysteries of Osiris and the secret brotherhood of knowledge, in preference to the Faith of his Fathers, the Patriarchs. God knew His servant needed the deterrent of crooked thinking as much as he stood in need of the thinking that would chime in with the Revelations at hand. By clearly showing his rejection of the first, he was now ready to receive instructions in the latter.

The rejection by the two fighting Israelites profoundly shook Moses. Was it possible that here, in his own race, he detected ever so faintly the traces of the same thinking he had rejected himself so completely? He needed time to think, and sort himself out in a profound and prolonged meditation.

'What was wrong with the thinking of the Israelites?'

God, Who knew that in the next 40 years Moses would get an answer to this fundamental question, allowed him to come to grips with the problem. Biding His time. Moses the mystical writer; Moses the prophet; Moses the law-giver; Moses the leader; Moses the teacher! On what Human Thinking was this towering tree of natural and supernatural beauty going to be implanted? What Philosophy was going to be the substratum and the foundation of this all-time record? A continuation of the 'right reason' that made him reject Satan's thinking encountered in the transient power of the Egyptian 'illuminati'.

The day of the burning bramble bush was drawing near ... and with it the day that Moses entered God's University to do a course. A course in what? In theology? No! A course in Philosophy. In the same philosophy that, some 3000 years later, would take the human mind to the edge of its potential, on the testimony of later Popes. And what is at the centre of this course? The future course of St. Thomas, as well as of this crash-course in the loneliness of the Sinai desert? The Existence of Absolutes.

When God revealed His Name to Moses, He did not give it in the theological definition and Revelation of the Blessed Trinity; but in the philosophical definition: the definition that clear human thinking can arrive at without the Supernatural Light of Revelation of the New Testament.

In stating his Name as "I am: 'I am'", God revealed to Moses that He is 'Being'. He is all there is. He is perpetual 'to be'. He is Absolute Existence. "Tell the sons of Israel 'I am' sends you", He tells Moses. And on that foundation, the knowledge of Absolute Existence; Absolute Holiness; Absolute Truth and Absolute Goodness and Forgiveness Moses sets out on the great adventure of his life; and on his own, and on all the world's future destiny. The same as Satan, and his seed, have embarked on their own destiny of ruin by denying Absolute Existence, and with the shallow knowledge of secret societies and the so-called 'illuminati', have made themselves out as the rulers of this world. And we can safely say that, if this is the thinking that God required in the man who was to lead His people out of slavery into the Promised Land, and if this is the thinking God wanted passed on to every Jew in preparation for the full Revelation in His Son, then this thinking will always lie at the foundation not only of human greatness, but also at the foundation of human sanctity.

Let us then briefly turn our attention to the history of enmity between this thought and the thinking that opposes it, over the last 600 years. If the human mind can scarcely rise higher than on the wings of St. Thomas, then it must follow that it can scarcely sink lower than in the contradiction of thomism, when it starts to chime in with Satan, and his seed: Antichrist.

William of Occam

When God revealed to Moses in the Sinai desert the existence of Absolutes: intellectual Absolutes first, to be followed by the Moral Absolutes later on, the Ten Commandments in the same desert, He revealed at the same time a foundation and framework of thinking that Thomism some 3000 years later, as a crowning effort of human thinking, formulated as follows:

"Human thinking cannot, by valid rational argument, come to any conclusion incompatible with Revelation."

This means that, if a philosopher arrives at a conclusion which contradicts, explicitly or implicitly, a Revealed Truth, it is a sign that either his premises are false, or that there is a fallacy somewhere in his argument, or both.

In the Sinai desert God revealed to Moses Truths about His own existence and about morality which are not impervious to the human mind; but about which a lot of human thinking can nevertheless go wrong. They are Truths the human mind is capable of ascertaining, but at the same time they are now also revealed

Truths, guaranteed to be always and everywhere true by God's own veracity. They are Supernatural Truths at the same time that they are natural Truths. Natural Truths guaranteed by God to be infallibly true. This means that philosophical speculations and conclusions at variance with these natural truths, are also at variance with God's Revelation.

Having said this, let us now direct our attention to Occam and the post-Thomistic era.

By way of introduction, consider the following remarks made by a world authority on the History of Philosophy, Fr. Frederick Copleston, S.J. in his monumental work *A History of Philosophy*, taken from Vol. 3, Part 1, pp 21-28, passim.

" ... a new movement, associated forever with the name of William of Occam, opposed the realism of the earlier schools and became known as 'nominalists'." (p 21).

As we will see later on, 'realism' in Scholastic Philosophy (Thomism) means not only that reality can be known, and can be known to exist, but also that the mental concepts of reality in the human mind, 'universals', are real.

" ... the nominalists left faith hanging in the air without (so far as philosophy is concerned) any rational basis." (p 21).

'So far as philosophy is concerned': that is, so far as proper human thinking is concerned, guaranteed by God to be capable of ascertaining objective truth and reality, as explained earlier.

"Ockham admitted indeed, that some metaphysical arguments are Probable. This substitution of probable arguments for proofs was connected of course with the nominalists' tendency to doubt

Chapter Six: The Nature of Catholic Philosophy (IV)

or deny the validity of inferring from the existence of one thing the existence of another."

"In this way, the whole metaphysical system of the 13th Century was discredited … St Thomas, e.g., was certainly convinced that valid metaphysical arguments can be given for God's existence. These arguments belong to the *Praeambula Fidei* in the sense that the acceptance of Divine Revelation logically presupposes the knowledge that a God exists Who is capable of revealing Himself, a knowledge which can be gained in abstraction from theology. But if no cogent proof or demonstration of God's existence can be given, the very existence of God has to be relegated to the sphere of faith … Ockham, by assigning to the sphere of faith the truth that there exists an absolute, supreme, infinite, free, omniscient and omnipotent Being, snapped the link between metaphysics and theology, which had been provided by Aquinas' doctrine of the provable Praeambula Fidei. By making the moral law dependent on the free divine choice, he implied, whether he realised it or not that without Revelation man can have no certain knowledge even of the present moral order established by God … This would imply the possibility of two moral orders: one established by God but knowable only by Revelation, and a provisional and second-class natural and non-theological moral order worked out by the human reason without revelation." (pp 23-25.)

Which means of course the beginning of as many 'moral orders' as there are human intellects working them out, by hit and miss methods, 'probable' arguments, and guess-work. Even on first acquaintance it must be conceded that the above description does not sound too good and it will become obvious that further explanations will not improve the bad first impression. No wonder, then, that Fr. Copleston could write a few pages further:

"When one looks at Renaissance philosophy one is faced at first sight with a rather bewildering assortment of philosophies." (p 28).

Let us now analyse in some more detail the historical fact that, when clear thinking had finally and at last been spelled out by St. Thomas in all its glory, Satan, who likes to work in secret through secret societies and 'brotherhoods', was forced to come out into the open and do something drastic quickly, thereby no longer being able to avoid showing his cloven hoof.

The facts of Occam's life are in keeping with the havoc caused by his attack on Thomism. Denounced to the Holy See for heresy, the Commission appointed to investigate the accusations accepted 33 of the 56 propositions submitted to it for condemnation, adding a few more of its own, altogether 51 propositions.

Some were definitely declared heretical, others, less important, as erroneous. When ordered to appear in person to answer the charges, he did appear, but then fled and took refuge under the temporal power of Emperor Ludwig of Bavaria. The Pope excommunicated the fugitives. From then on William was engaged in a long wrangle with the Holy See over papal powers, and his thesis 'that Papal powers should be constitutionalised ', that is restricted by, and more or less answerable to, a General Council of the Church, not only landed him in further hot water, but also became a powerful stimulus to the 'conciliar movement'. Although towards the end of his life steps were taken for him to be reconciled with the Church, it is uncertain if his excommunication was ever lifted in time of his sudden death in 1349.

Chapter Six: The Nature of Catholic Philosophy (IV)

Heresy, excommunication, head-on collision with the Papacy: these are the credentials of the man, an ex-Franciscan, who took it upon himself to provide the world with an 'alternative' to Thomism ...

"Like Macbeth, Western Man made an evil decision, which has become the efficient and final cause of other evil decisions."

With these words the late Professor Richard Weaver, professor in English at the University of Chicago, begins a most brilliant analysis of modern day decadence. It is so profoundly penetrating, that I continue it for a while longer, before giving a summary of Professor Weaver's analysis in his book *Ideas Have Consequences*.

"Have we forgotten our encounter with the witches on the heath? It occurred in the 14th Century, and what the witches said to the protagonist of this drama was that man could realise himself more fully if he would only abandon his belief in the existence of transcendentals."

If we replace the literary image of 'witches' with 'Lucifer', and replace 'transcendentals' by their synonym 'absolutes', we recognise that Prof. Weaver is here referring to what constituted the downfall of Lucifer, and the subsequent efforts of Satan to perpetuate the cause of his downfall in the human race.

"The powers of darkness were working subtly, as always, and they couched this proposition in the seemingly innocent form of an attack upon universals. The defeat of logical realism in the great medieval debate was the crucial event in the history of Western culture; for from this flowed those acts which issue now in modern decadence. I take the view here that the conscious policies of men and governments are deductions from our most basic ideas of human destiny, and that they have a great power to determine our course.

For this reason I turn to William of Occam as the best representative of a change which came over man's conception of reality at this historic juncture. It was William of Occam who propounded the fateful doctrine of Nominalism, which denies that universals have a real existence. His triumph tended to leave universals merely 'terms' or names serving our convenience. Ultimately the issue involved is, **whether there is a source of truth higher than**, and independent of, man; and the answer to the question is decisive for one's view of the nature and destiny of humankind. The practical result of nominalist philosophy is to banish the reality which is perceived by the intellect and to posit as reality only that which is perceived by the senses. With this change in the affirmation of what is real, the whole orientation of culture takes a turn."

We have already dealt with the essence of what Prof. Weaver singles out in this passage as one of the cornerstones of Thomistic Philosophy. To refresh the memory, here, once again, is a brief recapitulation of the essential points. The senses perceive some material object. Of this, a sense-perception is formed. This is received by the 'passive' intellect, where the mind, or the active intellect (the intellectus agens) abstracts from the details the nature of the perception: the concept or mental image. Because the Nature of humanhood is recognised in the individual man perceived by the sense, e.g., the mental image, or concept, is essentially Universal. 'Carhood' is recognised in individual cars, 'wheelhood' in the recognition of a particular wheel, etc. The mental image, or concept is not that which is known: the individual car, man, etc is known. The mental image is that by which we know the individual thing. It exists only in the active mind of man, as a universal abstraction of the sense-perception, which is individual and direct. In this whole process there are a few concepts that we can never escape; no matter what we do, or try as we may. The most important one of these is Truth. Even if we have to deny that this girl is the one we met yesterday, we believe this denial to be true; which makes truth an even more important concept that an ordinary universal. Truth seems to transcend visible reality as an ever-present, or absolute. Even if we try to make the existence of truth to be only probable, then we believe this probable existence of truth to be true: truth asserting itself, even in the denial of it.

If universal concepts have a real existence in the mind of man, then the concept of truth must be real; and since it is the concept of 'something' that cannot be denied, which defies denial, truth itself must be real. Since it transcends both man and every effort he may make to deny it, truth is a transcendental or absolute. The first requirement, therefore, in denying reality to the concept of truth is simply to deny reality or real existence to any universal concept in the mind of man by simply calling them 'names' or terms. Hence the word 'nominalism' as nomen is the Latin word for 'name'.

But God has guaranteed the existence of at least Four Absolutes in Holy Scripture: Absolute Good, outlasting Satan's evil; Absolute Existence: "I am: 'I am'"; an Absolute Moral Order; and finally Absolute Truth, otherwise we could not know or believe the other three Absolutes as Absolutes. It is illogical and unrealistic to confine the knowledge of these absolutes to the revealed knowledge of Faith. For one, the doctrines of Faith are contained in universal concepts which must be denied existence, since universals do not exist in Nominalism. But, more importantly, outside Faith and Revelation, relativism must then reign supreme, since absolutes apparently cannot be ascertained by the human intellect; which would make relativism absolute. Nominalism is shot through with these types of implicit and explicit contradictions; which means that poor Occam blundered into a minefield against which reason and Thomism have fortified themselves with invincible arms for their eternal protection.

In other words: correct human thinking can come to the knowledge of the existence of absolutes, and God's revelation of them only guarantees that this type of human thinking is correct. They are 'praeambula fidei', which facilitate the free acceptance of the Grace of Faith: that Supernatural Light and Faculty, by which we believe Truths that simply cannot be ascertained by the unaided human mind.

The popularity of Nominalism, and its ready acceptance in many of the late-medieval universities as an alternative to Thomism paved the way for the fragmentation of philosophy into 'philosophies'; and for the degeneration of these philosophies into modern agnosticism, relativism and atheism.

To summarise Prof. Weaver's observations and deductions:

"It is easy to be blind to the significance of a change because it is remote in time and abstract in character. Those who have not discovered that World View (Philosophy!) Is the most Important Thing about Man, as about the men composing a culture, should consider the train of circumstances which have with perfect logic proceeded from this. The denial of universals carries with it the denial of everything transcending experience. This denial means inevitably the denial of truth. With the denial of objective truth there is no escape from the relativism of 'man the measure of all things'. The witches spoke with the habitual equivocation of oracles when they told man that by this easy choice he might realise himself more fully, for they were actually initiating a course which cuts one off from reality. Thus began the 'abomination of desolation' appearing today as a feeling of alienation from all fixed truth." (p 4-5.)

This is a profound observation. Satan knew that he had only himself left over in Hell. So, with characteristic equivocation, he set man on a road which would end up with the loss of God, and only the possession of his miserable self, as if it was a road to full self-realisation … Man cut off from reality.

"Because a change of belief so profound eventually influences every concept, there emerged before long a new Doctrine of Nature …"

Here we must start our summary of Prof. Weaver's thoughts. Nature, up till now seen and accepted as a reflected glory of the Creator, now became looked upon as containing the principles of its own constitution and behaviour. Result? Rousseau's 'natural goodness of man' and the abolition of Original Sin. "And the end is not yet", continues Weaver. "If nature is a self operating mechanism and man is a rational animal adequate to his needs, it is next in order to elevate Rationalism to the rank of philosophy. Since man proposed now not to go beyond this world, it was proper that he should regard as his highest intellectual vocation methods of interpreting data supplied by the sense: Hobbs, Locke, 18th Century rationalists, who taught that man only needed reason". The question of what the world was made for now becomes meaningless because it presupposes something prior to nature in the order of existence. And that is inadmissible.

"It was at this stage that Religion begins to assume an ambiguous dignity", continues Weaver, and with no transcending truth and supernatural revelation accepted as possible, it degenerated into a man-made affair. It became powerless to bind in conscience.

"Materialism loomed next on the horizon …". Man became explained by his environment: Darwin, Marxism, evolution. Man became firmly ensconced in nature: biological necessity became the fundamental explanation of his motivation and behaviour. Survival of the fittest: abortion, euthanasia, genocide.

"Man created in the Divine Image, the centre of a great drama in which his soul was at stake, was replaced by man the wealth-seeking, sexual and consuming animal, free of everything except himself …"

And then we must depart from Prof. Weaver, with his final summing-up:

"His decline can be represented as a long series of abdications. He has found less and less ground for authority at the same time that he thought he was setting himself up as the centre of authority in the universe: indeed there seems to exist here a process which takes away his power in proportion as he demonstrates that his independence entitles him to power.

This story is eloquently reflected in changes that have come over education … If words no longer correspond to objective realities, it seems no great wrong to take liberties with words. Here be-

Chapter Six: The Nature of Catholic Philosophy (IV) 133

gins the assault on Definitions. From this point on, faith in language as a means of arriving at truth weakens ..."

And we have arrived at a new era of Babel where no one really understands the other, where meanings are lost and arbitrary, where universal truth is replaced by universal doubt, and where now 'might is right'. The cutting of the Gordian knot.

With this we have come full circle, for this is precisely the observation His Holiness St. Pius X made, recommending a return to Thomism, and I repeat:

"If such principles (of Thomism) are once removed or in any way impaired, it must necessarily follow that students of the Sacred Sciences will ultimately fail to perceive so much as the meaning of the words in which the Dogmas of Divine Revelation are proposed by the Magisterium of the Church." (*Doctoris Angelicic*, 1914.)

This must do to show conclusively by this whole train of fatal thoughts, translated down the ages into the whole train of fatal events, that Satan, forced to action after the brilliant truth of Thomistic Philosophy, picked accurately the beginning of this whole downward trend, when he found someone willing to deny existence to universal concepts; changing Logic from an art employed to arrive at truth to a means of speaking properly the meaningless words left over after the completion of the 'abomination of desolation'.

I could have stopped here, leaving you with the desolation of man in his utter and tragic loneliness, cut off from any higher Reality that counts. But God says 'that it is not good for man that he is alone'; and so we cannot let our story end here. For there are many Catholics who live with a de facto denial of absolutes, allowing only the transient impact of this world to absorb their time, interest and energies. In other words, there are many Catholics who are 'children of their age' and live by its philosophies. And they too are in effect lonely. I am not even speaking here of the modernists and Teilhardians: catholics who have abandoned their Catholic faith, and live wholly by the tenets of the consequences of Nominalism. They are nothing but 'nominal catholics': catholics in name only.

What we are trying to say here, of course, is that it must be possible, once again, to show that Thomism is of great practical value. Not so much to help us trace our steps back to its 13th Century glory; but to help us jump out of the senseless merry-go-round of 20th Century living. To help us acquire thinking that once again will 'chime in with Revelation' and Supernatural Truth.

The Saints have shown us what can happen, if the human mind lets itself be guided by absolutes, and in turn will guide the will and all the actions along the path of a realistic and logically compelling acceptance of God in everyday life.

The mind simply boggles if it considers what our planet would look like if, e.g., people would let themselves be guided by a realistic acceptance of the absolute holiness of God. If the human discovery of this Absolute starts to chime in with God's Revelation of His own Holiness, as it did in St. Ignatius, and earlier on in St. Michael ... If the Absolute Holiness of God dominated our lives as one of those preambles of the Faith ascertained by our Intellect, at the same time that it is a Revealed Truth, guaranteed by God; it would have the same effect on us that it had on Moses.

The Holiness of God. Totally worthy of our trust. Without any fear of 'ulterior motives', secret designs or vindictiveness. To what

Chapter Six: The Nature of Catholic Philosophy (IV)

human love could it inspire. Without any need for suspicion or a defensive attitude. The Holiness of God: capable of loving sinners; never to be doubted, never to be queried, always worthy of our Infused, Supernatural, Divine and Catholic Hope. The virtue that gives Glory to God. Faith in the Holiness of God. To what Hope and Love and endurance and trust is it capable. To what reverence and humility and finally tranquillity, and rest in God's security would it inspire. How profitable to us is this belief in an Absolute.

In His Wisdom, God has seen fit to leave us with a deterrent. Not only the example of Lucifer, and the fate that befell this Fallen Angel because of the infringement of this Absolute; but also – of all people – Moses! At one occasion, tried to the limit and probably beyond his human endurance, he refused to uphold God's Absolute Holiness before the rebelling Jews. And God's punishment was immediate and severe: Moses was not to lead the Jews into the Promised Land ... Moses took the bitter medicine with the characteristic greatness in sanctity he had reached, but his plaintive and charitable complaint in several places of the Pentateuch to his people, shows that he suffered nevertheless.

"Then Yahweh said to Moses and Aaron: 'Because you did not believe that I could proclaim my Holiness in the eyes of the sons of Israel, you shall not lead this assembly into the land I am giving them." (Num. 20:12.)

"Now Moses was the most humble of men, the humblest man on earth." (Num. 12;3.)

"Yahweh was angry with me too, on your account. 'You shall not go in either', He said." (Deut. 1:37, 3:26, 4:21, 34:4.)

But, as we all know, God loved His servant Moses, so much a prefigurement of His only Son, with a manly and deep and lasting Love. After he was shown on the top of Mount Nebo the length and breadth of the Promised Land in all its glory, Moses died in the arms of the God he loved and had seen so often 'face to face'. "And there He buried him ... but to this day no one has ever found his grave". (Deut. 34:6.)

" ... on your account ...". The example God made of His servant Moses is for our benefit! We are the products of our irreligious times, but in final analysis, if the restoration of Thomism is of such overriding importance, it is because of the envisaged Sanctity resulting from it is of such far-reaching consequence ...

To us, the seemingly unimportant, academic question of the existence of universal concepts may not be of great, practical value. But the existence of Absolutes is! What Occam envisaged: the acceptance of Absolutes in Faith only, without any logical and intellectual foundation for them, proved to be too much; and soon made Faith in them not only illogical but impossible ...

Therefore, pointing out as I did in my example with Moses, that it is the creative Will of God, that human beings come to the natural knowledge of an all-perfect and holy Supreme Being; Whose nature is to exist in all His perfections (Sinai desert), is showing at the same time its great practical value, for it makes the fulfilment of the saving Will of God: the acceptance in Faith of an all-perfect and Holy Trinity ever so much easier.

But there is more to it than this.

Moses was a preamble to Faith in Christ. That is, the Jewish knowledge of the great Moses (as Moses pointed out himself: Deut

18:18) was meant by God to pave the way to the acceptance of Christ; to facilitate Supernatural Faith in His Divine origin. That is why God could not tolerate a flaw in Moses. At one stage, in extreme exasperation, Moses conveyed to the sons of Israel the impression that God was not Holy enough, not Perfect enough, to love them. To really love that motley group of whingers and rebels before him.

"Listen, you rebels. Shall we make water gush from this rock for you?"

God knew how much the Israelites were in need of a rebuke; but not one that impaired an Absolute: the Holiness of God. God could not let it pass, and even 40 years later, God came back to it:

"Because you broke faith with Me among the sons of Israel that time at Meribath-kadesh, in the wilderness of Zin, because you did not display My Holiness among the sons of Israel, you may see this land only from afar." (Deut. 32:51.)

In the natural prefiguration of His Son, God could not tolerate a flaw in the integrity of an absolute, since it adversely reflected on the Absolute Holiness of God, that means on the perfection of his Love for sinners, to be completely revealed in His Son.

There is a great lesson in this for us Catholics. We are the preambles of the Faith of others. Through us, the acceptance of the Grace of Faith should be made easier. We, therefore, should be perfect 'as our Heavenly Father is perfect'. There should not be any flaws in us touching on Absolutes. For that we need great Faith, great Hope, great Love. The Holiness of God, the Love of God, the Goodness of God, the Truth of God, the Unity of God must shine forth from us, as it had to in Moses. As in Moses, it is to be built on the most correct, the most clear thinking possible. And for that we have the guarantee of God in Scripture, and of the teaching of the Church, that Thomism is indispensable.

The natural knowledge of an all-perfect Being, and the natural love for It, facilitates the transportation of the Human Mind to the truly Infinite: that one day we would come face to face with water gushing forth from the pierced Heart of God for the salvation of all the rebels, and all the whingers. To undermine Faith in such Absolutes, Thomism had to be destroyed. May its restoration return to Catholics what is their fullest right, for the salvation of All.

Chapter Seven

The Nature of Catholic Theology (I)

The Human Study of Divinely Revealed Truths

Introduction

The previous lectures in this series were meant to convince us that it is the Mind of the Church that only the proper thinking 'borne on the wings of St. Thomas' to heights scarcely capable of being matched, let alone surpassed, should not only be understood and practiced by everybody for the proper ordering of one's life; should not only be taught to everybody as a Preamble to the Catholic Faith, i.e. a most suitable preparation conducive to the embrace of this priceless Grace, but must furthermore be understood and put into practice by every Catholic for the support and the safeguarding of the Gift of Faith.

Holy Scripture bears out most strikingly this overriding concern of the Magisterium for clear and proper thinking as a foundation for the true Faith. In the 13th chapter of St. John's *Book of Revelation*, the holy author will assure us that there will come a time

" …that the whole world marvelled and followed the beast (Antichrist). They prostrated themselves in front of the dragon because he had given the beast his authority; and they prostrated themselves in front of the beast saying: 'Who can compare with the beast? How could anybody defeat him?' …"

If this means anything, it means that the whole world will come face to face with the consequences of centuries of crooked thinking: thinking that refused to 'chime in with Revelation', leaving people barren, and deprived of the graces so necessary to prevent the great and universal apostasy. As already explained, Thomism has been jettisoned not only by the scientific world, by the universities, politicians, big business, by the media and educators; but also finally even by Catholic scholars, and by everybody who came under their influence, accepted the lead given by them, and took over their thinking. In fact, not only are we not all that far removed from the reality expressed in the above-quoted passage from St. John: we are right in it. The one-world 'church' of Satan, the 'church' of the second beast 'that looks like the Lamb but speaks like the Dragon', the 'church' that will do everything in its power 'to extend the authority of the first beast', this 'church' is with us today; pointed out by Pope St. Pius X in *Our Apostolic Mandate* and identified for us, when he spelled out its marks and objectives. (1910.)

This question of 'who runs the world' is at present time of such tremendous interest, and the cause of such universal uneasiness and anxiety, clothed as it is in secrecy and darkness, that I am prepared to probe with you deeper into this whole business in order to bring out in great clarity the absolute power and glory of Catholic Faith: the study of which pertains to the subject-matter of this Lecture.

Chapter Seven: The Nature of Catholic Theology (I)

World Conspiracies

Books and stories abound trying to convince us that it is inevitable that the 'illuminati', i.e. Satan's seed, will eventually rule the world. And yet, these stories and the 'facts' they portray leave the truly consecrated to Our Lady stone cold and unmoved. There are several reasons for this.

For one, as already investigated in previous lectures, world conspiracies are the result of Crooked Thinking: thinking inspired by Lucifer. Just as Abraham and Moses, each in their own time, turned their backs on secret societies and their mysteries in order to concentrate their natural understanding and supernatural insights on the infinite expanse of Faith in the One True God, and just as Our Blessed Lord did not show the slightest interest in trying to follow the crooked thinking of the Jewish leaders in His days, leading directly to His Passion and Death, and did not even by a flicker of interest betray any curiosity to know the latest developments in that thinking, so also now the Catholic Church.

Secondly, God's ways and Light and thinking do not become clearer by trying to understand evil ways. In other words, a better understanding of the conspiracies does not make God's ways with the modern world clearer and more understandable. On the contrary: a better understanding of God's thinking gives us a better understanding of the deficiencies of our times and its evil ways. A great devotion to Our Lady of Fatima, by which we Stop Sinning, do penance, say our prayers, make reparation and stay at our post at all cost to perform our daily duties, makes one very sharp-eyed about what is happening now without any need to read books about conspiracies.

Thirdly, what the conspirators are secretly planning and plotting and saying, and what they want us to know, are two entirely different things. In other words, we never get the truth from them, and we never get to the truth following Lucifer's thinking and reading the conspiracy literature. As already said: we get a far clearer insight in what they are about from our Heavenly Mother saying Her Rosary.

Finally, following the thoughts and plots of the plotters is boring to the extreme, since their thinking is so manifestly shallow and wrong. The whole thing is one big yawn. Setting one's tide, as some Catholics nowadays do, to the ebb and flood of world conspiracies and catastrophes, is perpetually chasing one's tail, round and round in circles. If one crisis is not going to bring about a world conflagration, another will, and we are daily in a state of tension and apprehension, so unlike Christ. He and His Blessed Mother want us to go quietly about our daily business saving souls by prayer and penance and our daily duty. This will make us very sharp-eyed in the business of saving souls in all circumstances, and to make the most and the best of all circumstances. The Church goes quietly right through the time of Antichrist, just as Christ went quietly right through His Passion and Crucifixion. There was no need for Him to inquire about the latest developments of the plans of the plotters and sinners in order to make His Passion more meaningful and more adept to the needs of the times … The devil would love us to find his 'creation' so interesting and absorbing and important that we spend all our time analysing it and occupying ourselves with it.

The Heavenly Strategy

What is of tremendous interest is what Our Lady wants us to do at the present time to save souls. The Heavenly strategy: not in answer to the plotters, as if the plotters dictate Heaven's timetable, but ignoring the plotters since they have no part with God's saving plan with the world. To know Heaven's strategy, we do not have to know what the sinners are up to. All we have to do is meditate on the Mysteries of the Holy Rosary and be totally absorbed in Our Blessed Lady's plans and wishes. Like Moses, we will have to use our clear thinking and human resourcefulness 24 hours a day on the tremendous task of guiding souls entrusted to our care safely to the Promised Land, showing no interest whatsoever for the crooked thinking the 'Egyptian illuminati' may be engaged in to thwart our Exodus.

If Our Lord had been doing what is being advised in some quarters, He would have been concentrating on His own survival. He would have left Jerusalem as a dangerous place, and we would still not be redeemed ... And when Peter left Rome on the 'advice' of his senior counsellors, he met His Lord once again, carrying His Cross, telling Peter on the latter's query of 'where was He going', that He was going to Rome to be crucified once again.

The True Fascination ... The True Perspective ...

So, we too stay at our post, concentrating on our daily duty at that post and receiving from God all the insights and understanding necessary to carry the Holy Catholic Church safely through to the next generation. When we concentrate on God's Mysteries, we will receive abundant Light and He will not leave us in the dark about essentials: things we ought to know and pick up in passing, necessary for our work in His vineyard.

What hurts the plotters most is a strong, supernatural, infused, divine Catholic Faith, not exposes of secrets. Nobody cares a hang any more who knows who is a member of the 'Club of Rome' or what plans they have for the world. They disseminate all sorts of lies and falsehoods themselves, and the clear, supernatural insights of what they are about, is not obtained from studying their mysteries, but God's. It infuriates the devil if we ignore his tremendously important plots as totally unimportant, and boring and childish; and when, like the first martyr St. Stephen, we obtain far greater insights into what he and his seed are about than he has himself by staying close to Our Blessed Lady and the tremendous Light that gives. For close to Her we gather the supernatural insights and the ways by which God is going to thwart the plans of the plotters, making them serve His plans. And of this, the devil and the 'Club of Rome' have no nous.

We do not have to know how we are going to cope when we refuse the mark of the beast. It is far more to the point for the beast to know how he is going to cope when we refuse his mark and prefer to remain with God, resolved to have nothing to do with his childish empire-building. 'At the sound of my name, fearsome despots will be afraid', can truly be said of every child of Mary. This then is the true perspective and the fascinating discovery: far from being overawed and preoccupied by world domination and the one-world 'church', all built on crooked thinking, we put the fear of God into these empire builders and slave drivers by our Thomistic clear thinking as the best vehicle for the irresistible Light and Power of Supernatural Faith, bringing to nought the clumsy efforts of the unholy ones to rule this world as if it is theirs. Their efforts are not thwarted by the millions who mistakenly think that they ought to do what the devil and his seed secretly love everybody to do: to take their endeavours seriously. Taking the 'mysteries' of the so-called 'illuminati' so seriously that we think we do them a great damage by exposing them, is precisely playing into their hands. Studying what Abraham and Moses turned their backs on is a waste of time.

Let us then, instead, concentrate our attention on that with which Thomistic clear thinking chimes in: the Supernatural, and discover why a creature that shares the Life and Nature of God becomes so powerful that it is invincible, even if the beast is allowed to declare war on the Saints and to overcome them ... Just as the First Good Friday did not show the weakness of Christ but his invincible strength, so is it now with the Catholic Church. This Truth makes the study of Revealed Truth imperative.

The New Creation

Even in our run-down society, we can still see plenty of examples of how noble human nature really is and how richly it was endowed by the loving Creator. Side by side with the many examples of utter depravity and selfishness are the peaks and the heights human beings are capable of reaching. Time and time again we are allowed to marvel at the resourcefulness and originality the "human animal" is capable of, even in surroundings and conditions hardly capable of inspiring us to anything but the struggle for survival. And even that is more often than not done with a tenacity and endurance, betraying the existence of a nobility of soul truly created in the image and likeness of God.

It is a source of great sadness to see so much good and irreplaceable value suddenly brought to ruin and extinction by war, terrorism and abortion. If living according to the Thomistic principles, i.e. living to the perfection of one's human nature, living to the fullness of one's potentialities of intellect and will, and in the full recognition and appreciation of the Divine Absolutes, would already be of inestimable value for life on this planet, we can imagine what it would be like if such an existence was allowed everywhere to chime in with Revelation! Is it possible to even visualise what life here on earth would be, if the 'new creation' was allowed free reign, the light of the human mind was reinforced and perfected by the Supernatural Light of Faith, the human will strengthened and ennobled by the warmth of the Supernatural virtue of Love, and Christ would be King of every heart and hearth? If purely human qualities can be so strong that Carroll Quigley could write in

Chapter Seven: The Nature of Catholic Theology (I)

his famous work *Tragedy and Hope*, when, in one sentence, he summarises a novel by Burdick and Wheeler called "Fail Safe".

" ... the ultimate total catastrophe of making the human race resemble an antheap was avoided, because a few men at and near the top were able to assume the human functions of decision, self-sacrifice, love for their fellow man and hope for the future ..." (p. 886.)

What then, I ask, could be expected, if enough human beings decided to reassert the power of their supernatural faculties and potentialities, which they acquire sharing in the Divine Nature and Life of the Blessed Trinity?

That human beings here on earth can share in their created existence in the Divine Life of the Blessed Trinity: seeing what God sees and understands, loving and willing what God wills, hoping to acquire what God lives for and wants us to share ever more fully is Catholic Dogma. In Baptism we not only receive a share in that Divine Life: we also acquire the Supernatural Faculties to perform the actions that this Divine Life requires. These Faculties are the three Supernatural, Infused, Divine Virtues of Faith, Hope and Love. They have God for their immediate Object and Motive. One of the consequences of this New Existence is, that it is valued and treasured above and beyond our earthly existence, and that our earthly life is from now on only a means to an end, used solely for the greatest perfection of the new, divine life. The more matter-of-fact we become in this: the more we live in and from Faith; the more consistent we appear in subduing the old Adam to serve the new: the more we allow the Supernatural to take over our life here on earth, the more Light and insight we receive in the 'things of our Father' and the more efficient and happy we will be in achieving our ends. The old way of seeing this as 'The Ascent of Mount Carmel': (i) the Via Purgativa, or the Stage of purging ourselves from sin and from all earthly attachments; (ii) the Via Illuminativa, or the Stage of receiving great light and insights in the things of God; (iii) the Via Unitiva, or the Stage of total Union with God in His Mystical Life, will be the share of us all, if we take this New Creation and its responsibilities seriously.

It is the task and privilege of Theology to study all the aspects of this new life on the principles of Thomistic Philosophy. If at present time 'theology' seems to have gone haywire, it is solely due to the fact that it has abandoned its absolutely vital function of growing out of Thomistic, i.e. Catholic Philosophy. In other words, it has lost its roots. The previous six lectures not only have made us aware of that necessity, but also will have given us some insight into the reasons for this vital union between Thomistic Philosophy and Theology. There is only one type of clear human thinking, and that thinking must be used in philosophy and theology.

We are now ready to study the Heavenly Carillon, the necessary aspects of the Divine Life in God, with which the earthly carillon: Thomistic Philosophy, chimes in so beautifully to the eternal Glory of God and the enchantment of man. We will discover that nothing of the human thinking studied so far will have to be abandoned or modified in order to chime in with the eternal bells. To our amazement we will grow into the awareness that the Eternal Bells must have created the earthly ones in order to allow the earthly ones to chime in with them. Divine thinking, even done by humans in their capacity of adopted Children of God, does not destroy or bend human thinking, but perfects it. Catholic Faith, correct divine thinking performed by humans, is the crown and glory of Thomistic Philosophy: ordinary human thinking at its peak. This combination: the true discipline of the mind, (Lecture 10) is the most powerful thing on earth; and as far as the Enemy of Human Nature is concerned, invincible.

The Power of the New Creation

Right from the moment the New Creation got a foothold here on earth, God, in His wonderful Wisdom, and early Christians chiming in with it, wanted the Church to have a good idea of the power this new life possesses. Barely 30 years after the Death of Christ on Calvary, did the first Roman Martyrs under Nero go to their martyrdom singing. If it took some 15 years for 'The Word' to establish itself in Rome, then it took barely another 15 years for the first Christians to finish the Via Purgativa: divest themselves from all earthly attachment to possessions; finish the Via Illuminativa: making great strides in the understanding of the unworldly knowledge and Wisdom of God as preached by Peter and Paul; and even finish the via Unitiva: become united with Christ in eternity through their martyrdom, allowing their perfected human mind, intellect and thinking and their perfected will and love, take them to the peak of human perfection in 15 years. And those who escaped the persecutions took the same qualities and perfection with them to other regions to lay the foundation of the European Christian Civilisation.

In those 15 years there was no time to set up an elaborate Catholic School system; there were no Catholic hospitals or Churches. In fact, the Church could not have been established in Rome in a more unsuitable climate; with fornication, homosexuality and all the other signs of a decadent, run-down civilisation rife. And the Christians knew their job: to clean up the mess. And clean it up they did, for centuries to come. The first converts were totally unprotected in that hostile environment, and they had to learn fast. And if the signs are not misleading us, then the same conditions for fast learning, how to live by our natural and supernatural wits are with us again. Once again a mess is to be cleaned up; once again, there is no escape; and once again it cannot be left to the next fellow. We have to do it, and we will have to teach our children how to take over from us. Please God, they (and us) will make as credible job as the first Christians, when we are losing our Catholic Schools to the modernists, our hospitals to the abortionists, and our public institutions to the marxists. We too will have to rediscover the power of the New Creation.

[I like to continue and conclude this lecture on this note: "the power of the New Creation". Catholic Theology is so vast and complex, that it is impossible to reflect it, not even in its essentials, in one lecture. But that is not our purpose. Catholics know what they believe, and that they believe Truths the human mind could not unlock by its own power; Truths such as the Blessed Trinity in God, the Incarnation of the Second Person of the Blessed Trinity; the Divine Maternity and perpetual Virginity of the Blessed Virgin Mary; the participation here on earth in the Divine Life of God by adoption; the beatific vision; the resurrection of the body; the forgiveness of sins, etc. So, what I would like to highlight, and what you would like me to show, no doubt, is, that believing what the Catholic Church proposes to us to believe, far from restricting our human thinking, brings it to the peak of its perfection. In that way, the Thomistic Philosophy, far from being just a philosophy, becomes an integral part of that perfection: human thinking, chiming in with Revelation.]

Not Deceived

The Certainty of Catholic Faith ... That is the foundation of everything. Believing in a God Who cannot deceive nor be mistaken Himself. This means with absolute certainty that He left with us, i.e. within the history of human affairs, the Living Principle of that certainty, that impossibility of deception: the Catholic Church, headed by an infallible Pope, successor of St. Peter, and founded by His Son. It is good to reflect how this certainty, this knowledge on the Supernatural level, is the Crown and Glory of what we discovered in Thomistic Philosophy. In the Metaphysics of St. Thomas we came to the inevitable conclusion that the human mind can come to the knowledge of Absolutes: things that are absolutely true. Now, any religion which does not come to a belief in Supernatural Absolutes and allows its adherents to make up their own mind what they believe, cannot be the true religion revealed by God, since it places itself lower than Philosophy, which acknowledges the existence of absolutes that are ascertainable by the human mind without revelation. And any religion which claims to have its origin in the Revelation by God in the Person of Jesus

Christ, but denies that He left a visible principle of that certainty of Revelation co-existing within the human family in the authority of some infallible Magisterium, will find it absolutely impossible to maintain the fullness and integrity of that Revelation alive within their flock and will find themselves hard pressed in their endeavours not to let the belief of their flock sink below philosophy.

Only one Church has maintained belief in the existence of this principle of protection against error and deceit as an integral part of the Church founded by Christ, and has also maintained the Philosophy that underlies this Supernatural Reality as a Preamble to the True Faith and chiming in with it.

Any freedom of thought, therefore, claiming independence of this Faith and its underlying Philosophy, is not a true freedom at all, since only Truth will set us free. The New Creation does not have to fear this thinking, nor should it look wistfully toward it as something to be envied. The New Creation should always be very conscious of the fact that the salvation of everybody else depends on the Catholic Church and the Faith within it.

I Have Made Known to You Everything I Have Learned From My Father

The totality of Revelation ... Right from the start given to the Church, still in our possession today. The first Christian Martyrs knew what they were giving their lives for. They had the fullness of insight and understanding since, as the New Creation, they shared in the Spirit of God Who lived in them personally as well as in the community of believers: the Church. The Catholic Church teaches

Chapter Seven: The Nature of Catholic Theology (I)

that Tradition is an integral part of the Catholic Faith. Tradition shows how the Gift of Faith was understood, and lived and explained by the Magisterium down the ages. The Revelation of the New Testament grows organically from the one of the Old Testament, like a flower from its plant. Nothing can come in from the outside, nothing can be grafted on to it. As we will see more clearly in Lecture 9: "The Corruption of Catholic Thinking", 'evolution' and kindred weeds are poisonous plants which the enemy has sown amongst the Wheat of God's Word, trying to palm it off as pertaining to Revelation. Impossible, since it neither grows organically from Old Testament Revelation, nor from the New.

What the Catholic Church teaches, Theology explains. At any stage of the Church's human history, the New Creation was always and still is in the full possession of Christ's inheritance. And over the centuries, not only our supernatural insight into what this Treasure really contains, has grown, but also the knowledge of how it can be applied to the various stages of human development. But new applications are invariably in line with what has been revealed, and with what has been taught and explained by the Church previously. And here true Philosophy comes to the aid of Faith and Revelation: we never have to put up with Contradictions. The Principle of Contradiction not only guides true Philosophy, but also true Theology; since Theology is Human Thinking on Divine Revelation. Divine Revelation will never do violence to human thinking, but will respect it and make full use of it; and eventually will perfect it.

As with all these questions: a lot more can be said about any of them, but once the principle is understood and appreciated, prayer and study will bring the Catholic, and please God, many outside the Church, to the full knowledge of the powerful assistance this 'chiming in of Philosophy with God's thinking' gives to anyone who is required by outsiders 'to give an account of the Hope that lives within him'. (1 Pet. 3:15.)

The New Adam

Here we will come face to face with one of the greatest and most perplexing Mysteries of Divine Revelation: the Mystery of Suffering. The great Mystery, that the New Creation was born out of Suffering and Death. Much of human ingenuity has nevertheless fallen silent in the presence of great pain and inexplicable suffering. Will Philosophy? If Thomism has brought human thinking almost to the pinnacle of greatness, will it also 'chime in with the Revelation of the Cross'? The Redemption from Sin and liberation from the eternal Death were bought on the Cross and paid for in Blood? Is this a part of Revelation impervious to Human Thinking, where Human Thinking can no longer chime in with Revelation? Theology and devotional literature are resplendent with the development of this Sacred Reality, revealed to us in so much Love. We know its Supernatural Truth. The Saints and all the nameless great men and women have lived it, strengthened by the Divine Example. It is undoubtedly an area where Love reigns supreme. But is Truth altogether excluded? Must the Human mind fall here completely silent, and admit that the final word is to the inexplicable? That here a Word is uttered devoid of all meaning? That there is such a thing as a Divine Contradiction? Must the Human Mind admit that here, in truth, human thinking and Divine Thinking finally part company? Awesome thought.

Surprisingly, Ancient World Literature is so full of stories dealing with the struggle between Light and Darkness, Good and Evil, with Light and Goodness only gaining the upperhand through battle, endurance of hardships and even in noble death, that it shows that Humanity as a whole did more than simply (i) Live with the fact of this knowledge: it was prepared to go further and (ii) Accept the fact.

Even more surprisingly, the widespread acceptance in faith of some sort of existence and survival after death, a primitive preamble to a fuller realisation of the immortality of the soul must have strengthened the nameless masses, still under God's Fatherly care, to a belief that it is better to put up with hardships in this life than jeopardise peace after death in some union with the Deity. And belief, as we have seen, has a lot to do with intellectual conviction and with the acceptance of truth. So, when Christ gave us the parable of the two grains of wheat: one refusing to die, and so remaining alone, and the other prepared to give its life in order to produce fruit and offspring, He appealed to an accepted (iii) Truth found in the human store of knowledge. A truth which there and then was made into a preamble to the acceptance of a Revealed Truth: the way the Redemption was going to be achieved.

But there is still more to it.

What about the (iv) Love of this Truth? Was that totally unknown to Humanity? Did His very words spoken before Pilate: "I came into the world to bear witness to the Truth" not have an echo, one pealing bell, somewhere in humanity, however unworthy, humble and timid, but genuine? Trying to chime in with this profound Mystery of Divine Revelation? Was Christ's Love for Truth, a love so great that, on His own testimony, He came down from Heaven to bear witness to it, the first and only admission on this earth that Truth can be loved? No. Once again His Divine Love for sinful but nevertheless struggling Humanity had made allowance for a participation in this Mystery. There were bells in the distance pealing in supplication to be heard and acknowledged in Eternity. And once again, although not only, Philosophy, Greek Philosophy, the Queen of sciences, provided the earthly carillon. Here, at the peak of its knowledge, and of its love for knowledge, Humanity did bring to the threshold of Revelation that which was finally allowed to chime in with it. And, as with all peaks, this one too stands alone. Human genius shines forth in this: that the whole of what had to be stated is not related in an effusion of words, but is expressed in one word: Philosophy, or Love of Wisdom.

Love of Wisdom. Rising far above the love of sexuality, and above love of all the passions; rising above the love of material things, above everything that this life can offer, even prepared to sacrifice everything: is the crown and glory of man's hankering after God: Love of Wisdom. Which God did accept, as we know from the Revelation contained in the Old Testament Books of Wisdom, as a prayer for and a calling down of Redemption.

With this, the New Creation, drawing full knowledge from Theology in its aspirations to love and imitate our Crucified Lord, can nevertheless know and consider itself fully human, sharing with what we know to be most noble in Humanity: a great love and aspiration for Wisdom and Truth, prepared with all those who went before to sacrifice everything in order to gain it. In the full knowledge that this unworldly love has sanctified as far as possible human suffering in preparation for the great and all-embracing Sacrifice of Calvary.

In the matter of conversions, this will be of great practical value. The question of human suffering is not an easy one, and if we look for a preamble, to start people off on the road to Faith, we can try to inspire them with a desire for human wisdom as a motive for putting up with hardships in the pursuit of it. We can then be sure that this thinking and this love will never have to change radically in order to make way for the Supernatural, as, with God's Grace, this thinking and this love are already chiming in with the Catholic Faith, necessary to embrace the Supernatural Wisdom of the Cross.

Conclusions

Theology, then, is the study of the New Creation. Just as Thomistic Philosophy is the only recommended study by the Church of Human Nature, so Thomistic Theology is the only recommended study of our participation in the Divine Nature. Just as philosophy discovered and studied the human faculties in our soul, which enable us to live according to our human nature, so Theology studies the Supernatural Faculties of Faith, Hope and Love, which enable us to live according to our participation in the Divine Nature: to think like God, to love like God, to act like God would act.

Just as our Supernatural Nature does not do violence to our human nature, but brings it to perfection; and just as Catholic Faith does not destroy our human thinking, but brings it to perfection, so Catholic Theology does not destroy, or takeover, the role of Catholic Philosophy, but brings it to perfection. But by saying that, it becomes obvious that Catholic Philosophy must be there, otherwise it could not come to perfection. The Laws of Reasoning, the Rules of Logic, the Principles of Being are all needed and are fully maintained in order that the study of the New Creation can be a Proper Human Study. We will have a lot more to say about this in Lecture 9: "The Corruption of Catholic Thinking".

Just as Philosophy not only studies the human being, but also the human being in society, in his relationships with others, so Theology also studies the Divine Community: the Catholic Church and the Doctrines, the means of Salvation and the structures entrusted to Her care.

Finally, as promised earlier, a look at the proper relationship between Conscience and Faith. Conscience is a human faculty for the ordering of the right conduct for the safeguarding and the perfection of human nature. Faith is a Supernatural Light and faculty, given for the safeguarding and perfection of the New Creation: the divine Nature we share in the State of Grace. Faith, therefore, is the Superior Light, given for the guidance of Conscience. Catholic Faith brings conscience to perfection. Catholic Faith informs conscience. The Modernists, in their ignorance and their eagerness to destroy Catholic Faith as a pre-requisite for entry into their man-made 'church of darkness', would have us believe the opposite: that Catholic Teaching must give way to conscience, or better still: freedom of conscience. With Teilhard, they reject the Supernatural, and so there is only one order: the human order in evolution. And in that cock-eyed system, they think conscience reigns supreme.

Chapter Seven: The Nature of Catholic Theology (I)

We can leave them to their man-made religion and their man-made 'church': as long as there is but one Catholic left over on earth who knows better and believes what the Catholic Church always has taught, the salvation of the whole world will still be assured, and on that Faith, the Church will rise to see better days.

Chapter Eight

The Nature of Catholic Theology (II)

God, Man and the Moral Order

Introduction

In Theology, then, we study Supernatural Truths and Realities revealed by God. Although the knowledge of these Truths and Realities surpasses the powers and faculties of human nature, and so are inaccessible to the human mind; once revealed by God, their Study becomes subject to the rules and laws governing the human intellect. This means that Catholic Theology presupposes the only philosophy which perfected human thinking: the Philosophy of St. Thomas Aquinas. And this by the Will of God, Creator and Redeemer, wishing that no new Laws of thinking and rules of Thought would be necessary to switch over from the study of God's Creation (Philosophy) to the study of God's Redemption (Theology). Only a new and more powerful Light would be added: the Light of Catholic Faith.

For simplicity's sake (because the subject is so vast), I introduced Theology as the human study of the 'New Creation': redeemed Man, sharing God's Divine Nature here on earth through Sanctifying Grace. Furthermore, because times are bad, and each day resembles more the conditions in which the early Roman Martyrs found their Faith, I used the study of Theology to highlight the Power of the New Creation. When the whole world is gradually becoming convinced of the power of the conspirators and the one-worlders, and their seed: Antichrist; Catholics and other Christians will have to be equally and even more convinced, that the true Power, the Power of God, the Power of Redemption, lies with them and extends over the whole world.

The Catholic Church teaches, and Theology explains, that Catholics possess that power because they have (i) the Certainty of Faith, (ii) the Totality of Revelation, and (iii) the Fullness of Love, by which they not only share in the merits of Christ, but also in His Passion. In bringing this out in my previous Lecture, I was at pains also to stress that each of these had a preamble to Faith in human thinking, brought to perfection in true Philosophy, so that it is true that no new thinking is required, but only thinking on a higher level, with new and more powerful light and faculties.

For (i), the certainty of Catholic Faith, Philosophy has the knowledge of Absolutes. The certainty of human thinking is not destroyed but elevated. For (ii), the totality of Revelation, Philosophy brings its Principle of Contradiction to the rescue. If the Catholic Church possesses the fullness and totality of Gods' Revelation, then it is clear that Nothing New can be offered to the Church or it must contradict what is already there. So, if a theologian offers us some new doctrine, then it can either be shown to have grown organically from the Deposit of Faith already in the Church's possession, and so not contradicting Church Doctrine; or else, if it is so new that the Church never had it, it must contradict something in the Deposit of Faith since the Church is already in the possession of the totality of Revealed Truth. For it is a contradiction to have the totality of something to which something can be added.

Chapter Eight: The Nature of Catholic Theology (II)

As for (iii): the Catholic Church's Love for the Cross, here too, by God's Providence, we are able to point to a preamble in Philosophy to this Faith, where Philosophy can point out in humility but in Truth, that it too had already discovered and taught that the greatest love on earth is the love for wisdom and truth; and so, if the cross is true Supernatural Wisdom, then Philosophy will encourage Christians to embrace it with all their heart and mind.

And once again we may appreciate the fury of Hell and of Modernism against Thomistic Philosophy: far from being a hindrance to Supernatural Faith, it is its greatest advocate and protector.

We can now continue our theological studies of the New Creation.

God

Now that the Supreme Being of Philosophy: Absolute Existence, Absolute Truth, Absolute Holiness and Perfection, has been totally revealed to us as the Blessed Trinity, Father, Son and Holy Spirit, of Christianity, and now that the Human Being of Philosophy has been fully revealed to us as the New Creation of the Redemption in Christ, it is fitting that we look with the eyes of Faith and Theology to the Triune God Whose Divine Nature we are allowed to share.

The Mystery of the Blessed Trinity in Whose Life we partake, Whose Thoughts are now ours and Whose Life of Love we are privileged to enjoy. The Father Who created us, and Who sent His Son into our world to redeem us and teach us all there is to know, and Who sent His Holy Spirit to sanctify us and to remain with us as His adopted children: nimis sero te amavi! 'All to late have I loved You!' (St. Augustine.)

This Great God of ours, we know Him as the Revealing God. The God Who took the veil away and showed us His adorable face in the Birth of His Son. He revealed Himself as the God Who wrote a book: a Book without mistakes or deception. A Book about Himself and His works. A Book about us, and our relationship with Him. A Book that, now that we are fully His Children, He reads to us, and we can understand. He has held nothing back.

We know Him as the Creating God. A God Who loved to be with the children of men, and Who loved to have us forever with him in Paradise. We know His as the God Who runs and governs things to perfection. Who looks after His creatures, even when they disobeyed God and lost his friendship.

We know Him as the God Who respects free will and so allowed the Mystery of evil to invade His Creation. We know Him as the God Who respects the Laws of His own creation; Who respects the Laws of Thinking to such an extent, that He is not afraid to let people live with the consequences of their actions in the full realisation of His own Omnipotence which includes the power to draw good from evil.

We know Him as the God Who Redeems in His Son Jesus Christ. We know Him as the God Who conceived and gave to us the altogether incomparable Blessed Virgin Mary. We know Him as the God Who died for us on the Cross so that we might live for Him.

Chapter Eight: The Nature of Catholic Theology (II)

We know Him as the God Who restored Grace and our share in His Supernatural, Divine Nature. With the incomparable faculties of Faith, Hope and Love, by which we are also capable of seeing one another as brothers and sisters.

We know Him as the God Who founded His Church and made it the visible and irreplaceable sign of the extension of His Redemption in time. We know this Church to be infallible in matters of Faith and Morals, governed by a man who is truly the Vicar of Christ, the Eternal Shepherd and Head of the Church. We know that Church to be a Mother, modelled on the Blessed Virgin Mary and to remain here on earth to do God's saving will in spite of hatred and opposition. Sanctifying Her children as far as they wish to go and enter into Her saving work of Redemption. The Catholic Church, which we know as "the pillar and mainstay of Truth". (1 Tim. 3:15.)

We know Him as the God Who sanctifies us through the Seven Sacraments of the Church. Who so enters into every stage of our life and our journey to Him, that we never have to be without the healing touch of His Hand.

We know him as the God Who gave us the clearest precepts about our moral life. Who gave us the certainty of where we are going and how to get there. The God Who sanctified our daily life and work through the Life of His Son and the Holy Family here on earth, so that no work is too menial to be done for the Glory of God and the salvation of souls, no offering too insignificant. We know Him as the God Who sanctified our daily crosses, since He sees in them the Cross of His Son.

This, then, is the God we are asked to love "with all our heart, with all our soul, with all our mind and with all our strength". (Mk. 12:30). If this is our God, Who wants us to be with Him for all eternity, then, even if we meditated on Him as He revealed Himself to us for the rest of our lives, then this retreat must not be considered too long, as it will continue in Eternity ...

These, then, are the saving Truths believed by our Catholic Faith and explained to us in the Catechisms and Theology. This is the Powerful Reality encompassing our world, the True Power, by which every other pretence to power pails into insignificance. "Yahweh derides them." (Psalm. 2:4).

This, then, is the whole saving Truth. Nothing can be added: no evolution, no soul-of-the-world, no cosmic christ, no omega-point or any other pseudo-scientific clap-trap, rosicrucian mumbo-jumbo or secret-society 'profundities' ... "God just laughs at them." (Psalm. 59:8).

Man

Man too has passed from the way he was known by Philosophy, true and noble as that knowledge about himself is, to the way he is known by God and to us in Faith.

In Faith, we see Man endowed with a share in the Divine Nature, and we turn to Sacred Theology, based on true Philosophy, to see what this knowledge holds in store for us.

If we know our God as a Revealing God, and we share His Nature, then we too must reveal Him to others. We must make Him known, so He will be loved and revered through us, His children.

Chapter Eight: The Nature of Catholic Theology (II)

If we know our God as a creating God, and we are His children, then we too, out of the nothingness of our existence, must bring forth acts which merit redemption and eternal life for others.

And so we can go on. Like our Father, we must respect others. We must respect their free will, but always be on the look-out to see if we can do good, undo the damage done, and help good to come out of evil.

We must carry our cross, pay our share of the human debt in prayer and suffering and patience, like our Brother, Christ. Restore Grace where it got lost and work with Our Lady to undo the knot of Eve of our days.

Like our Heavenly Mother, we must be a model of the Church wherever we are. Through us, the Catholic Faith and the Catholic Church must spread where it is not yet established: in individuals, families and groups. The Church is the pillar of Truth, and we must defend Her Truth and dissolve ignorance and darkness. We must use the Gifts of the Holy Spirit as God gave them to us, for the building up of the fullness of Christ on earth.

This is obviously living according to our nature, our New Nature as a child of God. Making use of the Sacraments to help ourselves as well as others. If it is Divine Law that every creature must live according to its nature and according to the perfection of its nature, then this must have a profound meaning to all of us who have been called to share so abundantly in the Divine Nature of God our Father; and of Jesus, our Brother; and of the Holy Spirit, the Sanctifier. This is not a take-it-or-leave-it package deal: this is Divine Law; the Law of the New Covenant, built on Love, Love freely given. There is a Divine Economy of Grace: Grace given to some for the salvation of others. It is God's Divine Nature to give us Grace: do we, although sharing in that same Nature, now refuse to pass it on? Or to merit it for others?

We have the founts of Eternal Life welling up inside us. If these Living Waters are not freely given, then the parched souls who were in vain entrusted to our care, will tear us apart and break us open, to drink the living waters that were rightly theirs. That is what is happening in persecutions. That is what persecutions are all about.

The Moral Order

We have had ample opportunity to convince ourselves that in elevating human nature to a participation in the Divine Nature, God did not destroy or nullify any quality, power, faculty or principle of human nature. Nothing of human nature got lost so that the Divine Nature would take over its role.

We saw that the human mind is still required to play its fullest part in the question of Catholic Faith. The rules of clear thinking and of logic are not to be abandoned. The human will is still to be incorporated in any action the New Creation is going to take in its Life in God. Philosophy is still required to underlie any thinking on the Supernatural, i.e. to support Theology. In fact, any 'theology' which does not base itself on the principles of Thomistic Philosophy, is not a theology at all and is not recognised by the Church as having any validity in making assertions in the matter of Faith and Church doctrine. Even in the most recent times we have examples

Chapter Eight: The Nature of Catholic Theology (II)

that the Church is prepared to take away from such 'theologians' the qualification 'Catholic'.

So, it should therefore not come as a surprise, that in the Moral Order God and the Catholic Church have followed the same line. Human morality, the absolute moral order, discernible by the human mind as the Ten Commandments did not get displaced to make room for the 'New Morality of the New Creation'. Anyone who maintains that the Ten Commandments have been abolished to make way for the new 'Law of Love' wants the Ten Commandments out of the way so they can break them, as we know every Modernist and Teilhardian does. The modernists cannot produce a scrap of evidence for their assertion that the Ten Commandments are no longer to be taught, as the new law of love has superseded them. But then, they cannot produce evidence for any erroneous assertion they make, but that does not worry them, as they never give the Church time to make an objection; or, when She makes it, they do not read it or listen to it. It is one of their infantile ploys to label 'old' everything they object to, to make it appear old fashioned, stultified and stuffy. But the Ten Commandments are as young and fresh as the latest new-born baby, for in that little heart they are engraved with the same loving Hand of God Who will give the self-same creature its Supernatural Nature in Baptism. The Law of Love does not find the Ten Commandments incompatible, nor do the Ten Commandments exclude Love.

Whoever sees the Ten Commandments as some external straight-jacket, totally divorced from the essence of human nature, is being deliberately obtuse and almost certainly has taken up this point of view in order to do away with the straight-jacket and be free to do as he pleases, even to the extent of breaking the Ten Commandments as he sees fit. Such a person cannot have any high idea of the Love of God, and can at most see in love only 'Luv': some well-known brand of dog food. Whoever has been subjected to the type of 'luv' the modernists and teilhardians are capable of will know what I am talking about. One shudders at the thought that this is the type of 'love' one will be subjected to in the coming 'church of darkness', their great man-made dream … The only love without the Ten Commandments is self love. And that, after all, is all that they preach … Assert yourself. Free yourself. Fulfil yourself. Find yourself. Love yourself. It is all there in the *Melbourne Guidelines*. The 'gospel' of the 'church of darkness' is in no need of the Ten Commandments. For a little while, their 'gospel' will sound exciting and new to the innocent young, until people see the face of Satan behind this 'freedom' and find what ruthless consequences are in store for anyone who is in the way of the total freedom of a modernist. In the dark 'church' of no Ten Commandments the preacher of the abolition is just as much a victim of the abolition of the 5th commandment as the one who learned the 'gospel' and puts it into practice. A dictatorship, far more oppressive and intolerant than God's Ten Commandments were supposed to have been, will be necessary to curb the passions and maintain law and order.

A supernatural without a nature to be raised is just as fanciful as love without the Ten Commandments. It is necessary therefore, in view of the widespread misconceptions about morality, to briefly examine the relationship between the natural morality, binding all men in conscience: the Ten Commandments; and the Law of Love, binding the New Creation.

Chapter Eight: The Nature of Catholic Theology (II)

For a start, it is true, that the Ten Commandments get a more profound understanding in the Supernatural Light of Faith and Love. But that is nothing new. That has been the case with everything else human. The emphasis now is keeping the Commandments out of love for others. That includes our enemies. We are never permitted to give false witness against our enemies, but now the emphasis is on keeping this Commandment out of love for him. Many people have the impression that an act of intercourse between two consenting partners (of the opposite sex, naturally) is not a grave sin because it is such a natural expression of love. But the Higher Law of Love demands that keeping the 6th Commandment fully intact, is seen as an act of higher love for the partner, than breaking it. For the sacrifice required to keep the Commandment is of immense spiritual benefit for the other, and that is a greater sign of love than keeping the Commandment for the sake of the Commandment.

Furthermore, Christ has specifically stipulated that the Commandments should be kept out of Love for Him. His Love is a Crucified Love, and so the Love of the New Creation, His Bloodbrother and sister must also be a crucified Love. The first aspect of that crucifixion is keeping the Commandments out of Love for Him.

It is obvious that this way of looking at the Ten Commandments is seeing them in their Sublimation, i.e. in their sublime role of pointing beyond themselves to a higher state of being: a state of love. They are no longer kept exclusively for the benefit of the one keeping them: they are being seen and used as expressions of love for God and fellow man. They are no longer exclusively being regulated for an ordered life here on earth, for an ordered and well regulated social existence: they are being used for the Redemption of others, i.e. they are being used to bring others into the state of being a New Creation themselves. They are being used for the Apostolate. Because Love is by its very nature fruitful, and the Supernatural Love that is being used to keep the Commandments will be Supernaturally fruitful; will produce New Creations. That way, the whole Church is 'in mission', is being missionary, is making converts. Christ has blessed that attitude. In stipulating the keeping of the Commandments, He has acknowledged their great value for Supernatural Love and fruitfulness. At the same time that the keeper of the Commandments is using them for the conversion of others, the Justice of God is seeing to it that the rewards for keeping them are not lost on the one who keeps them out of charity.

Great and necessary as these requirements of God, Nature and Love are: they are not the final word on the heights that the New Creation can reach in love of moral nobility. But they are the Foundation to any other heights that one can and may aspire. Consequently, further heights will need them as stepping stones and basis for further advancement. Further advances in holiness and perfection need a solid foundation of humility, obedience and prudence; not only is 'keeping the Commandments' the best school where to learn and practice those virtues, but they will need constant application in any higher state of holiness.

There is a way of living which is more direct, i.e. by its very nature, aimed at the perfection of the New Creation as well as its Supernatural fecundity: the conception and generation of Children of Grace around the world. The Ten Commandments – as we saw –

Chapter Eight: The Nature of Catholic Theology (II)

are directly related to the perfection of human nature and the attainment of that perfection in God. By Sublimation, a virtuous life according to the Ten Commandments, is meritorious in the Supernatural Life of Grace. Meritorious for the salvation of others. But the Height of Perfection, which here on earth conforms to the crucified state of Our Lord and to a share in His Mystical Life of the embrace of "Poverty, Chastity and Obedience" for the redemption of mankind, is lived in the life of the Evangelical Counsels of the Vows of Poverty, Chastity and Obedience.

Like with everything else that they have touched, the Modernists and Teilhardians have tried hard to twist this life of holiness and the perfection it always aimed for, into some unrecognisable caricature of it, in the hope it will mask their transition to the embrace of the world. So was one Sr. Kelly allowed to write in the Melbourne *Advocate* of 4th May, 1978, in an article reporting top-level discussions on Religious 'reform', under the heading: "Canon Law on Religious Mostly Good" (luckily for the good nuns!):

"Participants also discussed Changing Interpretations of the religious vows of poverty, chastity and obedience."

[For 2000 years they have always meant only one thing. Now hear how this eternal meaning is being changed into its opposite, and through the 'philosophy of sameness' is being held up as still meaning the same today.]

"Formerly, (i.e., for 2000 years ever since the days of Our Lady and Her Son) poverty meant 'do without' Sr. Kelly said. Now it means 'transcend material things' (but, if it no longer means 'do without', then transcending material things is very easy for every one having the pleasure of, say, motor car). Chastity meant: 'stay away from'. Now it means 'loving availability of service' (whom does the good nun think she is fooling here!). Obedience meant: 'don't do this or that'. Now it means 'mutuality (between community leader and member) in discerning the Father's Will'. ...."

I realise that we are not concerned here with yet another example of corruption of Catholic thinking: that belongs properly in the next lecture. "I am sorry, Father Rector, Mother Superior, but 'obeying' no longer means what it used to mean: Obeying. So, now that I don't want to do this or that, let us mutually agree that what I want to do is the will of God ..." Is that what Vatican II teaches? This is what we read in the most important document of the Council: *The Dogmatic Constitution on the Church*, Lumen Gentium, Ch. 6, Religious:

"The teaching and example of Christ provide the foundation for the Evangelical Counsels of chaste self-dedication to God, of poverty and obedience. The Apostles (one cannot go much further back) and Fathers of the Church commend them as an ideal of life and so do Her Doctors and Pastors. They therefore constitute a gift from God which the Church has received from Her Lord, and which, by His Grace, She always safeguards." (#44).

So far none of Sr. Kelly's 'formerly and now' business. Vatican II goes straight back to what it formerly meant: what Christ, the Apostles, the Fathers, the Doctors and Popes of the Church always have taught us about them. Furthermore, Vatican II specifically mentions that the Church has always been at pains to safeguard that meaning.

"The Bonds by which he pledges himself to the practice of the counsels show forth the unbreakable bond between Christ and His Bride, the Church." (#45).

"Furthermore the religious State constitutes a closer imitation and an abiding re-enactment in the Church of the form of life which the Son of God made His own when He came into the world to do the Will of the Father and which He propounded to the disciples who followed Him."

From this we conclude that the many misconceptions about the Moral teachings of the Church, have extended far into the state of perfection, the Evangelical Counsels, as well. People who have the audacity to call the Vow of Obedience a euphemism for 'doing your own thing in the religious life' can have no qualms about extending this idea to the moral order of the Ten Commandments. Unless these attitudes, and their preaching of it, change, the Religious Life will not receive many vocations and adherents; as the above way of 'explaining' the Three Vows shows clearly that their proponents have not left 'the spirit of the world, the flesh and the devil'.

Chapter Nine

The Nature of Catholic Theology (III)

The Corruption of Catholic Thinking

Introduction

This Lecture will finally link all that went before with what is still to come. It is meant to reinforce the subject-matter of the previous 8 Lectures, vividly bringing home the importance of what was studied there, by employing the well-tried method of "teaching by contrast": inspiring a greater love for Catholic Thinking by showing what has happened if sound Catholic Thinking was abandoned. When all the positive and negative aspects of present-day Catholic Thinking have been studied and grasped, then is the final analysis shown in this Lecture in a much better position to prepare us for the final one: Lecture 10, on the Discipline of the Mind.

Apart from the obvious didactic reasons and the pedagogical values of such an approach, demanded by sound educational principles, this study of the Corruption of Catholic Thinking recommends itself to us for its own intrinsic value as well in the never ending-battle for the mind of man and the salvation of souls. Even from this point of view alone, I am sure that many of my readers and listeners would like to know more about the deterioration of Catholic Thinking and Practices, simply to be better equipped to come to the aid of the many distraught souls, who first would like to know 'what is wrong', before they are willing and prepared to take our solutions and remedies as valid and effective.

As we all know: there have been serious deviations from clear thinking in the long course of human history, but none have been as serious as the deviations from Revealed Thinking, i.e. from Catholic Thinking. To the Catholic Church alone, and to the Catholic Faith within it, have been entrusted the salvation of humanity: the continuation of Christ's redeeming work on earth. All major deviations from Catholic Thinking have been disastrous, causing splits and divisions of such magnitude that they have lasted for centuries. In all those upheavals, the Catholic Church has always been able to show from Her past teachings that the causes of these splits and divisions were known to Her; and that She had warned Catholics of the serious consequences if these causes were allowed to run their courses unchecked, or were met with means and methods not inspired by Her previous teaching and Tradition. She was always able to show that there never was a need to go outside the Catholic Church for necessary reforms: She Herself possesses the totality of Redemption within Her, including the Redemption from whatever was causing the need for reform. But the irresistible pressure of the Holy Spirit has invariably proven to work against those who tried to force from within reforms unacceptable to the Church. Time and time again such reformers found themselves working from the outside, where of course they belonged, as the reformation envisaged by them was not inspired by the Holy Spirit and was alien to true Catholic Thinking. No matter how much Catholic Thinking may have been in need of correction …

Chapter Nine: The Nature of Catholic Theology (III)

In the course of Human History, containing the myriads of examples of spurious thinking, there have occurred three Corruptions of Thinking of such vast magnitude, that they have left a lasting effect on Humanity as a whole, because of the totally unexpected use that the Almighty has made of it for the work of Redemption.

The first one of these is the Corruption of Jewish Thinking, which deviated from the God-inspired Jewish Tradition; resulting directly in the Death of Christ and in the Salvation of the Gentiles.

The second one is the Corruption of Western European Thinking through Nominalism; resulting directly in the destruction of Thomism and the subsequent enslavement of the whole world under tyranny, being used by God for the Glorification of the Mother of God, the Blessed Virgin Mary.

The third one is the present-day global Corruption of Catholic Thinking; resulting directly in the almost-death of the Catholic Church, the Bride of the Lamb of God, leading almost certainly to the Conversion and Salvation of the Jews.

The first one mentioned is obvious, and certainly worthy of our deep meditation and private study. The second corruption we have already partly studied in Lecture 6, and the subsequent envisaged glorification of the Mother of God is the constant consolation of all the true lovers of Our Lady of Fatima. The third one mentioned is the one proposed for study in this Lecture 9. And right at the beginning of this important discussion, we must be clear in our minds what is meant here by Catholic Thinking. It obviously cannot mean the corruption of All Catholic Thinking. I have consistently shown to believe with Catholic Faith, i.e. from Revelation, that the Catholic Church cannot go wrong, even if millions of Catholics take up wrong thinking. Wrong Catholic Thinking therefore must mean corrupted thinking in many, even maybe in a majority of Catholics; which thinking is being presented and portrayed as Catholic, which it is not, and which thinking can only be rectified by the uncorrupted Catholic Teaching and Doctrine proclaimed by the Church, even if no longer believed by a majority of theologians and faithful. If they hold and propose a doctrine contradictory to one professed and believed by the Church, then we are fully entitled to refer to such doctrines as corrupted catholic thinking. It is significant to realise that immense psychological, physical and moral suffering has resulted from each of the three major corruptions of Catholic Thinking; and that God has allowed this suffering so that a Greater Good could be drawn than if the suffering was not there. This is obvious in the case of the suffering and death of Christ; and, in the Light of Catholic Faith, the same will be found true in the other two cases. Study and meditation will bring to light that this is so because of the Revelation of the Deep Love lying at the Heart of the one who is undergoing the Suffering. Unless God revealed it we would never have known, or even suspected, that more Redemption and Restoration would be forthcoming from this Love-in-Suffering than would have been the case had the corruption not taken place. It is all-important that this is **understood and believed, for it lies very close at the heart of that elusive entity:** Catholic Thinking. O Felix Culpa! Exclaimed one of the most beautiful Catholic minds ever produced: St Augustine's. O happy guilt that deserved such a Redeemer and such Redemption.

Chapter Nine: The Nature of Catholic Theology (III)

And so, finally, at the end of this Introduction, we must define Catholic Thinking as thinking with the Catholic Church. Sentire Cum Ecclesia (St. Ignatius). Catholic Thinking is at home with Dogma, with Catholic teaching and great loyalty to the Holy Father and the Magisterium, in the certainty that Catholic Teaching is logical, satisfying, certain, and in no way against reason. Indirectly, therefore, as we have seen, Catholic Thought is at home with Thomism. It is directly at home with Catholic Faith and with the moral Teaching of the Church.

Catholic Thought rejects any accusation of 'not being free', or of being 'inferior'. On the contrary: Catholic Thought is convinced that any deviation from it injures the sublime status of the New Creation, and constitutes a turning back to the World, the Flesh and the Devil. If Restoration and Redemption through Love shown in Suffering lies at the heart of Catholic Belief, then that is the reason why Catholics right through the centuries have suffered and sustained incomprehension and hostility gladly for the salvation of the world, leaving to God to draw more good from that suffering, than they hoped to achieve even by missionary activity and works of mercy. And we will find that the greatest corruption of Catholic Thinking lies precisely in this area: when this unworldly, supernatural and redeeming Love is no longer understood and appreciated and is being perverted to a liberation from anything else except Sin and Hell.

Section I: The Origins and Manifestations of the Corruption of Catholic Thinking

It is my intention in this Section to shed some light on the disturbing fact of Catholic Thinking gone wrong in our midst. The Lecture will then be concluded with some three examples of this tragic phenomenon, taken from the Australian scene, and analysed in Section II.

The Abandonment of a Truly Catholic Philosophy

As we know from what went before: the Holy Fathers were right in claiming that the disuse and final abandonment of Thomism would have the most savage consequences for the Faith. The corruption of Catholic Thinking does not start with the Faith: that is where it ends. It starts at the lower level of ordinary, human thinking, clear thinking: Philosophy. From there the cancer will spread to the rest of the body, finally claiming as its victim the New Creation in God, the Supernatural Life and its faculties. This means that the true origin of the deterioration in Catholic Thinking must be found in what we discussed in Lecture 6: the Corruption of Human Thinking as a whole. Ironically, Nominalism, as we saw, was a corruption of 14th Century Catholic Thinking, which, through the Renaissance, spread to the secular world as well; paving the way for Marxism, Communism and Evolution, which, as Modernism are now being taken up by the greater part of Catholics who so far had resisted any affinity with the poisonous offspring of Nominalism.

Chapter Nine: The Nature of Catholic Theology (III)

Without going over the ground covered in Lecture 6, which dealt with the gradual abandonment of Thomism, it is for the understanding of what follows of the utmost importance to see what sort of 'philosophy' has taken its place. This can only be done successfully with the iron logic of Thomistic ruthlessness. We must always show mercy and compassion with the sinner, but never with sin and error. For in order to be merciful and kind to the sinner, we must, from this alien philosophy, uproot its First Principle and hold it up against the light of reason, and the Supernatural Light of Revelation and Faith. For, if the Popes are right, then it is there, in an alien 'philosophy', where all the trouble with modernism has its origin.

Some Examples of Thinking Seriously Proposed as 'Catholic'

"In the present state of Theology and Science it cannot be proved that Polygenism conflicts with orthodox teaching on Original Sin. It would be better, therefore, if the Magisterium refrained from censuring Polygenism." Fr Karl Rahner in "The Evolving World and Theology", *Concilium*, Vol. 26. [The quoted words are taken from Fr. Rahner's chapter to this article, which chapter was titled: "Evolution and Original Sin". Previous to this contribution in *Concilium*, a magazine edited by Fr. Schillebeeckx, O.P, Fr. Rahner had written "Hominisation" with Fr. Overhage, S.J, and the Introduction to "Teilhard and Creation of the Soul", by another Jesuit, Fr. R. North. In doing so, Fr. Rahner gave much more than moral support to the ideas expressed in those two works.]

"Mysticism has often been considered embarrassing, threatening and irrelevant to the study of theology. Yet mysticism, from St. Paul to Teilhard, has been an experience profoundly shaping theology ... Whether or not student enthusiasm is a fad, it is clearly related to the drug-orientation of the present time. The question is how. I read the works of the famous and the unknown in this turned-on world, from Alan Watts, to some of my more intelligent students, and find that they seek, and in some small measure discover, the experience which men of faith have found before them. The experience, sadly, has been kept under cover and unheard for too long. Current student enthusiasm may also be a healthy reaction against what might be called 'second-hand theology'. Second-hand theology (she means Thomism here) is the kind which, when translated into teaching or catechism, answers questions which have never arisen in the religious experience of the students, or even perhaps that of the teacher. Teaching on the Trinity falls into this category most of the time. To some who have never experienced the Holy Spirit in action, the question of whether the spirit is God or not is meaningless." [April Oursler Armstrong in "New Dimensions in Religious Experience", the 1970 proceedings of George Devine's series of *Proceedings of the College Theology Society*, Vol. II.]

"In these discussions there are no set answers which the group must discover. The work of each group will depend on the situation of that group and the type of material members contribute. Each member will probably learn different things and at a different rate. Our primary aim is not to find answers, but to clarify issues (?) that confront us. We hope (!) for increased understanding, new

Chapter Nine: The Nature of Catholic Theology (III)

commitment and strength to live." [From "Notes for the Leader in the conduct of the Meeting" confidential instructions to "Our Living Faith", Growth in Faith series, Part I, to consolidate the fruits of the Melbourne Eucharistic Congress, 1973.] Imprimatur Card. Knox.

"One model (of 'faithing') which many teachers have found useful is that contained in the book: *Will our children have Faith*, by John H. Westerhoff III, [an American Protestant minister of religion], published in Australia by Dove Communications. He speaks of 'searching faith' – which involves Doubts and/or critical judgement, Experimentation (p. 96-7)." (*Melbourne Guidelines*, Overview, p. 7). Imprimatur Archbishop Little.

"Christ is present in the bread and wine." (*Melbourne Guidelines*, Senior Primary, p. 111, last line.) Imprimatur Archbishop Little.

What have all these quotations in common? As can be seen, they come from various parts of the world: Europe, America, Australia. Yet they sound strangely alike and familiar. Not only do they come from catholic authors and sources: they are meant to convince us that they contain Catholic Doctrine! They are meant to transmit Catholic teaching. And on the strength of the last quote: they mean to transmit Catholic Dogma, the Deposit of Faith. Each and every one of these quotes attacks, mutilates, distorts and falsifies Catholic Teaching, even including Catholic Dogma; yet they are presented as Catholic teaching, as if it is the same as authentic Catholic Teaching from way back. By what principle can a Contradiction of the Truth be presented and believed as the Truth? By what principle can the official teaching of Pope John XXIII: "Contrary 'Truths' cannot exist" (*Ad Petri Cathedram*, 1959, No III) be contradicted and still held up as being the same 'catholic teaching'? Not by any Thomistic principle. By the principle of Identity. The first one to adopt this fundamental of First Principle within the Catholic fold as an absolute prerequisite for his untenable 'evolutionary system' was, as I have already shown in a previous work, *Teilhard de Chardin and the Dutch Catechism*, Pierre Teilhard de Chardin himself. It must by necessity underlie all modernism: that contradicting Catholic Doctrine and Dogma, and holding this up as 'catholic teaching' is the same, identical. Illogically, many well-meaning Catholics will try to defend the perpetrators of the evil by saying: 'Yes, but these people are very sincere'. I agree that they are very sincere in what they are doing: they want to destroy Catholic Faith and substitute in its place the 'faith' that will give entry into their man-made 'church of darkness'. By all means: let us maintain that these people are very sincere, otherwise they will not be taken seriously enough …

It is necessary to go quickly through these quoted words of the neo-modernists, to bring out with Thomistic ruthlessness the enormity of what is being attempted: the abortion of Catholic Faith.

Fr. Karl Rahner S.J.

That Fr. Rahner is fully aware of what he is doing, and of the consequences of his actions, becomes apparent from his own words, when he continued:

Chapter Nine: The Nature of Catholic Theology (III) 187

"The decision of the Biblical Commission of 1909 about the 'formation of the first man' is no longer tenable in the exclusive literal sense if one accepts in general with Pope Pius XII the evolutionary origin of man, which basically conflicts with this decree. We cannot think of 'Adam' in terms of evolution and deny this to 'Eve' ... One cannot accept evolution for Adam and reject it for Eve. Polygenism can therefore no longer be rejected in the case of one couple." (Op. Cit).

This not only contradicts Two Popes: to say that Pope Pius XII accepts evolution for Adam constitutes calumny. To quote one Holy Father against the Biblical Commission that another Holy Father covered with Papal Authority, is again making use of that frightful non-existing 'principle' of 'identity': it is all the same catholic teaching if we accept and reject the Biblical Commission, and the authority it received from the Popes.

This is what Pope St. Pius X wrote in his Motu Proprio of 1907 fully known to Fr. Rahner and Pope Pius XII, and upheld by the latter:

" ... but we observe that some persons unduly prone to opinions and methods tainted by pernicious novelties ... have not received and do not receive these decisions (of the Pontifical Biblical Commission) with a proper obedience. Wherefore We find it necessary to declare and prescribe, as We now declare and expressly prescribe, that all are bound in conscience to submit to the decisions of the Biblical Commission which have been given in the past and shall be given in the future in the same way as to the Decrees which appertain to Doctrine issued by the Sacred Congregations and approved by the Sovereign Pontiff. Nor can they escape the stigma both of disobedience and temerity, nor be free from grave guilt, as often as they impugn these decisions either in word or writing and this over and above the scandal which they give, and the sins of which they may be the cause before God, by making their statements on these matters which are very frequently both rash and false."

If Evolution stands or falls with polygenism, as Fr. Rahner is forced to admit, and if polygenism is ruled out by the Biblical Commission, and forbidden to be held by Catholics in Pope Pius XII encyclical *Humani Generis*, then evolution of man is doomed, as indeed the teaching of the present Holy Father Pope John Paul II has settled the matter. As per usual, Fr. Rahner does not bring out even a scrap of evidence to show how and why he has weightier reasons than two Holy Fathers, not only for disregarding the Pontifical Biblical Commission, but also a Motu Proprio and an encyclical, and even to publicly contradict them. And so we are not too rash and not too harsh on Fr. Rahner, when we accuse him of having abandoned Thomism in favour of an untenable, non-existing philosophical 'principle' allowing him to rashly and with temerity set aside a Biblical Commission and an Encyclical, and of having corrupted his human thinking to such an extent that it has affected his Faith and so has corrupted his Catholic Thinking as well.

Forgive me, if I went into this matter in unusual detail. The pattern has repeated itself a million times over, and it really breaks our hearts to see so much talent wasted and used for destruction and scandal. But it proves the Holy Fathers right who stated with so much conviction, that the attack would come not directly on the Faith, but through the Human Mind; not through Theology, but

Chapter Nine: The Nature of Catholic Theology (III)

through Philosophy: philosophy so-called. "Those false evolutionary notions", wrote His Holiness Pope Pius XII in *Humani Generis*, "paving the way for a Philosophy of Error …". (1950) It is an everlasting pity and enigma, that all this was wasted on Fr. Rahner.

George Devine's "Proceedings …"

The "Proceedings of the College Theology Society" is an annual publication of the theological papers from various American theology faculties. They are the most accurate reflection of the destruction of true theology, caused by Modernism. Every conceivable modernistic sin and disease is contained in these papers: from irrational and illogical reasoning all the way to unbelief and blasphemy. I have selected Mrs. April Armstrong's contribution as a good example of all of these, leading directly to the same contagion in the quoted Australian examples.

First, we must be grateful to April for showing us the fingerprint of the 'master mind' when she mentions Teilhard. As I have analysed in previous articles: Teilhard has taught his disciples how to hold up and portray a caricature of true and official Catholic Teaching, which April does here, by clearly relating 'mysticism' with drugs, and then, in the process of dismantling and doing away with Catholic Thinking held up to ridicule, a few foundation dogmas are slipped in as well, so that they too suffer the fate of dismissal with the 'caricature'. Her statement that the students, under drugs, experience the same mysticism as the holy men of old, is completely gratuitous, unfounded, unproven, but necessary for the abortion of the Faith in the Trinity and the Divinity of the Holy

Spirit which follows immediately. Her destruction of 'second-hand theology' is a deliberate false positioning of the Catholic Church's teaching. Not only has the Church never related "teaching the Truth" to "private subjective experience", which April does here, but the Church has never confused Thomism with Dogma. Even when expressed in Thomistic terms, Dogma ceases to be Thomism and becomes Verbum Dei: the Word of God, Eternal Truth. But this destruction through ridicule of Thomism is necessary for the subsequent abolition of True Catholic teaching, which follows immediately in her quoted words: "teaching on the Trinity ...". The strokes are deft, expert and almost painless. The supernatural Zombies are now ready to accept that the 'spirit' is in the drugs, because he can be experienced there. Experience is all that is necessary. Just as human abortion techniques have improved over the years, so too have the techniques for the abortion of the Faith in Catholic children and students. Force students to attend this sort of 'theology' class (catechetics class) and sure enough, you will have them all experimenting with drugs to experience the 'spirit' on "April's sound catholic teaching", and "on April's First-Hand 'Theology'". This micro-cosmos accurately reflects the macro-cosmos of modernism around the world.

The Australian Scene

There is little doubt that the great unification of evil in Australia under Modernism is being achieved and consolidated by the *Melbourne Guidelines For Religious Education*. The greatest proof of this before God is the fact that all who have been concerned with their promotion – from the bishops who permitted and defended their distribution down to the enthusiastic teachers and recipients – no longer see any evil at all in its Twin Corrupter: the immoral and depraved Sex Education courses in Catholic and Government Schools. We can learn from the latter what the first does to the mind. If ever we want from Almighty God a reason why He allowed the terrible scourge of unrestricted abortion in the world of our time, we may learn from His reply that it is dwarfed in evil by what Modernism does to the Faith of a child …

As can be seen from the quotation taken from an official Melbourne publication "Our Living Faith": the Modernists are determined to kill the Catholic Church as we know it. There are no set answers to be found. Anything goes. Situations and experiences (April) differ from person to person. It is all the same. And this is the exact content of the *Melbourne Guidelines*: there are no set answers to be found. All they provide the teachers and children is a welter of Experiences. But they do teach that Catholic Faith is to be doubted … If we ignore the millstone, God certainly will not.

The Stages of Catholic Corruption

Whoever read Philip Trower's penetrating analysis of the inroads of Modernism into Catholic circles: "The Church Learned and the Revolt of the Scholars", *The Wanderer Press*, 1979, will understand my impossible task of rendering in a few pages what he so ably expressed in sixty. Yet, the Popes demand that every effort be made to restore everything in Christ, so an attempt must be made at this stage to collect from the foregoing some intelligent understanding of what happened and what can be done about it. Modernism is like a giant derailment. There is only One Way in which the train could have stayed on the line, and everyone is interested in that. It is idle and futile, at the scene of the devastation, to speculate in how many ways the train could have broken up, and how far the bits and pieces could have been flung. The mess simply has to be cleaned up, and the wounded attended. In context, it is no good chasing after every heresy that Sister, Brother, Father or Catechist can come up with: we never know what they will come up with next. We must learn from the devastation in general how to prevent any repetition, and how not to get caught up in it. Once off the track of orthodox Catholicism, a derailment is inevitable however slight the deviation in the beginning.

The First Signs

The first sign of a pending derailment is going through the red light ordinary human thinking, perfected in Thomism, has placed along the track. Of that we are now convinced. Temptations have been put to Catholics to indulge in crooked thinking, in order, as we now know, to get at their Catholic Faith. In order that these temptations were recognised as temptations, Grace was absolutely necessary. And so, from the enormity of the devastation, we may gauge that the prayer life and the life of sacrifice of many Catholics was not what it should have been. It is remarkable that the Catholics least affected by Modernism, are the ones closest to Our Lady, to the daily recitation of the Rosary, sharing in the full understanding of what Her Fatima apparitions were all about. A more remarkable feature is that these are also the people who have kept sound judgement and a lot of ordinary common sense, which prevented them from going on fancy flights with the teilhardians. Evolution is crooked thinking at the ordinary human level. If rejected, it will never be in a position to do damage at the Supernatural level of Catholic Faith. All derailed Catholics, without exception – which includes bishops who allowed the *Melbourne Guidelines* in their schools – have first sacrificed clear thinking, which shows that there was not enough spiritual capital to resist temptations in that direction. In other words, the grave warnings and earnest pleas of the Holy Fathers with regard to the safeguarding of Thomism were not heeded.

The Second Hurdle

Evolution is not the only example of crooked thinking put to Catholics by the teilhardian modernists. There are hundreds of deviations from sound judgement, clear thinking, common sense, logic, by which Catholics can be tempted to give up adhering to the known Truth and fall into error. Even if the Supernatural Light of Faith was dim, and people were not very well trained in the use of ordinary logic and reason, there was a Second Barrier the Enemy had to ask the individual Catholic to remove, before any entry into the Sacred Domain of the Supernatural and Catholic Faith. This barrier is known as the Sensus Catholicus, the Catholic Sense, by which a Catholic could Sense more than anything else, that what was being proposed to him contradicted Catholic Teaching: Supernatural Truth. Here we clearly recognise once again, how, by the Will of the Creator and Redeemer, the Human Mind is at the service, not only of its own protection as in the previously discussed first hurdle, but of the protection of Catholic Faith. Seeing and sensing a contradiction is done by the human mind. Seeing and sensing a contradiction of Revealed Truth, is the human mind coming to the aid of Faith.

If, as we saw, a diminished Light of Catholic Faith was revealed to exist behind the weakening of the resolve at the first barrier: not to go along with spurious thinking in whatever form; what, then does weakening of resolve at this second barrier show, where we are asked not to go against our Sensus Catholicus? Weakening here shows unmistakably a diminished Supernatural Love-Life. An absence of Sensus Apostolicus. Absence of the Love for the Catholic Church and Her Mission. Modernists and Teilhardians are invariably cold, hard, cruel and insensitive. From the devastations caused at both sign-posts, we may now start to understand how much in need of correction the pre-Vatican II Catholics were, and what God intended when He convened that unbelievably timely Council. When, during the Council, the Infallible Catholic Church, ever sensitive to the wishes of Her Bridegroom, the Lamb of God, showed Her Catholic children once again how the whole world was their concern, the teilhardians took it as a sign to go out and identify themselves with the world; but Her true children understood Her better, and embraced the world like Her Founder did: in a Crucified way. And the gulf between the two, the Schism, has been widening ever since. The ones who resisted the temptation to go over to the modernist camp at the second barrier, and kept their Catholic Sense intact, did so for the love of the Church, for love of

Chapter Nine: The Nature of Catholic Theology (III)

their neighbour, as they realised more and more that on their Catholicity the salvation of the world depends. And gradually their Faith grew stronger and they were able to use their stronger Supernatural Light to come to the aid of their natural light. And in renewed prayer and penance they were better equipped to understand the idiocies of Modernism and how fortunate they were in having been preserved from falling for it. And of being now in a position to call others back from it and from the brink of disaster

From this it can be gauged, that it is not necessary for the average good Catholic to analyse in detail what the modernists offer us as poison: e.g. as in the *Melbourne Guidelines*. If their ware does not immediately insult your intelligence, at least listen to your outraged sensus catholicus, and for the love of others, reject it out of hand. When the time comes, your insight into their assault on your intelligence will grow.

Section II: Analysis of Some of the More Important Examples of the Corruption of Catholic Thinking in Contemporary Australia

The First National Conference of Catholic Laity, April 1976, Sydney

The fact that no other National Conference of Catholic Laity has been convened since, that none of the resolutions taken at that first Conference have been carried out, and that by 1981 we still have not got a National Pastoral Council, the most important resolution to come out of that Conference, are all solely due to the fact that Crooked 'Catholic' Thinking was employed to prepare the Conference, and Sound Catholic Thinking to undo its attempts.

The Facts

1. The Sydney-based organisers did not exactly endear themselves to most other delegates by their pre-conference 'banner': "The Catholic Church in Australia", a booklet so unrepresentative, that the Melbourne Conference Executive sent the whole parcel of 400 copies straight back to Sydney.

2. In line with the sentiments and the spirit of this literary misadventure, the Melbourne Diocesan Conference convened in preparation for the Sydney National Conference, was told by a Planning Committee member from Sydney 'not to expect a Conference as the one we had just finished here in Melbourne, with general sessions and an orderly agenda. You frightened me with that'. In the 5 minute talk this member was allowed to enlighten us, it became clear to the initiated that Sydney was planning an exact copy-book replica of the notorious Bangkok World Conference on Missions, run by the WCC in 1973: fragmented, innumerable workshops and only one general session.

3. The Melbourne Conference Executive decided to contact all delegates to the National Conference to protest against two glaring deficiencies in the planning: (i) that an unrepresentative, anonymous group should dictate to the National Conference what format to accept, and (ii) that the format envisaged would be exclusively one of fragmentation; and

Chapter Nine: The Nature of Catholic Theology (III)

to ask the delegates to request an early plenary session to allow Conference the freedom to decide its own format.

4. The first plenary session was granted, but so grudgingly as to be a waste of time. There was hardly a 'chair'. People were allowed to jump up at will and speak at will and at length, even non-delegates (observers). The 'chair' did not put the question straight; there was no explanation from the 'chair' that a conference is entitled to choose its own format; there was no warning against fragmentation; there was a 'free for all' and 'let the spirit drive us' atmosphere. In other words, there was a total absence of an outline of Balance, Perspective, Framework and Choices. Only a tenacious driving to the Planning Committee's ideal: fragmentation.

5. That there was an absence of even a basic honesty, did not only come out from the above: it was even more spectacular in the way the members of the 8 groups were to be selected. Delegates were asked to pick, from a bag that was doing the rounds, a piece of a cut-out picture, and to form a group with people who had the other 7 cut-outs. This method is obviously wide open to being rigged. If you want a certain person on each of the 8 groups, all you have to do is make sure beforehand that each has a cut-out from one of the 8 pictures, and they become 'automatically' distributed over 8 groups. So, 8 delegates from Melbourne refused to take a cut-out, with the result that they eventually became distributed over the 8 groups. From the posted composition of the groups it became immediately apparent that this precaution

had become necessary: each group had at least one radical catholic in its make-up. From these groups the steering committee and the agenda committee had to be selected, and because of the Melburnians-in-the-know, the back of the radical grip on the conference was broken. Care was taken to have every workshop well attended by orthodox Catholics, so that none of the important ones would become lop-sided in the direction of radicalism and modernism.

6. One more item of interest emerged. On Saturday Morning, the first working day of the conference, the radical element secretly circulated a "Manifesto to the People of Australia", urging them to accept the conference decisions. No decisions had yet been taken: so sure were the plotters of having pulled the wool over the eyes of the unsuspecting delegates. Luckily, within 5 minutes of circulation, one such circular fell into the right hands ...

[They said it took two years to plan this conference ... It is extremely hard to believe, that during those 2 years of preparation it never occurred to the organisers to run an honest conference, which would take care of all the glaring omissions mentioned above. Anyone who wants the Truth to come out of a gathering like that, sees to it that means are being employed to facilitate the maximum emergence of the Truth. It now has become painfully obvious What took 2 years to prepare: How to Run a Conference for the Triumph of something other than the Truth. And to make sure that this is accepted ...]

Chapter Nine: The Nature of Catholic Theology (III)

Why bring all this up?

For the simple reason that this paper is not only concerned with the symptoms of Modernism, but, even more so, with the aims and objectives of the plotters. If we were allowed to believe by the Divine Son of the Almighty, that 'things just happen', and that marxist catholics, radicals and modernists are sincere but misguided do-gooders, who only have to be shown their 'mistakes' and they come running back to the Father, we would only have been told by Jesus to be 'as simple as doves'. But He did tell us to be also 'as circumspect as snakes'. In other words, He expected us to be constantly in a hostile environment, where violent people would take away the Kingdom of God.

To understand what happened in Sydney during those memorable days of the First (and only) National Conference of Catholic Laity in April, 1976, it is absolutely essential to understand two things thoroughly:

1. Marxist Catholics are deadly serious about one thing: they want power. They are the articulate, polished, cultured commissars of the new-breed modernism, which has clearly shown them the way to obtain this power: through the Sacred. Through the 'church', through the parish councils, through diocesan and national conferences, through bishops, which they meet in their most cherished dream: the National Pastoral Council, the only thing worthwhile they hoped would come out of the Sydney conference. They used the Sydney conference as they use anything else: to

firm their grip on the Sacred, to be recognised everywhere as the new Fuehrers. These people are already convinced that they impress bishops; they now want to appear to dominate them by invading their territory and sit with them as equals: a National Pastoral Council, like it is in Holland.

2. The second thing that must be thoroughly grasped is more difficult to understand. The power that they crave is not so much 'church' power, but real power, political power, temporal power. Power to lead to their Utopia: a one-world 'church' for a one-world government. What is so difficult to grasp is this: the feeding ground of these radicals is not the Catholic Church (never mind the pious invocation of the Holy Spirit every five minutes!); it is not Our Lady, nor the Blessed Sacrament, nor the Rosary, nor the Communion of Saints, nor prayer and penance. Instead, they are being fed and sustained from a totally different background, which is menacingly real and uncomfortably close, but hidden. Since these people are visibly on the scene, they prove by their very existence that their marxist breeding ground is equally real; just as alive and real as the products it produces everywhere (inside and outside the Church that is, for Marxists transgress Church boundaries as easily as national boundaries). The real breeding ground of all Marxists are the Dissenters, and this is no exception for catholic marxists.

Chapter Nine: The Nature of Catholic Theology (III)

What, then, was at stake in Sydney?

Since the real power base for radical catholics within (the visible confines of) the Catholic Church are Dissenting Catholics, what was at stake in the Sydney conference was the Status of Dissenting Catholics. Those 'catholics' must at all cost be kept within these visible confines of the Catholic Church to remain the feeding ground for marxists within the same confines. It is the avowed intention of radicals that dissenters from Papal teaching must be given equal status with believers. On any National Pastoral Council organised by radicals, there is the distinct possibility that a bishop will find himself with one orthodox priest and two marxist ones, and with one orthodox layman and two marxist ones, in the one workshop, in mortal combat about this very point: the Status of Dissenters from *Humanae Vitae* within the Catholic Church. Even if the bishop and his two orthodox supporters oppose the workshop view, they will be outvoted 4-3 on the report adopted. The plenary session will then carry the workshop report as 'obviously inspired by the Holy Spirit' ... Bangkok '73 showed that it could be done: hence the 2 year planning for a Bangkok style Sydney Conference.

But from beginning to end, Crooked Catholic Thinking, fraud, deception are underlying this type of manipulation. That is why it found its place in this study. The battle over the status of dissenters from Papal teaching is far from over; that is why Thomistic Thinking must be brought in at every stage of the battle to oppose and overcome any undesirable grip on the Sacred. The Sydney Conference shows by its result: the defeat of the radicals, that this is not an impossible task.

A Second Analysis: The Thinking Surrounding Spurious Catechetics in Australia

What facts have emerged in this whole area?

1. Before they were marketed, such 'catechisms' were conceived by catholics, discussed by catholics, written and printed by catholics, approved by catholic bishops and even given Imprimaturs.
2. After they come on the market, they are promoted by catholic education offices, by diocesan coordinators of religious education, sent to catholic schools by catholic instances, where they are received and read by the schools' R.E. coordinator, R.E. instructors and principals, and subsequently passed on to Catholic children as the Catholic Faith.
3. Nowhere along the line of these various stages are/were Catholic parents consulted or even informed. Only where a Catholic Bishop refused entry into his diocese/area to this explosive material, were Catholic parents and children relatively safe from corruption. (For even good Bishops are aware that they are not always obeyed in this matter.) In all other cases parents have been unsuccessful in having this corruption removed from the schools their children attend.
4. Hand-in-glove with this sort of anti-catechesis came into catholic schools its twin-evil: Classroom Sex Education.

This too found its way into the presence of Catholic children along the same putrid pipeline of deceit as the 'catechetics' which supports it: conceived, discussed, written, printed, marketed, approved, distributed and finally taught by catholics unbeknown to Parents.

5. One Bishop, Bishop Bernard Stewart, of Sandhurst, Vic, is known to have publicly resisted entry of this sort of catechesis into his diocese, and has gone out of his way to make sure that everybody understood what was and what was not to be taught.
6. No Australian Episcopal Conference is known to have supported Bishop Stewart in this Duty.
7. No Australian Episcopal Conference is known to have spent its major part on analysing the innumerable complaints from Catholic parents, or to write an analysis of the *Melbourne Guidelines*, or even to have given detailed instructions to caution against spurious Catechesis.
8. Episcopal Conferences are known to have their own 'silent minority', bishops who perform their God-given duty in their own dioceses, but who are unable to influence an Episcopal Conference. From the facts that have emerged so far, it is to be taken, that Australian Episcopal Conferences are in favour of the destruction of Catholic Faith in innocent children, and are in favour of the corruption of Purity in Catholic schools and in innocent Catholic children.

The question is not: what damage can be prevented by a conscientious religious instructor, forced to use the *Melbourne Guide-*

lines. The question is not even in the first place: what do the *Melbourne Guidelines* omit? The question is: what do the *Melbourne Guidelines* state, recommend and teach, encourage and infer which is Corrupted Catholic Thinking, and can only be recommended, taught and defended by equally corrupted Catholic Thinking. And by a grave loss of the Sensus Catholicus, even in Bishops.

Anyone connected with the writing, distribution, recommendation and teaching of the *Melbourne Guidelines* and Sex Education in schools, will have to face Our Blessed Lady. Where will they hide from Her?

A Third Analysis: Psycho-babbling

Psycho-Babbling is the self-inflicted curse of all modernists, and of all who go along with them. It is the direct result of their adherence to Existentialism, caused by their departure from Thomism. It is also a punishment from God. God is at present asking a veritable Cross from His true followers, but not deception. Psycho-babbling gives the enemy away: the pseudo-catholic who pretends to be a catholic; but in reality, inwardly, has succumbed to modernism, or, out of human respect, goes along with it.

Psycho-babbling is: 'becoming incoherent', or 'not making sense'; not because of a bodily impediment (somatic, from the Greek 'soma', body), as in the normal development of a child, when the body is not yet equipped to be a perfect instrument for the child's mind, but because of a psychological impediment, (from the Greek 'psyche', soul). It is therefore caused by a defect or disease of the soul, and will manifest itself when the afflicted person is trying to give 'food for the soul'. This means that a psycho-babbling modernist or fellow traveller can hide his or her affliction when they talk about the weather, or the motor car; but not, because of their inner conflict, when they try to communicate about, say, religion. That is why most of them try to steer clear of the subject and immerse themselves in Social Action where they think they become less incoherent when they speak out on social injustices, and revolutions. (Modern Episcopal Conferences.)

Psycho-Babbling in Catholic clergy, religious and laity invariably shows some corruption of Catholic Thinking. Since no Catholic thinking can be corrupted, unless clear thinking, logic, sound reasoning: in fact Thomistic Philosophy, have been affected first, followed, as we saw, in the more severe cases also by a loss of the sensus catholicus and apostolicus, and in the worst cases by the loss of Catholic Faith altogether, it is clear that the loss of clear Thinking is shown up first, especially in the area where the person has an inner conflict: psycho-babbling in religion.

But try as they may: psycho-babblers do not even make sense in the area in which they take refuge: the social and political action arena, because of their fundamental link with Existentialism.

Existentialism versus Thomism

Existentialism is the exact opposite of Thomism. As we know, St. Thomas maintains that the human mind extracts from the data supplied by the senses, the Nature, i.e. the Essence of the objects perceived. When we are looking at a car, we are aware that we are not looking at an incomprehensible mass of parts, which fail to make sense in some 'whole': no, we are aware that we perceive a car, a 'whole' that makes sense of the individual composing parts. The nature of the thing we perceive, its essential element, is that it is a car.

Existentialism, as the name already implies, denies that the human mind can do that. We are only aware of 'existences', to which we give Names: Nominalism. We know nothing about what they are, and beyond the senses, we do not even know if there are 'other existences'. There are of course many modernists and fellow-travellers who suit themselves when they are 'thomist', i.e., realist, e.g. when they talk with the bank manager and do not want to be given fictitious money; and when they are 'existentialist', i.e. agnostic, e.g. when it comes to keeping the Ten Commandments. It is precisely this mixture of two totally incompatible philosophies, which makes clerical psycho-babblers so incoherent in their sermons and addresses. They want to be 'with it', without altogether being totally agnostic. And so they prattle on about 'luv' in total oblivion of the Absolute Majesty and Holiness of God. They prattle about God as if He is a kind of Santaclaus, a weak sort of do-gooder without any demands and rights. They babble and prattle about human relations as if we live in a sinless world, from which we have nothing to fear, and from which we go straight to Heaven after death.

And again, these clerics will one day have to face Our Lady, who came all the way down from Heaven at Fatima, to bring us Her first and most important request: Stop Sinning. This is never repeated by the clerical and religious psycho-babblers.

Psycho-babbling is not restricted to Australia of course, and not even to Australian bishops. It is in full swing in Rome, during the Synod of Bishops, if we are to believe the *Osservatore Romano*. No wonder the last few Synods have not even left a ripple, only more agony in the souls of the faithful. And once again Pope John Paul will have to go it alone. May God bless him, and all his true children.

Chapter Ten

The Discipline of the Mind
(Pope St. Pius X)

Introduction

We have come a long way to the commanding position of this final lecture: the synthesis between Reason and Faith, found in the true Wisdom of "The Discipline of the Mind".

Prompted by initial misgivings occasioned by what is sometimes loosely referred to as 'the state of the Church', ranging all the way from uneasiness in some to downright perplexity in others, we were at first met by a certain incomprehension, to further our difficulties. For, on opening the Church's most important documents, Her marvellous Encyclicals, for the last 100 years, we found that, in the defence of Catholic Faith, the Holy Fathers unanimously stressed the importance of St. Thomas Aquinas. And we were told by way of example, that his Holiness Pope Leo XIII has reputedly said that, if all his Encyclicals [and he wrote more than 80, amongst them 13 on the Holy Rosary], were to be placed in order of importance, then the one he wrote way back in 1879 on the Restoration of Christian Philosophy, *Aeterni Patris*, would have to be placed on the top. So sure was this Holy Father, that even the love for, and the Faith in, the Holy Rosary would dwindle, if crooked thinking were allowed to seep into the minds of the faithful flock entrusted to his care.

We read what these earlier Popes had written about this restoration, and we looked to the subsequent ones for understanding and explanations. And as the Lectures progressed, it became clear to us, what a wonderful and infallible Institution the Holy Catholic Church is, and what a true miracle of God Her continued presence among us really is. For we not only came to understand that it is Her Teaching that the Human Mind can only 'chime in with Revelation' in one way; that only one way of clear thinking is a preamble to the Faith: that necessary condition and preparation for the reception of so great a Grace, and that only one Philosophy will support and firmly anchor the Catholic Church's true Theology: not only did we gradually come to understand this, but we became convinced that this teaching is true. That it is borne out by irrefutable Evidence. And with growing admiration for the Papal vision and accuracy, and for the development and consistency of this teaching, we thanked God for the Infallible Teaching, expressed so surely and convincingly in the pages of the Ordinary Magisterium of the Catholic Church.

And now that we have not only enjoyed and analysed this sure and sound teaching, but have also been made aware more fully of the frightful derailments and devastations, caused in the lives of many contemporary Catholics, when this sound teaching was not adhered to, was contemptuously discarded in the embrace of its opposite, and was held up with ridicule in the pages of theological books and journals, and even of the most perverse catechesis ever given to innocent Catholic children, we are now in the proper disposition of mind and heart to analyse the final synthesis of this twofold area and source of knowledge: the natural level of the Human Mind and the Supernatural level of Revelation and Faith.

"... a proper disposition of mind and heart ..."

I said Thomism is not an intellectual edifice, towering impassively above the ebb and flood of human life at its base. Far from it. Thomism is a passionate and burning love for the Truth. It is the only true-blood "Philosophia Perennis", the only everlasting "Love of Wisdom". And it is this love of the Truth, which is seen by all the Holy Fathers, inherited from Christ before Pilate, as of such immense Redemptive value. So strong is this Tradition in the Catholic Church: to see Love of Truth as the foundation and inspiration of all apostolate and missionary action, to see Love of Truth as having immense Redemptive value, that all these Holy Fathers, under the Inspiration of the Holy Spirit, simply had to show the hatred for human beings the Evil One has revealed in his attack on Thomism over the centuries, culminating in the destruction of Thomism in our own times. According to St. Ignatius of Loyola, the devil has a veritable hatred for human nature. The Nature taken up by the Son of God used for the Redemption he, the evil one, had irrevocably excluded himself from. A Redemption that would fill the places in Heaven vacated by him and his fallen angels. And in order that human beings too would miss out on the valuable Redemption: to prevent the elevation of this hated human nature to a participation in the Divine Nature; in order then to destroy the Initium (the beginning), the Fundamentum (the foundation) and the Radix (the root) of that elevation, [which three terms we recognise are the true definition given by the Catholic Church to Catholic Faith], all the Devil had to do, and has in fact done, was to destroy

Thomism; for no other Philosophy, i.e. no other system of thought, would chime in with Revelation, or would provide a preamble to the Faith. Hence the concern of all those Holy Fathers who became aware of this plot; not a concern for the preservation of the intellectual achievement or supremacy, but a concern emanating directly from the Sacred Heart of Jesus in His Divine Love for the fullness of His very own Redemption, paid for in His Precious Blood. Try as you may to convince a teilhardian of the wretchedness of his ways and state, and the correctness of the Catholic Church's Thomistic Philosophy, and you will see if an intellectual conviction is of such little importance for the eternal salvation of only one soul ... Philosophies are loved! That is why it is so impossible to take the wrong ones away from people.

"This devil is only cast out by prayer and fasting..."

are the very words of Christ we are constantly reminded of in this work of the apostolate of the intellect, because it really is so very much an apostolate of the heart. And Christ's words are put into practice by thousands of men and women for the sake of their seduced and perverted children and of other unfortunate contemporaries who cling to their erroneous and illogical convictions with a grip of iron.

Seemingly, then, our only hope at present appears to be to prevent still free and loyal Catholics from going over to the other camp, which is nothing but a mental and spiritual concentration camp, no matter how hard the emaciated minds and the parched souls at the wrong side of the barb wire are trying to convince us that we are the captives and they the free and emancipated ones. And we will let the coming persecutions be Gods' instrument of salvation for all the ones we could not bring back by intellectual and spiritual reasoning, nor by prayer and fasting.

For our own safety, then, and for the sake of the apostolate, so dear to the Maternal Heart of Our Blessed Lady, and to Our Holy Mother the Catholic Church, we will find ample motive to tackle the last part of this study, and come to grips with the Synthesis between Intellectual Understanding and Supernatural Insight. This divides the final lecture naturally into Three Sections:

1. A synthetic revision of the first part of St. Anselm's famous dictum: "Fides quaerens intellectum", or 'Faith in search of an intellect, in search of understanding'.
2. A penetration into the meaning of the second part of the Saint's famous saying: "Intellectus quaerens fidem", or 'Intellect in search of Faith'; human intellect in search of a higher and more powerful light, the Light of Faith.
3. The Synthesis between the two. The True Wisdom of the 'Discipline of the Mind'. The Glory of the New Creation. The Power of the New Creation.

Section I: "Faith In Search of Understanding"

Very few things initially touch directly on Catholic Faith. Long before Catholic Faith is invoked – or should be invoked - to make a final decision as to whether or not something should be believed as true, Catholic Faith is searching for an intellect to do an initial appraising for it, in a proper and orderly manner.

The initial meaning of 'Faith searching for understanding' is thus not: Faith in search of Being Understood. That comes later. What Faith perceives it would like to understand; that is true. But in the ordinary humdrum of everyday life, the practical and first meaning of 'Faith in search of understanding' is: Faith telling the human intellect to do its homework. To get on with the job of initiating a proper investigation first at the level on which it is competent, and to come to grips with a reality, whatever it is, at its own human level. Before willy-nilly dragging Faith into it.

The examples of what is meant here are numerous. Let us take just a few at random to show what is meant here by 'Faith is search of understanding'. We could take Pentecostalism, Marriage Encounter, Marian Movement of Priests, One-World Week, the Victorian Council of Churches, etc. The trend nowadays is just to go along with these things because it is the fashion, because we trust the spirit, because the bishops encourage it, because ..., because .... This is a typical example, then, of the Existential Act: the aimless act, the unsubstantiated act, the act-for-act's-sake. The acts that make up 'drifting along' in the group: the group that refuses to do a proper investigation into the nature of things, and, through the group-action, reinforces the false security of the individual members that 'all is well'.

Once having drifted into such a situation, Catholic faith now gets invariably directly involved; and if the drifting is in the wrong direction involving falsehoods, Catholic Faith gets knocked about, dragged along and pushed around, being at a distinct disadvantage, because the intellect, not having done its homework in the first place, is now being dragged along itself by the Will, which has as-

Chapter Ten: The Discipline of the Mind (Pope St. Pius X)

sumed, on no intellectual conviction, and on no intellectual evidence, that it is good to belong and go along with it.

This means, as we clearly established in Lecture 9, that the first hurdle, the first barrier, the first checking post, the first red light, has been ignored: i.e. The Intellectual Understanding of Things, and that from now on it depends entirely, and quite unfairly, on the person's 'Sensus Catholicus', the Catholic Sense, if he will eventually break with the drifting-in-the-crowd, when it starts to become more distinct, that the originally assumed good is by no means a true good; and so is detrimental to the final end and the Catholic Faith of the individual. For anything false is injurious to the final end, and to the moral end, and to the Faith of a human being.

Faith, then, is constantly in search of an intellect, some intelligence, that will give a First Approximation of the meaning, the nature, and so the Understanding of a thing. Long before Faith itself becomes involved at the second barrier through the Catholic Sense. If a proper investigation into the thing under observation reveals contradictions, rejection of Absolutes, rejection of Thomism as such, of its fundamental principle, or of its secondary teaching, then belief in the thing will be withheld by the intellect; the will does not get the green light, and, through non-involvement from then on, not only is intellectual integrity saved, but also, and more importantly, the Catholic faith is much better safeguarded because of the proper ordering on one's life.

"Before you involve me", the Catholic Faith, according to St. Anselm, is saying to the human mind, "get a line on this thing, and see if it is worthy or ordinary human credence. Use the clear thinking and reasoning techniques, the laws of logic and inference, appropriately taught by the Philosophy of St. Thomas Aquinas. If found defective, have nothing further to do with it".

First and foremost, then, St. Anselm's maxim "Fides quaerens Intellectum", 'Faith looking for understanding', means Faith asking the human intellect to establish the nature and the Truth of whatever will eventually involve Faith in making an Act of Faith. The Act of Catholic Faith is not to be given lightly and with Credulity, for it has God for Object and Motive, and this priceless Gift and Possession may not be put at a disadvantage in the pursuit of objects which have no truth-value and do not come from God. And for the safeguarding of this Faith, the human believer must make sure that he/she has a proper understanding of the Nature and Truth of things, before giving an intellectual assent for the guidance of the actions. The Existential Act, the act without a proper investigation into the Nature and the Truth of things, is totally unworthy of any human being, and is in great danger of jeopardising the Faith.

Examples of matters commonly accepted nowadays and drifted into, without much thought and investigation:

Pentecostalism, Charismatic Renewal, False 'apparitions', Marriage Encounter, Marian Movement of Priests, Deep Sharing Weekends and 'Retreats', Freedom-of-conscience, 'Intercommunion and false ecumenism'.

and the more serious manifestations of endangering Catholic Faith:

Chapter Ten: The Discipline of the Mind (Pope St. Pius X)

Modernism, Teilhardism, Evolution, Permissiveness, Absolute Freedom of Conscience, Sex Education programs in schools, Spurious catechetics courses culminating in the *Melbourne Guidelines*.

Any proper investigation into the nature and consequent activities of these matters, done with Thomistic thoroughness which excludes any wishful thinking and make-believe, will not only reveal the deficiencies of any of the above, but also, in some cases, the grave defects and even corruption inherent to their composition and purpose. That heresy and heresy teaching are now rampant within the City of God, is almost solely due to the fact that Catholics discontinued the age-old practice of properly investigating anything first with clear thinking and common sense, before allowing matters of importance to intrude into the domain of Faith. And why this practice always was of such overriding importance can be gleaned from the fact that His Holiness Pope St. Pius X has made the absence of the discipline of the mind a hall-mark of the looming 'Church of Darkness' ...

"Faith in search of understanding of itself" is another meaning quite often given to the first part of St. Anselm's famous adage. This meaning can also quite easily be read into the quoted words in Latin, and they have been quite frequently quoted as a working definition of the study of Theology. Faith in search of an intellect that will make Faith better understood, is a ready made principle that can be followed by any God-fearing theologian or catechist, to whom the minds of God's children have been entrusted for the growth in Faith. The frightful betrayal of trust that has taken place in this area alone through the cowardice of bishops and other people in charge, will be to the eternal condemnation of this generation by all who went before, or are still to come.

The same revolting 'kiss of friendship' by which the Son of Man was betrayed into the hands of sinners is now being used to betray the Bride of the Lamb of God into the hands of all who hate Her with an implacable hatred. The only use the teilhardians and the authors of the *Melbourne Guidelines* have of 'explaining the Faith' is to explain it away … and the only use an 'Imprimatur' has on this sort of religious pornography is to make the betrayal of trust more effective … and more official …

Section II: "Intellect in Search of Faith"

The great apostasy of our times of which Pope St. Pius X spoke in his celebrated encyclical letter *Our Apostolic Mandate* of 1910, and which he saw organised in every country of his days in preparation for the 'church of darkness' which he foresaw so clearly that he was able to describe its marks for us, this great apostasy then, is the direct result of the 'pride of modern man'. Through pride, 'modern man's' intellect is no longer in need of Faith – so he thinks – and consequently his intellect is no longer 'quaerens', i.e. searching, for Catholic Faith.

But what is 'modern man'?

It is good to remind ourselves once again in this context of the definition of 'modern man', given by one who not only prides himself on being one, but who also worked unceasingly to make others conscious of that glorious privilege.

Chapter Ten: The Discipline of the Mind (Pope St. Pius X)

"What make and classifies a modern man?" asks Teilhard de Chardin. And his answer to his own question in the pages of the *Phenomenon of Man* is absolutely classic:

"Having become capable of seeing in terms, not of space and time alone, but also of biological space-time, and above all: of having become incapable of seeing anything otherwise, anything, **not even himself**." [Teilhard's stress] (p. 214).

This reduces 'modern man' to nothing more than the pathetic end-product of a faked evolution. Incapable by will and design of seeing himself as The New Creation in God. Incapable of seeing and appreciating the powerful light of Supernatural, Infused, Divine, Catholic Faith: God's greatest Gift to finite little man. A Gift to enhance and augment the Human Intellect at the same time that it is given to increase its power. No wonder, then, that this caricature of man, as he was created in the image and likeness of God, will one day lay hands on the Saints, and break them open in violent persecutions, in order to drink the Life-giving waters, denied him by all the teilhardians and modernists, by the marxists and communists, in their relentless drive for world domination. In order to succeed in their quest for power, and in order to reduce all opposition to a pitiful state of incompetence, 'modern man' had to be made into such an imbecile, that he even would be proud to carry the title. Satan's greatest ever slave-labour camp houses all those who have reached such a degree of absurdity and such an advanced stage of delirium, that turning one's back on God to commit and teach every sin in the book is considered the greatest freedom of them all ... So much worse is this last state of man than the first, that the destruction of Thomism is considered the greatest intellectual achievement on the road to complete emancipation from God. And inside the City of God the modernists are vying with the zombies outside for the 'honour' of who should carry the prize for having caused the greatest devastation. The Humanists can claim as their global conquest that their efforts in education have produced a whole generation of semi-illiterates; while the Modernists can proudly point to their achievement of having aborted the Catholic Faith from the minds and hearts of countless youthful victims. Both groups hoping and plotting, that the combination of these twin perversions will produce the global utopias envisaged: the 'one-world church' of darkness followed by the total enslavement under one-world government.

And once these goals have been achieved it will be the stone-end of permissiveness; and the ugliness of the distorted Satanic features under the heel of communism and antichrist will be but onestep away from the eternal reality in Hell. But for one all important difference: a return to Thomism and sanity, a return to 'chiming in with Revelation', and thus a return to 'Intellect in Search for Faith' will be possible and accomplished only in the living hell this side of the grave, to the complete and everlasting glory of Our Lady of Fatima. In Hell, this will be impossible; but in the living-hell-on-earth under Anti-christ, this Marian dominance will be the beginning of the end. But since Thomism does not have to return to some minds now, and since 'chiming in with Revelation' is still being practiced and adhered to now, and consequently, since there are still 'Intellects in Search of Faith' now, it is now, in the heroic achievements of our times, that Our Lady of Fatima has already started to crush the head of Satan now, for it is through Her

Chapter Ten: The Discipline of the Mind (Pope St. Pius X)

Children that the Catholic church continues Her Existence and Her saving work here on earth now. The power of that Church is once again being manifested and realised in the greatest weakness this earth has seen since the apparent weakness of Her Founder on the last day of his mortal Life on earth: a weakness so strong that it saved, in One Man, the whole world.

It is against this formidable background, against the self imposed incapability of 'modern man' to see beyond 'biology', against the ever-growing menace of the 'church of darkness', and against the greatest display of strength-in-weakness this earth has witnessed since the First Good Friday, that the second half of St. Anselm's dictum must be assessed: 'Intellect in Search of Faith'. For no Discipline of the Mind will be complete without it.

The astute reader will – from the foregoing – have already come to the correct conclusion, that once again we have here come face to face with a true Mystery. Where, in ordinary daily affairs, one person, cornered by a hostile mob, would gratefully welcome the timely arrival of the police, another, in similar circumstances, would brand this as interference. Where one human being, in great financial difficulties, would be grateful for an offer of assistance from a friend to alleviate his plight, another would reject it with scorn as an insult. And where finally one creature, struggling to get by with the dim light of his created intelligence, welcomes the arrival of the Son of Man bringing with Him a new order of Grace and Light, another will criticise the Redemption as interference in human affairs, as an insult to human dignity and freedom, and as a restriction on human intelligence …

If this last example is clearly yet another instance of the 'Mysterium Iniquitatis', the Mystery of Iniquity, already met in Lecture 6, the former, i.e. 'intellect in search of Faith', is concrete evidence of the Mystery of Salvation and Election. But since the Catholic Church rejects rank determinism and any helpless predestination as totally incompatible with the freedom of the individual to accept or reject the Supernatural Light of Faith and the Gift of Grace, the Mystery of Evil and the Mystery of the Number of the Elect may never be portrayed as being some sort of cause for the eternal destiny of souls.

This teaching of the Church clearly shows that the acceptance of the Superior Light of Faith by the created light of human intelligence is open to acceptance unless, by some clear but inexplicable Mystery of Pride, it is rejected until even beyond the grave. This means that the human mind, even the ostensibly recalcitrant human mind, must be considered inclined to grope for, and eventually willing to yield to, the Superior Light of Catholic faith if properly handled ... Anima naturaliter christina, said already Tertullianus (b. circa 160 AD), or 'the soul is christian already by nature'. It is natural for the human mind, then, to be drawn to the Supernatural Light of Faith.

If properly handled ... It is here that once again the Philosophy of St. Thomas Aquinas sparkles in all its human glory and perennial brilliance, for it is precisely this Philosophy which the infallible teaching of the Catholic Church has recognised and singled out for us as the "Preamble of the Faith": just as "Wisdom has built a house" where she is at home (Prov. 9:11) so Faith has built herself a

Chapter Ten: The Discipline of the Mind (Pope St. Pius X)

human dwelling place in the *Philosophia Perennis* of St. Thomas, where she feels at home while on earth.

What is meant here, is best illustrated by using as an example what another Catholic genius has written: the Thirty Day Retreat of St. Ignatius Loyola. There is not the slightest doubt that at the end, St. Ignatius throws the retreat wide open, allowing the generous soul the Infinite Expanse of the Majesty of God as the sole criterion for his devotion, love and service. But this should not be done at the beginning. The First Week is exclusively written for the conversion of heart, for sorrow, compunction and expurgation. Yet the end of the retreat is too powerful a drawcard to be left out altogether. And it is the genius of St. Ignatius as a Spiritual Leader to weave into the beginning just enough of the powerful ending to arouse, not interest or intellectual satisfaction which would have destroyed even the end, but nostalgia, in order to unleash from the tight little knot of the selfish human heart the first genuine tears of repentance and contrition on the Royal Road to Perfection. Christ on the Cross is such a Mystery of Infinite Love, it surpasses the intuition of even the greatest Saint, yet in its humility and silence it is appropriate to let the sinner kneel before it after the First Meditation of the Retreat. Earthly suffering, the preamble to the tiny human mind and heart taking flight into the divine domain of Understanding and Love. The end of the retreat is there at the beginning, but because of the Ignatian genius, it is there at the beginning, and no more. Like the end of the plant in the seed, vigorously growing towards its fulfilment and final end, which would have been impossible if it had not been there in the first place, not as the end, but as the beginning. Yet, the seed is a true part of the plant, not only the start.

For 'Intellect searching for Faith', the Philosophy of St. Thomas fulfils an identical role. The genius of St. Thomas lies precisely in this undefinable but exquisite quality that he without a shadow of a doubt wrote a Philosophy for the human intellect, entirely for the satisfaction of the human intellect, precisely because in it he weaves the elements that point beyond it. There is just enough Supernatural Light concealed in discrete places, but entirely to the satisfaction of the human mind, to make the whole a dazzling unit, an interplay so powerful that the echo and response from Eternity are not only missed, but welcomed when they are there.

And so we have completed our journey. We are back at our starting point: the Philosophy of St. Thomas, but now no longer as a starting point, a beginning, but with the end firmly within our reach. These are the two components of the Discipline of the Mind: 'Natural Understanding', perfected by the Philosophy of St. Thomas, and 'Supernatural Insights' provided by the Catholic Faith, as one, glorious possession of the tiny Human Mind, an interplay so powerful that nothing on earth can compare as its equal.

Allow me then, in a final section, to bring out more clearly the meaning of this; especially for those who, because of difficulty with abstract reasoning, would like to see the ideas come to life, preferably embodied in persons who, after having once grasped the ideas revealed, are now capable of putting them into action.

Chapter Ten: The Discipline of the Mind (Pope St. Pius X)

Section III: "Fracto Alabastro ..." (Mk. 14:3)

This unity, this subordination to the higher Light of Faith as well as the freely given share of the role to be played by the human intellect: a genuine contribution, because it could be refused, is ultimately played out in Love between the Bride, the human soul, and the Groom, the Son of God, Jesus Christ. 'Fides Quaerens Intellectum' is then the Word of God, the Light of God, coming down in search of a Bride, a human mind where He would be recognised and received. And 'Intellectus Quaerens Fidem' would then be a soul, in search of something to love, something higher than its own created light, something that, in love, would perfect it and make it fruitful. The Word of God in search of a soul with whom He could share His Wisdom, His Knowledge, His beloved Truth and His Love; and the tiny human mind, in search of Him Who would take it into His arms in order to lift it high above itself and fill it with knowledge it would love to share for its own perfection and enjoyment.

It is the women in the Gospel who have shown us by their spontaneous behaviour that they, more than the men, have understood the desire of the Lamb of God to share with individuals as well as with His people and His Church, what was rightly His in the infinity of His 'equality with God'. (Phil. 2:6).

"When He arrived at the Pharisee's house, and took His place at the table, a woman came in who had a bad name in the town. She had heard He was dining with the Pharisees, and had brought with her an alabaster jar of ointment. She waited behind Him at His feet, weeping, and her tears fell on His feet, and she wiped them away with her hair: and she covered His feet with kisses and anointed them with the ointment."

For one brief moment, the Creator and the creature were wet together from the same tears, and He and the woman "who had a bad name in the town" smelled alike in the sweet scent of the perfume poured out with so much love. The Creator searching for a creature to share His Love with, and the creature searching him out among all the other guests as the one who had the Supernatural Light she craved for.

"Six days before the Passover, Jesus went to Bethany, where Lazarus was, whom He had raised from the dead. They gave a dinner for Him there: Martha waited on them and Lazarus was among those at the table. Mary brought in a pound of very costly ointment, pure nard, and with it anointed the feet of Jesus, wiping them with her hair; the house was full of the scent of the ointment."

The same natural understanding of this woman to know what to do, the same hankering after the spiritual union in love, and surrender to the higher Light that is leading her from then on. It was Mark's little addition to the text: "She broke the alabaster jar ..." which in Latin is 'Fracto Alabastro' which holds the key-note of finality in this beautiful little episode, which I have chosen as the heading of this final section. Fracto alabastro. Until it is done, there is no scent. There is no brief unity of Creator and creature being engulfed in the same wave of aroma, symbol of the surrender of the Creature and the acceptance of the Creator. And ever since the example given by these two women, one on the Via Purgativa, the other on the Via Iluminativa, how many countless creatures have broken their pride and their self-will, and have surrendered to the Superior Light of the Son of God which He left behind in the humility of His Church, and have filled Heaven with the scent of their love.

"Near the Cross of Jesus stood His mother, and His mother's sister Mary, the wife of Clophas, and Mary of Magdala."

We all know how tradition has depicted the presence of the latter kneeling at the foot of the Cross, her head pressed against the Sacred Feet and the cruel nails. And here, for a brief moment on the Via Unitiva, where Creator and Creature are once again wet and streaked by the same fluid, this time the Blood of the Lamb of God, after He had broken for us the pure white alabaster of His Virginal Body. Once again human understanding, brought to the peak of its natural power and helpless in the face of such an all-out Mystery of Love, begging to be taken further into the Supernatural Insights of the Son of God, in order to be equals in the union of Love, demanded by so much Divine Extravagance.

We may never reach such heights in the Mystical Union of the soul with her Spouse, but the road is the same for all. Fracto Alabastro. Let human ingenuity take you as far as it can in finding ways and means of breaking your pride, your self will, and all the bonds of your sins, and then use your intellect in search for Faith, in search of the Supernatural Insights and Wisdom the Catholic Church has stored up, for whoever is eager to learn, in the teachings of the great Saints and Doctors of the Church, and in the pages of Her own Encyclicals. And once on the road, this marvellous interplay between Human Mind and Supernatural Faith will never cease. Never will the human mind cease to exist, or cease to find new ways to please God, or show her love, or grasp the need of the poor. And always will the Supernatural Light be there, to show the soul in love in ever clearer detail, the way God sees the world and every detail of every human life. And what started off as an investigation into Papal preference for Thomism, ended up – need we be amazed? – as a blue-print for perfection ... With neither Thomism or the human mind destroyed, but kept very much intact in order to sustain, know and enjoy Perfection ...

Appendix A

Modernism, Modernists; Teilhardism, Teilhardians

Modernism

Although Pope St. Pius X has been the most articulate Pontiff in exposing and condemning Modernism inside and outside the visible confines of the Catholic Church, he was by no means the first one to do so. Modernism is the general name for the doctrine which attempts to subject 'the Supernatural' (i.e. that which exceeds human nature and powers) to 'the natural' (i.e. to that which is in the power of human nature). Rationalism, Positivism, Naturalism are all examples of this attempt. There are various Supernatural entities on this planet: the Catholic Church is a Supernatural presence in this world, because Her Head, Our Lord and Saviour Jesus Christ is Divine. Within the Catholic Church we recognise the Seven Sacraments, the Infallibility of the Pope, and the Dogmas of the Church as Supernatural Entities in the life here on earth, exceeding the understanding of the unaided human intellect.

As explained in the text of the Lectures, in order to accept the existence of the Supernatural presence in this life, we must have received from God a Supernatural Faculty, which is called 'Catholic Faith'. Only in the Supernatural Light of Catholic Faith will Supernatural Revelations by God be accepted and adhered to.

Proud men who have not got this Supernatural Light and Faculty, because they either deliberately lost it or refused to accept it, cannot tolerate the fact that there are things here on earth which exceed their natural powers of understanding, and consequently, they want to suppress God's Revelation and bring it to submission under the control of human understanding and the human intellect, admitting only to what can be understood. From this it becomes immediately obvious that the main thrust of Modernism is directed towards the eradication of Catholic Faith: that Supernatural Faculty and Light by which Supernatural Revealed Existences are recognised and accepted. As explained further in the text, Catholic Faith is undoubtedly the most precious Gift, Supernatural Gift, of God to finite little man, because it is only in the Light of Catholic Faith, and with the Supernatural, Infused, Divine Faculty of the Virtue of Catholic Faith, that all God's Supernaturally Revealed Truths can be 'seen' and accepted. Hence the vehemence of a Saint and Pope, Pope St. Pius X, in resisting this thrust of Modernism. In his most famous encyclical *Pascendi Dominici Gregis* of 1907, the Saintly Pontiff goes to amazing lengths to hold up the various *strands* from which modernism was composed and by which it could be recognised. The encyclical is readily available from orthodox sources, but no longer from so-called 'catholic' bookshops and publishers. It is a 'must' for the understanding of our times.

Appendix A: Modernism, Modernists; Teilhardism, Teilhardians

Modernists

A modernist is first and foremost someone who readily accepts and tries to diffuse the tenets and maxims of Modernism. They live by those beliefs and promote them in all sorts of catechetical, theological, and philosophical publications and seminars. Since many of them pretend to be still Catholics and Christians, they come closest to what St. John describes in his *Apocalypse*, Ch. 13, as the Second Beast: 'which looks like the Lamb, but speaks like the Dragon': a 'system' and people, preparing directly the way for the reign of Antichrist.

In a broader sense, we could refer to 'modernists' all those who, because of the weakness of their Faith and an inadequate knowledge of it, seemingly live according to the tenets of the modernists, without much understanding of what it is all about. It is just convenient to them to make use of the general confusion to drift into the easiest way out and stay there without any investigation into proper Catholic Teaching. Although not going as far as promoting the state of modernism in which they actually live, they will nevertheless defend it, and resist any attempt by the Holy Father to reconsider their plight and stir themselves out of it. Their prayer life is moribund.

Since it is impossible for active modernists not to have at least deliberately Doubted a Dogma of the Catholic Faith, and since many have gone much further and are not only openly denying Dogmas of the Catholic Faith, but are actively engaged in promoting the abolition of such Dogmas and the Faith in them, it is clear that All active Modernists have lost the Priceless Possession of their

Supernatural, Infused, Divine Gift of Catholic Faith, and have become modern apostates. For Catholics who have kept untrammelled this powerful Light and Faculty, it is altogether inconceivable that Bishops, Priests, Nuns and Theologians who constantly either promote, or actively allow the consistent promotion of anti-Catholic doctrine in their schools and Seminaries, that such people would still possess that Supernatural Light and Faculty by which it can be immediately seen that Catholic Faith and the promotion of Modernism are absolutely incompatible.

De Facto Modernists, i.e. modernists out of convenience, the fellow-travellers and the great bulk, which make it appear as if the Catholic Church has become 'modernist', these people are all on the way of eventually losing their Catholic Faith and are consequently in the gravest of danger. And yet, as the author of *Pascendi* remarked in another of his encyclicals "… how tranquilly they repose there …" And yet, assisting the Holy Fathers in their untiring efforts to rouse them out of their mortal danger by proclaiming the Truth, is seen (by necessity, of course) as uncharitable and a flaming nuisance by not a few bishops, priests, nuns, catechists and lay folk alike.

Teilhardism

Teilhardism is the most outspoken exponent of Modernism extant today. This means that all that can be said of Modernism must now be applied to Teilhardism. It is directed to the abolition of Catholic Faith by making the Supernatural totally subjected to Evolution: an unproven, pseudo-scientific system which catholics are asked to accept in surrender of their Supernatural Birthright: the priceless possession of their Catholic Faith ...

A French Jesuit Pere Pierre Teilhard De Chardin (1881 – 1955, and an acknowledged Freemason and Martinist), for the reasons entirely inspired by Modernism, decided that the time had come "to reformulate the whole of Catholic Dogma and to initiate a new religion as postulated by the requirements of Evolution". These very words of intent are actually used in: his 1929 article *The Human Sense*, his formal break with the Catholic Church; in a 1936 letter to one of his lovers, Zanta; and in his 1953 article *Stuff of the Universe*. This he intended to do, "not by changing institutions and ethics, but by laying the axe to the root of Catholic Faith itself" as he wrote himself in 1950 to an ex-priest. Teilhard sought to transform Catholic Faith itself by advocating the wholesale reformation of Catholic Dogma since, according to him, "*a hitherto unknown form of religion* had gradually germinated in the heart of 'modern man', in the furrow opened by evolution". (*Stuff of the Universe*, 1953).

Although, as was to be expected, he managed to accumulate over the years and after his death no fewer then fourteen known interdicts, prohibitions and outright condemnations from competent Superiors and Church Authorities, including one encyclical *Humani Generis* (Pope Pius XII, 1950), his private works were nevertheless disseminated and avidly read and discussed by hundreds of Jesuits and theologians all over Europe since the 1920's. It was heady stuff, and the thrust was of course not immediately evident.

That Catholics are asked outright to surrender their Catholic Faith can be immediately gleaned from his fundamental thesis: in order that a breach could be made for the introduction of evolution within the body of Catholic Teaching, the Dogma of Original Sin as taught and understood by the Catholic Church had to be abolished. This was condemned by *Humani Generis*, which means that Pope Pius XII condemned Teilhardism in no uncertain terms! In Teilhard's system of evolution, Original Sin as a historical fact could never have taken place. Adam and Eve, as First Parents, never existed, and can at most be taken as symbols for all humanity. Instead polygenism or polygenesis had to be taught: an evolutionary theory that the human race developed from lower animals, and originated all over the globe at once. Scientifically disproved by the world-authority on genetics: Professor LeJeune. The 'theological systems' which have adopted this fundamental postulate of the non-existence of Original Sin have in the span of fifteen years unhinged all other Dogmas of the Catholic Church, as was already logically demanded by Teilhard himself.

That Teilhardism is Modernism, i.e. determined to subject the Supernatural to the natural, becomes clear from the *Phenomenon of Man* where Teilhard expressly states "that the Kingdom of God is a prodigious Biological operation". This was to underline, and to make sure that people correctly understood, what he had written earlier in the same book:

"What makes and classifies a 'modern man'? Having become capable of seeing in terms not of space and time alone, but of biological space-time; and above all: of having become incapable of seeing anything otherwise, anything NOT EVEN HIMSELF." [Teilhard's stress]. (p. 241 – 242).

'Biology' is the ultimate reality to which the Kingdom of God is now subject. 'A prodigious biological operation: that of the Redeeming Incarnation' (Epilogue of the *Phenomenon of Man*). 'Redemption passed on by Sex ...' The exact opposite of Catholic Teaching for 2000 years: Original Sin passed on by Propagation.

It is obvious from this what happened in the 40-odd years separating the two great encyclicals *Pascendi* and *Humani Generis*: the Strands of Modernism became so closely intertwined to form the system of Modernism: Teilhardism. And what has this totally un-Catholic system got, to recommend itself as 'catholic' to the millions of catholics who fall for it, and who accepted it in exchange for their genuine Catholic Faith? Teilhard's evolution is being relentlessly portrayed as ending up inevitably in god-omega. That message was balm for tired and weak catholics of the West who were looking for a way out from the Cross and from Sacrifice. They were invited to 'let go of the cross', and take an armchair ride to god-omega-point. To leave the storm-tossed Barque of St. Peter and board a jolly cruise-ship 'lolly-pop'. And with this everything that has plagued ordinary catholics no end falls into place: no sin, no confession, only a meal, no Sacrifice, etc. Ecumenism takes the place of an Infallible Pope. To keep this up, Teilhardism and his marvellous evolution must be maintained at all cost ...

Teilhardians

Teilhardians, as with Modernists, come in two groups: the adherents and promoters of the 'system'; and the weak, thoughtless and hopeful followers of this modern brand of catholicism so-called. The first ones advocate 'the embrace of the world' and of marxist ideologies as solutions for our problems; the latter simply embrace and follow the world and the false ecumenism, thinking to render a service to God and the Church. Hoping that all this is the genuine interpretation of Vatican II. They all behave as if they are on a cruise ship. You do not worry about the direction of the ship: it will end inevitably at its destination: omega point. No need to atone for sins, or to worry about them. Enjoy ship board romances. Have regular meals (Mass seen as a meal). And above all else: maintain a pleasant camaraderie with everybody else on board: the false ecumenism. No more Missionary activities and conversions: everybody on earth is bound for Heaven with this evolutionary ship, bound to end up with all creation in omega-point. Nice of all those new theologians to call this 'the new catholicism'. Saves us from feeling guilty about it ... and if you sometimes do, well, there are enough priests on board to give 'general absolution' ...

Appendix B

The "Melbourne Guidelines"

After no fewer than 12 prints and reprints, the *Melbourne Guidelines For Religious Education in Primary and Secondary Schools in the Archdiocese of Melbourne* (Victoria, Australia) are today easily the most sophisticated and up-to-date 'guidelines for subversion' ever conceived by Modernism. They will guarantee the loss of Catholic Faith in teachers and pupils alike. Conceived in Hell, they are written in hatred and taught with malice. The conspiratorial secrecy surrounding their introduction into a diocese is to be seen to be believed. For parents it is easier to buy a ticket for a flight to the moon than to obtain a copy of the *Melbourne Guidelines* (M.G.). No one can ascertain for sure if they are in a school or not. And if they are, no one can find out which of the hundreds of recommended books a particular teacher is using.

From the long list of its heresies it is easily shown that the whole production is subversive. Referring catechists to specific pages in non-catholic books written by non-catholic authors, the M.G. teach:

1. That Catholic children must be taught to Doubt their Catholic Faith in order to advance in it! Whereas the official Catechism has always officially taught that a deliberate doubt of the Catholic Faith can be sufficient to extinguish that Faith.

2. That children must be taught to experiment with other faiths …
3. That children must be taught to Move Away from the Faith of the Catholic community to a 'faith' of their own.
4. That Catholic children must be taught that the Authority for the 'faith' is found in the community, whereas it is Catholic Dogma that authority is vested by Christ in the Papacy, independent of the approval of the 'community'.
5. The M.G. boldly declare 'that Genesis is a collection of myths', which are compared with the myths of Aboriginal folklore.
6. The M.G. teach throughout its various books 'that revelation is on-going', and is found in the life-experiences of individual persons, which only the individual can unravel and give meaning to through Private Interpretations. (It cannot be more 'Protestant').
7. The M.G. teach expressly 'that Christ is present in the bread and wine', which is a heresy of the First Order.
8. With regard to the Sacrifice of Christ, the M.G. teach a proposition which has been expressly condemned by the Church as being totally inadequate.
9. The M.G. teach that Baptism is but an initiation Ceremony receiving the recipient into the 'faithing community', since the authors categorically refuse to teach anything on Original Sin and Christ's atoning Death …
10. The *Book of Revelation* is dismissed as 'science fiction' (sic!)
11. Etc. 12. Etc. 13 …

Appendix B: The "Melbourne Guidelines" 239

... to mention only a few of the innumerable distortions, deviations, lies, errors and downright heresies contained in these demoniacal pages.

All the ingredients of the Teilhardian 'Jolly Cruise-Ship' corruption are present:

I. It does no longer matter what you believe;
II. There is no longer any mention of Sin, Sacrifice, Atonement, Conversion, Penance;
III. One can pass the time of day on board ship by making one's own altar bread from condemned recipes which make the Consecration invalid, preventing Transubstantiation. This last Dogma is not taught: preference is given to a heretical explanation of Christ's presence;
IV. A pleasant camaraderie is assured through the removal of every specific Catholic Dogma and Teaching, as requested by the World Council of Churches. The broad liberal Protestantism that is left over is supposed to be the implementation of the requirements of 'ecumenism'.
V. In the sure knowledge that the ship will take you and everybody else on board inevitably to god-omega, there is no longer any need for a Catholic Church, a specific Catholic Faith, an Infallible Teaching Authority (Magisterium) requesting assent to its teaching in Faith and Conscience. No need for the Catholic Mass, Confession, Obedience. All you need is a meal ...
VI. Just enjoy yourself, make sure you do not forget Number One, that very important, unique person that continually

receives revelation from God, which is open to any fancy explanation, which your whim, feelings and changing situations will tell you infallibly is coming from the Holy Spirit ...

It is impossible to maintain that the M.G. just happen to be in almost every diocese of Australia without the express consent of the Bishop of the diocese in which they are found. That being so, the consenting bishops must be of the strong conviction ('opinion' is not enough in this all-important matter) that the M.G. are orthodox Catholic teaching, taught by the Catholic Church for 2000 years and reducible to Christ's teaching and that of His Twelve Apostles. Since from the quoted sample it is obvious that they are NOT, the question is: "What went wrong?" In the *Advocate* of March 19, 1981, one of them – Archbishop Little of Melbourne – went so far as to invoke his divinely given teaching authority to impose the M.G. on the conscience of his hapless flock ... This has now set a precedent for the whole of Australia; which, of necessity, must have put other bishops in a spot.

Book II

The Hedge of the Vine

Frits Albers, Ph.B.

Published

1991

Foreword

In Hell nothing makes sense! This is not hard to substantiate. In her memoirs Sr. Lucia tells us the following about the vision of Hell granted to her and to her two little cousins Jacinta and Francisco on July 13, 1917:

" ... and we looked as into a sea of fire, in which were huge numbers of devils and damned souls in human form, like transparent coals of black and bronze embers. They would be raised in the air by the flames, floating and swaying in clouds of flame and smoke, then falling back on all sides and in all directions, without weight or equilibrium and unable to control their contorted movements. On fire within and without, they floated and showered about like sparks in a great conflagration, amid shrieks and wailing screams of fiendish terror, pain and despair, which filled the fiery atmosphere."

In the 'checklist' found in Chapter 25 of St. Matthew's Gospel, Our Blessed Lord tells us how Catholic Bishops, priests and laity become part of this terrifying scene:

"Depart from Me with your curse upon you into everlasting fire, which was prepared for the devil and his angels. For I was hungry and you gave Me nothing to eat. I was thirsty and you gave Me nothing to drink. I was a stranger and you did not take Me in; naked and you did not cover Me; sick and in prison and you did not visit Me." (Mt. 25: 42-43)

If this is a clear reference to the eternal punishment even for the <u>careless</u> neglect of the corporal works of mercy, how ever more deserved, in the Divine Mind, must the punishment of eternal damnation be for the wilful neglect of the spiritual works of mercy by the innumerable programs, courses, books, 'guidelines' of twenty five years of undiluted Modernism which, like the Tasmanian RENEW, boastfully nail to their masthead:

'No Divine Truths! No answers to moral problems! No Catholic Teaching! No Catholic doctrine! We will not allow Papal and Marian Catholics to pester us with these in our deep-sharing 'faith sessions'!'

And then the divine condemnation of the RENEWED reads like this:

1. "I was hungry for solid Catholic doctrine and you would not give it to Me. Instead, you fed Me poisonous programs, and you tried to ruin the reputations of those who came to My aid."
2. I was thirsty for the Truth, and you refused to give it to Me. In fact you gave Me lies to drink, and the least of Mine lost the use of their God-given Catholic Faith. And once again, you discouraged those who came to My rescue by bringing odium on their reputations and intentions."
3. "In the least of Mine I was naked, devoid of all virtue, and you refused to cover Me with the riches of My Holy Church! In fact you made fun of My helplessness in those RENEW churches when from the pulpit and with placards, banners, slogans, gimmicks and literature, you paraded your own nakedness before Me. And you ignored the ef-

forts of those who came to My aid to restore the dignity due to My sanctuary as well as to the least of My brothers."

4. I was a stranger in your Modernist 'RENEWED church' and the least of Mine could no longer find their way out of it. But you, far from helping them out, you pushed them deeper and further into error with an endless stream of follow-up programs. And you hated and thwarted the efforts made by all those who came to My aid."

5. "I was sick when the least of Mine were sick with the sin of contraception. And you, not only were you the cause of their sickness by saying they had nothing to fear from a healthy conscience: in their wretched state you left <u>Me</u> totally alone. And on this Day, the Day of Judgement, I shall reveal by what means you encouraged My people to 'stay in their sin', what labels you attached to those who came to My aid and how you thwarted them."

6. "When the least of My people were in Satan's prison, caught up in a web of lies and shackled to their sins of impurity, it was Me who was left there with them, and that is where you left us. And if it had not been for the Marian Catholics who came to the rescue with prayer and penance and the Truth of My Church, then the least of Mine would be where you are now: on My left."

That Modernism with its crop of poisonous weeds like CROPP and RENEW are totally empty of Catholic Truth cannot be written off as a product of an overworked imagination. It is (i) self admitted, (ii) known to bishops, priests and laypeople who push these programs and (iii) <u>willed</u> because the absence of Truth is <u>by design</u>! But then, when the Modernists and their RENEWED, by their own design and on their own free admission, deliberately leave the hungry starving, the thirsty unquenched, the naked uncovered, strangers unsheltered and lost, the sick in their sins and the prisoners in Satan's clutches, then the end result associated with this ultimate evil, eternal damnation, is also enforced by the Modernists and their RENEWED 'catholics' not only on themselves, but on all those who out of fear or 'loyalty' "have become partners in their wicked works". (Second Letter of St. John.)

The Purpose of this Book

In this my most recent book I want to bring out and discuss, that an important aspect of Divine punishment in Hell is already inflicted on bishops, priests and laity here and now, when they enforce their Modernism contained in their 'homilies' and in programs like RENEW, MELBOURNE GUIDELINES, PARISH 2000 on the sheep entrusted to their care! It is the terrible tragedy, so clearly brought out in Sr. Lucia's vivid description of her vision, that in Hell nothing makes sense and nothing ever will make sense! In that dreadful place there is no longer any purpose and everything is aimless and chaotic. Nothing will ever have value or even meaning!

That is was the Divine Will that this particular aspect 'of no longer making any sense', associated with the pain of damnation, should already be suffered by those on earth who would be found willing to do the Devil's work, God Himself made clear when He pronounced sentence over the devil after the fall of our first parents. The first recorded curse by God, the one pronounced against Satan after the temptation and fall of Adam and Eve in the Garden, is exceedingly important as the punishment meted out there to Satan, <u>involves human beings</u>.

"And the Lord God said to the serpent,

'Because you have done this, be accursed beyond all cattle, all wild beasts. You shall crawl on your belly and eat dust every day of your life. I will make you enemies of each other, you and the Woman, your seed and Her seed. She shall crush your head, and you will strike at Her heel'." (Gen. 3 : 14-15)

'Because you have done this ...'

"There is no mistake as to the reason for the curse", writes Pember in his book *Earth's Earliest Ages*. "It is no accident but the deeply burnt brand which testifies to God's abhorrence of him who brought sin into creation!"

'Because you have done this .... Because you engineered the first apostasy; because you were successful in making the woman believe you and doubt God, extinguishing in her the supernatural Light of innocent Faith in God: be accursed beyond all cattle. And the punishment is absolute and forever: <u>never</u> will the devil succeed in producing anything of real or lasting value. For as long as this world will last he <u>and his seed</u> are condemned to be satisfied by crawling around in the dust of dark places ('workshops'), eating dust and producing nothing but dust! Never, for one moment, will the divine curse allow them to produce anything of real human value, of lasting satisfaction, or permanent beauty, or even something that has meaning and makes sense ...

What awesome thoughts for our contemporaries.

How often in the course of history have bishops, priests, teachers and parents repeated the first apostasy? Enforced heresy on those entrusted to their care? Made people believe them, and made them doubt the Voice of God as it became known to humanity in the teachings of the Catholic Church? How often have they extinguished innocent Catholic Faith? Has the curse been mitigated so that they got away with it? Has History truly nothing to say about what is rampant in our days? Is it silent about 'the vengeance of God' over the wilful destruction of innocent Catholic Faith?

No, History has been far from silent. It has told us again and again: 'There will be no mistake: God's pronouncement is indeed a deeply burnt brand!' No matter how encouraging the popularity of a 'RENEWED catholicism' is to bishops and priests: it will turn out to be merely dust coming from those condemned to live in dark places. The 'easy catholicism' of our times, the revolt against *Humanae Vitae*, the contraceptive pill, the Modernism that teaches 'freedom of conscience' to do one's own thing: RENEW, 'Women priests', 'Married priests'; and the 'deaneries' to form the framework for the smooth transition of all the 'benefits' of Paul Collin's anti-Hierarchical church into the RENEWED 'local churches': it will all prove to be dust, condemned to be empty of any real value, of human satisfaction, of lasting joy.

A deeply burnt brand: 'Psycho Babbling' ...

And one of the visible signs of the 'brand' here on earth is 'psycho-babbling': the insanity and inanity of Hell breaking through the surface and becoming manifest in the speech of those determined to carry out Satan's work of deception. That is the sole essence and the whole meaning of the terrible phenomenon: 'Psycho-Babbling'.

Psycho-babbling is a self inflicted mutilation on Modernists, a punishment from God, but is open to scrutiny. At present, Almighty God is putting a veritable Cross on the shoulders of His true children and followers, asking them to imitate the sufferings of His Son in His Sacred Passion and Death, and to patiently endure the indignities associated with being ruled by deceivers. But God is <u>not</u> asking them to submit to deception or to fall for it! Psycho-babbling sounds the alarm and gives the enemy away: the pseudo-catholic who pretends to be a catholic, but who inwardly has succumbed to Modernism or out of fear and human respect goes along with it.

Psycho-babbling is an outward manifestation of inner chaos and conflict. It is 'becoming incoherent' or 'not making sense', when the minds of the Modernists and their RENEWed have to go through endless contortions trying to make sense of their soothing conviction that leaving Catholics comfortably in their sins must now be accepted everywhere as 'the new catholicism'.

Psycho-babbling is caused by a defect, a disease of the soul, and occurs when the afflicted person tries to make 'catholic sense' from a no-longer-catholic mind; from a catholic mind in turmoil, in dissent, and so in open conflict. That is why programs of dissent like RENEW, which suppress Catholic content while claiming to be Catholic, no longer make Catholic sense and are nothing but psycho-babbling all the way from beginning to end. And this dissent, and the inner contortions to hide it become the very reason why Catholics who enforce such programs of 'easy catholicism': bishops, priests and 'leaders', or those who accept them with glee, become equally incoherent and irrational, and no longer make sense to orthodox Catholics. And the longer the deception is maintained and the inner contortions go on, the more manifest the outward signs of the final damnation become, and the more the terrifying senselessness of Hell breaks out into the open in the speech and the lives of all those who are afflicted.

As will be made clear in the main body of this book, psycho-babbling in Catholic clergy, religious and laity invariably shows up corruption in Catholic thinking. Since no Catholic thinking can be corrupted, unless clear thinking, logic, sound reasoning, in fact Thomistic Philosophy, have been affected first, the stigma of psycho-babbling must also be seen as an act of God's mercy towards sinners, because the affliction can be noticed by the sufferers themselves. Those afflicted (as will be shown on the Last Day of Judgement) should have caught themselves out as no longer making any Catholic sense at all in their public utterances (e.g. 'homilies').

But is 'self-awareness' of this sign of approaching damnation enough? The discussion of the main theses of this book will make it clear beyond doubt why St. John gives an emphatic 'NO' to this question.

So there it is. The mind which has been forced by an evil will 'to uproot the Vine': one's own and other people's Catholic Faith, will by Divine punishment be a mind in chaos from then on, a mind condemned to be satisfied with mere dust. If the clear thinking of the *Philosophia Perennis* has been declared by the Church "to be truly the hedge and fence of the Vine" (Leo XIII in *Aeterni Patris*, 1879), then the Vine cannot be trampled underfoot unless this hedge and fence have been destroyed first. But there is a Divine Rider to this:

"He that uproots a hedge, a snake will bite him." (Ec. 10: 8)

It is this 'bite of the serpent from Hell' which has our intense and undivided interest in this book.

Introduction

St. Thomas Aquinas is adamant: "There is only one truth". And because his Catholic Faith <u>is</u> 'this One Truth', he was convinced that nothing discovered in nature could ultimately contradict the Faith. And vice versa: because the Faith is the One Truth, nothing really deduced from the Faith could ultimately contradict the facts.

If Catholic Faith would contradict what appeared to be 'facts', then time would prove that they were not true facts at all. It is an expression of the supreme Thomistic confidence, that scientists can freely go on exploring nature, because in Faith we know that they will never discover a 'fact' or 'truth' which will contradict Facts and Truth we know from Revelation.

So strong is this belief in the Oneness of Truth that even if man would discover something that appears to contradict, what we know to be True in Faith, then further investigation will eventually bring to light that this seeming contradiction of Catholic Faith clearly involves contradicting facts and truths accepted as true by the ordinary human intelligence.

It is the purpose of this book to bring out the unbelievable importance of this last sentence. Anything that is stubbornly held up as contradicting the Truths of Catholic Faith, does not have to be refuted from the supernatural standpoint of Faith. In many cases this would be impossible, and thus a futile exercise, simply because of the absence of the supernatural Light of Faith in our adversaries, either because they lost it or never received it. But the oneness of Truth can always be relied upon to show that, what <u>seems</u> to contradict the Faith, does <u>in reality</u> contradict truths and facts ascertainable or already ascertained by the ordinary human intellect. *The Crumbling Theory of Evolution* is one example that springs to mind as the due reward for that very astute Catholic mind of the late J.W.G. (Wallace) Johnson.'

In his little biography of St. Thomas, G.K. Chesterton gives the reason why, at the height of his once-and-only anger with an opponent, in his controversy with Siger of Brabant, St. Thomas let loose such thunders of purely moral passion. It was because the work of a lifetime was being betrayed behind his back by those, who had used his Aristotelian victories over the Medieval reactionaries to split up truth is such a way that one truth would contradict another. And the way the cornerstone of Thomism was presented to the Sorbonne in Paris made it appear as if St. Thomas agreed with the twisted shambles! Chesterton:

> "And yet, even in this isolated apocalypse of anger, there is one phrase that may be commended for all time to men who are angry with much less cause. If there is one sentence that could be carved in marble, as representing the calmest and most enduring rationality of this unique intelligence, it is a sentence which came pouring out with all the rest of this molten lava. If there is one phrase that stands before history as typical of Thomas Aquinas, it is that phrase about his own argument:
>
>> 'Behold our refutation of the error. It is not based on documents of Faith, but on the reasons and statements of the philosophers themselves.'

Introduction

Would that all Orthodox doctors in deliberation were as reasonable as Aquinas in anger ... At the top of his fury, Thomas Aquinas understands what so many defenders of orthodoxy will not understand. It is no good to tell an atheist; or to charge a denier of immortality with the infamy of denying it; or to imagine that one can force an opponent to admit he is wrong by proving he is wrong on somebody else's principles, but not on his own. After the great example of the Doctor Angelicus, the principle stands ..."

We may now begin to understand 'the bite under the hedge of the Snake in Hell', after the clear enunciation of this principle: how not only 'the Vine' had to be destroyed on earth, Catholic Faith, but 'the hedge' as well, the human mind guarding the Faith, so that it would become impossible to argue from any standpoint at all, or in any 'light', neither natural nor supernatural. "If then the light inside you is darkness, what darkness that will be!" (Mt. 6: 24)

With this so clearly established, both the purpose and the subject-matter of this book are laid open before us. The history of 'the Vine and the Hedge' is six thousand years old. What it teaches is just as relevant today as it was then.

Chapter One

The Vine

There really was ever only one Message:

The Message of the 'Everlasting Enmity'. (Gen. 3: 15)

Those whose desire it is to be on the wrong side of it, will have to be satisfied with for ever 'eating, gathering and producing dust' in defeat, no matter how spectacular and permanent the splendour of their illusionary technology and 'mastery' may appear to be.

Those who by a holy and inexplicable urge, wish to be on the right side of it, will have to be satisfied with everlasting watchfulness and readiness in battle, now matter how their victories and effectiveness may be cloaked in apparent feebleness and defeat.

Those on the wrong side are forced to look forever over their shoulders to identify those most likely to stab them in the back.

Those on the right side are continually "looking up to Heaven whence comes their salvation".

Those on the wrong side are forever engrossed in this world, in all its comforts, riches and pleasures.

Those on the right side behave like pilgrims, in search for their Fatherland, their true and eternal Home.

Those on the wrong side are "your seed".

Those on the right side are "the Seed of the Woman".

Since the treasures of God's hidden designs are there to be found in His Creation, we can be sure that 'the adversary of the Woman' has done everything in his power to unlock God's hidden code without a Key, in order to twist the Message for the seduction of those to whom it was given to read and understand it. From the way the devil behaves we can gather what his superior mind has read into God's Revelation; and from the twisted versions of the devil's ways, and his attempts at 'reconstruction', we many get a clearer picture yet of why the devil failed, and Mary succeeded, in reading what God had intended for discovery by all 'the children of Wisdom', 'the seed of the Woman of Genesis', whose sacred image God has forever incorporated in the blueprints of His eternal Secrets.

For who is there to maintain against overwhelming evidence, that God did not keep to Himself a long line of faithful servants whom he made His confidants in the true meaning of the mysteries of His hidden designs? And is it not equally beyond dispute that a future 'Mystery Woman' played a most prominent part in the implementation and power of these designs? That Her role and mystique became unerringly implanted in Tradition, to become the indelible code in the spiritual chromosomes of God's faithful strain?

Thus the hand of God planted a tiny Vine, His very own, at the origin of the human race, when humanity was only 'two people' old. It was an invisible Vine, for although in this world, it was not of this world. It was a Vine that was meant to carry God's strain, the New Covenant after the Fall, from generation to generation, a Living Tradition that would keep the 'Everlasting Enmity' alive, free from any oblivion or corruption. And deeply encoded in the chromosomes of its spiritual nature, to guarantee this Uncorruption, is the mystery of the promise of the Woman of Genesis. Ini-

Chapter One: The Vine

tially no more than human longing for Her and for 'the Fruit of Her womb', it would one day break out into full bloom in a future Church of which this Fruit would be the Head and this Woman would be the Mother and Type.

Thus it came about that with this Vine God established True Faith on this earth never to disappear again, as in the Fall, even when eventually it would be kept in only <u>one</u> family.

"Faith without which it is impossible to please God."

(Hebr. 11: 6)

And inseparable from Faith something else had been grafted onto this Vine as a hallmark of the Divine strain: Obedience to the Faith.

"Obedience is better than sacrifices." (1 Sam. 15: 22)

Thus sentence had been passed. The Great War had been declared: 'The Everlasting Enmity' between 'Satan and 'his seed' and 'the Woman of Genesis and Her Seed'. The battle lines had been drawn, the conditions clearly laid out, the final outcome made absolutely inevitable. And from the way this War was fought in the beginning we may receive some light on the way it is being fought in the world of our times, 'the Last Days'. Let us pick up the threads.

Earliest attacks on the Vine

Writes Ben Adam in a major commentary of the previous century, entitled *The Origin of Heathendom*, about the first twins Cain and Abel:

"Now Satan, however cunning and sagacious he may be, of necessity could have known nothing of God's purposes beyond what had been revealed. Doubtless the Promise in the Garden meant more to him than it did to Eve, but he would know only what had been revealed: that the Deliverer who was to crush his head was to be the Seed of the Woman. Was Cain the promised seed? He might have been, but then so might Abel. As the twins grew up together, and their respective characters became manifest, it would be plain to Satan with his knowledge of God's ways, that a man of Cain's type could not be the promised seed. On the other hand Abel, the man of God, might be. Satan was taking no chances: he had too much at stake. Hence Abel's premature death. Satan found a convenient and suitable instrument in Cain, 'who was of the wicked one, and slew his brother' (1. John 3: 12).

Though Abel was not the promised seed, he was the first of the line [which we have called 'strain'] through whom the Promised Seed was to come. For, when Seth was born, Eve said he was to be called Seth which means 'Appointed', because God had appointed her another seed 'instead of Abel whom Cain slew'. 'Instead of Abel' indicates that he was meant to be a continuation of Abel's righteousness. When we read the generations of Adam in Chapter 5, which gives the long line from which the Promised Seed was to come, Seth heads the list. Hence Satan, from his point of view, did quite the correct thing in engineering the death of Abel."

Chapter One: The Vine

We may well pause here for a moment to give an expert in biblical exegesis an opportunity to explain to us in more detail what all this means for us and or our times.

In a remarkable book, first published in 1876 by Hodder and Stoughton, *Earth's Earliest Ages*, the author, G. H. Pember, M.A. goes to considerable lengths to do just that in a truly magnificent fashion. After drawing our attention to the fact that Holy Scripture reveals to us the different pursuits adopted by the twins, Cain a tiller of the soil, Abel a keeper of sheep, he points out to us the significance of the latter by making us realize that the sheep were not kept for the production of food, which was as yet forbidden (see Gen. 9: 3, when permission was given after the Flood), but solely for sacrifice to God and for the production of clothes. He then proceeds to analyse for us the reason why God accepted Abel's offering but rejected Cain's, as the reason for this clear difference "is fraught with the deepest interest to us. For there are many in these latter days who, according to the prophesy of Jude 'have gone in the way of Cain', (Jude 11), indicating, that the 'theology' of the first murder has been adopted by a large and perpetually increasing school of our times".

Cain's 'theology' recognised in our own times.

Pember explains that Cain neither denied the existence of God, nor refused to worship Him. He recognised Him as the giver of all good things, and brought Him an offering from the fruits of the ground in recognition of His bounty. But that was as far as Cain was prepared to go. He was prepared to give God only what he, Cain, had decided what God ought to have asked, but not what God actually did demand. He was willing to give God from the fruits of the field, which God had not asked for, but he was unwilling to bring the necessary obedience with his warped 'faith', and to offer the sacrifices God indeed had demanded, above all 'a humble and contrite heart' to go with his offerings. (Ps. 51: 17)

Like the Modernists of our days, he could well have passed among those with whom he dwelt as a good and even religious man, but he failed to satisfy God. The reason Pember advances for this divine rejection is frighteningly modern. Being yet in his sins, Cain presumed to approach the Holy One without the shedding of blood. He was willing to appear on the outside as taking the place of a dependent creature, but he would not confess himself a sinner guilty of death, who could be saved only by the sacrifice of a Substitute. In this he is the archetype of many a Teilhardian in our own times. They too will prattle indefinitely about the love and goodness of God, claiming the benefits of these divine attributes for themselves without any reference to their own unworthiness and sinful condition, without a thought of that perfect Holiness and Justice which are as much elements of the Mind of God as His Love.

But the Most High rejected the gravely defective 'sacrifice' of Cain, for none may approach to worship Him except through the Blood of the Lamb "slain from the foundation of the world" (Apoc. 13: 8), which He has provided in the daily Sacrifice of the Mass. The sin-offering must come first, only then the offering of thanksgiving. We can enter the Holy of Holies, and cast ourselves before the Throne of His Mercy only by passing through the torn veil of Christ's Flesh. And therefore Woe, Woe, Woe to all who only see in the Mass a 'meal' to sustain them on their journey to an eternal encounter with God, which in the conceit of their hearts they see as inevitable. But, "having gone in the way of Cain", they will miss God. For, as Scripture says so clearly: "without the shedding of blood, there is no remission". (Hebr. 9: 22)

Abel knew something of this and confessed it. He sacrificed the firstlings of his flock and poured out their lifeblood in humble avowal of his own deserts. God accepted his offerings, showing that in a type His wrath with regard to Abel would one day be satiated upon a Substitute.

And so with the fearsome act of the first murder and the subsequent banishment of Cain, our first parents were deprived of both their sons in the one day. How vividly must they have realised the terrible consequences of their own disobedience, producing poisonous fruits in their offspring. But "the God of all consolation" was merciful and in time and gave them another son, Seth, who would follow the slain Abel in putting into practise the growing understanding of the urgent demands of the coming deliverance.

Cainites – World – Modernists

From that time onward we find a twofold development in the human race. The Sethites and the banished Cainites remain securely separated for a while, thus representing the Church and the World. Once again we are struck by that striking parallel between the antediluvian Cainites and the ultra-modern Teilhardian Modernists.

The Cainites, with the restlessness of men alienated from God, were ever striving to make the land of their exile a pleasant abode, a replica of 'Paradise Lost'. Ceaselessly trying by every means to palliate the Curse, they made it their main pursuit in life to reproduce their new Eden artificially.

Cain their leader who had been condemned to wander, was the first man to build a city which he called Enoch, after one of his sons, the first attempt at avoiding the toil and to settle comfortably upon the blasted earth. Beyond the mere listing of names we have no further record of Cain's posterity until we come to his descendants of the fifth generation. The few particulars concerning Lamech and his family present us with a vivid picture of human corruption and of the way of the children of this world. We see the onset in a sensuous life that involves the loss of the God-consciousness, and of all fear of breaking Divine Laws. We trace it as it goes on to make present circumstances as comfortable and as indulgent as possible; substituting arts, sciences and intellectual pursuits for spiritual aspirations. As in other ages of unbridled human passions and great corruption 'Truth was flung to the ground and trampled underfoot' (Dan. 8: 12), wholesome thought was banished by excitement with the aid of divers amusements and pleasures. Predictably it all ends up in a thorough concentration upon self, defiance of God and violence! (Gen. 6: 11)

Lamech broke the primeval law of marriage, the first one on record to have scotched monogamy, thus giving proof of the utter godlessness into which the Cainites had lapsed. Of his sons, Jabal became a shepherd-king, Jubal invented music and Tubalcain became the first technocrat. Here we see combined in Holy Scripture the three ingredients of our modern corruption: wealth, pop music and unbridled technology. The boasting spirit of self-reliance, violence and revenge of the time have been preserved for us in 'the song of Lamech', which is in the form of some address to his wives. It is of interest to us, as it reveals what Christ had in mind when He instructed His followers "not to forgive our brother seven times, but seventy seven times". For Lamech's 'pop-song' ends like this:

"For sevenfold shall Cain be avenged, but Lamech seventy and sevenfold." (Gen. 4: 24)

This is the last we hear of 'the family of Cain' as separated from the rest of the world. Its first ancestor was a murderer, a man who refused to acknowledge his dependence on God for the forgiveness of his sins. And it disappeared in the person of a polygamist, murderer and open worshipper of the god of brute force and violence.

This same ending is to be expected for all those who followed Teilhard de Chardin in his 'embrace of the world' when, in their passion, they too were not prepared to render God the service He did request but decided like Cain, that their worldliness is what God ought to have asked and is now getting anyhow. But before the Revolution will turn on its own children to wipe them out like the Deluge, the violence is bound to erupt first against the Catholic Church at the centre of the last and most terrible persecutions under Antichrist, as foretold by the Mother of God at Fatima in 1917.

Sethites – Church - Orthodox

Turning now briefly to Seth's posterity we see there an altogether different scene. Envy, strife and deeds of licence and violence are no longer before us. Our ears cease to be assailed by the strains of shrill music, the clatter of anvils, the vauntings of proud boasters and all the mingled din that arises from a world living without God and Sacrifice, but struggling to overpower His Curse. We see a people poor and afflicted, toiling day after day to procure food from the ungenial soil according to the appointment of their God, patiently waiting till He would be gracious and humbly acknowledging His chastening hand upon them.

They have no share in earth's history: that is entirely made up by the Cainites. As strangers and pilgrims in this world they abstain from fleshly lusts; they build no cities; they invent no arts; they devise no amusements. For they are not mindful of the country in which they live, but seek a better, that is to say a Heavenly one. (Hebr. 11: 10, 14-16)

Conscious of the Curse, they kept also the Promise continually before them. How can we know? Here is why we know: the Bible tells us. In contrast to the boasting Lamech, Seth called his son Enos, that is 'weakness', a humble confession of the feebleness and helplessness of man, which is then naturally followed by the next sentence in Genesis 4: 26 -

"This man was the first to invoke the Name of Yahweh."

Now 'Yahweh' is the Name of God as He is in Covenant with man. At the heart of this renewed Covenant of God with man is the Promise. Thus, when Sacred Scripture tells us expressly that men began to call on the Name of Yahweh, it is teaching us that men were calling on the God-Who-had-made-the-Promise. 'Yahweh' and the 'Promised Deliverer' were inseparable. From this it follows that as long as mankind is in this frame of mind, calling on God in Covenant with it, mankind is also praying for the arrival of 'the Woman' who would bring the Deliverer into the world. At night their hopes were lifted up at the sight of the Sign of Virgo; and the Fear of God, the Coming Judge, was kept alive at the sight of the Sign of Leo. The Woman and the Judge were also kept inseparable.

How do we know this? Because, again, Holy Scripture tells us. Of the most famous of all the Sethites, the patriarch Enoch, Scripture tells us he was a prophet, which means that he went around 'walking with God, preaching repentance from sin'. And what was his central message? According to St. Jude it was this: "that the Lord [the Deliverer, the Seed of the Woman] would come as the Judge with thousands of His saints [the other seed of the Woman] to pass Judgement on the ungodly". Thus when Enoch comes back to preach to the world at the time of Antichrist, he does not have to change his message: it was and still is 'spot-on'. Because, coming from God, it is Eternal and in no need of 'updating'.

This sharp cleavage between Cainites and Sethites is still with us today in the Church in the form of Modernists and Catholics. The former, having 'discovered' a by-pass of the Curse and a short-cut to Paradise in their embrace of the world through the abomination of 'Evolution', have eliminated Catholic Faith and the Sacrifice, exchanging it for the certainty of arrival; thereby clearly showing that they are outside 'the strain of God'. The latter, in staying with 'the Woman' to become Her other seed, have opted to help Her in Her struggle 'to undo the knot of Eve' and 'to crush the serpent's head'.

The first group has abolished altogether the Sacrament of Penance as superfluous in view of the certainty of Heaven; the other 'are still working out their salvation in fear and trembling', (Phil. 2: 12), lest the corruption and deception that befell Teilhardians and the Cainites before them might become their lot as well. We must see in the abundance of global corruption now, and as it was at the time of the Deluge, the adoption of a new strategy of Satan in the light of a further unfolding of the mystery of the 'everlasting enmity'.

Two Universal Corruptions: Two Universal Frustrations

The Deliverer was to be the son of a woman. That much was known. At first the conviction had prevailed that the Deliverer was to be the son of Eve herself. But later, as we see from the words of Lamech (the other Lamech, the father of Noah) in Gen. 5: 29, it had become evident that the words 'her seed' were to be understood in a broader sense, and might apply to any of a woman's male descendants. So, appropriately, Satan's next effort is nothing more or less an attempt to corrupt the whole of Adamic womanhood, thus rendering the coming of the Promised Seed impossible. God's way of dealing with the new threat was to keep <u>one family</u> free from the prevailing sexual corruption and to destroy all the rest of humanity by means of the Deluge.

In order to succeed it was necessary for the Devil to approach a universality in evil akin to the one apparently still to come and foretold twice in The Book of Revelation:

"And <u>the whole world</u> ran after the Beast" (Rev. 13: 3,8)

Was such a consensus, such a unanimity achieved before the flood? What do we read? In Gen 6: 11-13 it is stated:

"And the earth was corrupted before God, and was filled with iniquity. And when God had seen that the earth was corrupted –

Chapter One: The Vine

for <u>all flesh</u> had corrupted its way upon the earth – He said to Noah: 'The end of all flesh has come before Me ... Make thee an Ark' ..."

Yes, with such a record of universal corruption behind us and ahead of us as well, the advice of St. Paul to the Philippians quoted above: "Work out your salvation in fear and trembling" seems to have lost none of its force. But in both these instances God has a Refuge ready, an Ark to carry those who found grace in His eyes to safety. The earlier one is the prototype of the second, the only difference being that in the first universal flood the Ark was man made whereas in our days the second Ark, the Catholic Church modelled on Our Blessed Lady, is of divine origin, untouched by human hands.

There is a profound mystery underlying all this. St. Paul calls it 'Mysterium Iniquitatis': the Mystery of Evil, (2 Thess. 2: 7). For, in order to corrupt the whole world twice, Satan had to find a way for the perversion of the God-fearing Sethites before the Flood as well as God-fearing Christians prior to the reign of his most prominent seed: Antichrist, in order that the Bible can point twice to the universality of iniquity: 'all flesh', (Gen. 6: 12) and 'the whole world', (Rev. 13: 3, 8).

The seduction and perversion of the good and righteous is a great mystery. But equally inscrutable, and reserved to God's knowledge alone, is the mystery of how and why some of the just, His elect, did not succumb but where preserved from global corruption and the subsequent wrath of God. 'Entering the Ark', i.e. 'staying on the right side of the Everlasting Enmity' has a lot to do with it, and ultimately constitutes the decisive sign of this preservation in either situation. The question thus is: 'Who may enter?'

The Mystery of Perseverance

In his book already mentioned, Pember deals with this question in a very astute way. In an effort to isolate the elements which led to the first corruption of humanity, in order that we may learn how to read 'the signs of the times', when we come face to face with the second occurrence in our own times, he has managed to extract from what has been revealed to us in Genesis some of the underlying causes, which he recommends to our prayerful consideration. Here they are with my comments:

I. A tendency <u>to keep God remote</u> and removed from human affairs so that we can manage on our own without any divine 'interference'. A condescension to worship God, but only as Elohim, i.e. merely as a remote Supreme Being to Whom we offer only what <u>we</u> choose. No need for acknowledgement that we must worship Him as the covenant God of Mercy, dealing with human beings as sinners appointed to death, but finding a Ransom for them. No need to deal with Him as a God Who is close enough to us so we humbly acknowledge His supreme Rights and Demands, a Father to Whom we <u>owe</u> love, gratitude and obedience in return for Salvation.

Chapter One: The Vine

Comment

This description fits our 'educated and enlightened' western world like a glove. According to the Freemasons who are past masters in this attitude to religion, Teilhard committed the unpardonable sin in the eyes of Rome: 'he elevated Man to the altar' to be adored in place of God! But modern atheistic 'liberated' man, whether Communist or Capitalist, agrees with this. There is no longer a need for a Sacrifice since we are quite self-sufficient to look after ourselves. It fits our own Teilhardians, allocation to 'god' his place and role in a non-existing 'evolution' while deciding unilaterally that the Mass is merely a meal on our journey to an inevitable heaven.

II. An undue <u>prominence of the female sex</u> coupled with a supreme disregard of the primal law of marriage.

Comment

Pember draws our attention here to the fact that in the biblical genealogy of Seth's family there is no mention by name either of wives or daughters. Lamech's ungodly brushing aside of the primeval laws of marriage, and the introduction of his 'wives' names in his genealogy, which is an abomination in God's eyes – for no man can have two 'wives' at the same time – could be a strong biblical indication that women were unduly prominent among the Cainites, and that physical beauty and sensuous attraction were the only valued qualities, going by the names Lamech gave his wives and daughter. That we have an exact replica of this situation now, coupled with the contempt of God with which it became associated in antediluvian times, is in no further need of elaboration.

III. An <u>inordinate progress in technology</u>, the arts, inventions of 'labour-saving devices', whereby the hardships of the Curse were mitigated and life became more and more indulgent. Leisure and sloth help to captivate the minds of men with the concomitant evil of a gradual but pronounced oblivion of God and His service.

Comment

Of the fact that leisure and luxury corrupt just as easily and effectively now as in the past we do not have to speak here. Of their power to produce arrogance together with complete absorption in the material things of life only, we have daily the most tragic examples before our very eyes.

IV. An inevitable '<u>alliance of consensus</u>' between increasing numbers of 'nominal' Sethites with the 'World of Cain', and a steady exodus from the former 'lifestyle' into the embrace of the other.

Comment

This is the mystery of the evil of corruption of the righteous mentioned earlier! The lure of splendour and achievement, of 'progress' and indulgence found 'in the world of Cain', proves in the long run to be too strong for nominal christians, who are easily led to believe that all this is a visible blessing from God, even if it does not need much meditation to find out that <u>none</u> of this was ever preached by the Gospel. In our days, this 'nominal gospel' of 'building the earth' is the alliance between the Marxist 'church' of the World Council of Churches and the 'church of darkness' of the Modernists

V. The rejection of the preaching of <u>Enoch and Noah</u>, both by the Cainites as by the corrupted Sethites.

Comment

This constitutes the penultimate in the Sins against the Holy Spirit: Obstinacy in Iniquity. The hardening of impenitent man almost to the brink of no return: 'Final Impenitence', the last and irrevocable Sin against the Holy Spirit ...

In the days of Noah and Enoch, this hardening of impenitent men in sin resulted in universal lawlessness and violence: "And the whole earth was filled with violence" (Gen. 6: 11). Is it any different today? Modern hardening also comes from sins against the Holy Spirit in the rejection of that same message, but in our times held up to us by "The Woman of Genesis" Herself: Our Lady of Fatima. A heavenly reminder to give up sin and to practise prayer and penance.

The rejection of this divine command coincides with the rejection, by an ever increasing number of modernist (i.e. nominal) Catholics, of the true Church which continues to keep before the people this fundamental requirement of the Gospel. And in our days too, the universal rejection of prayer and penance, of sacrifices and atonement, has resulted in the same universal lawlessness and violence which swamped the earth before it was flooded by the Deluge.

No salvation outside the Ark

Whenever the Word of God is faithfully preached it cannot return to Him void. "Yes, as the rain and snow come down from the heavens and do not return without watering the earth, making it yield and giving growth to provide seed for the sower and bread for the eating, so the Word that comes from My mouth does not return to Me empty without carrying out My Will and succeeding in what it was sent to do". (Is. 55: 11) It must have some effect on those who hear it. As St. Paul explains: "We are Christ's incense to God, for those who are being saved and for those who are not; for the last, the smell of death that leads to death; for the first the sweet smell of life that leads to life". (2 Cor. 2: 15)

No one can assert that the Word of God was not faithfully preached to the antediluvians, or that it did not accomplish what it was sent out to do: a sweet smell of life to Eight, a smell of death that led to Death for the rest. Nor can it be maintained that that same Word of God, that same Message encoded in the Vine, has not been faithfully preached to our world too, before the onslaught of a 'second universal deluge' of fire and disaster. Or that this Message too 'did not accomplish what it was sent out to do': a sweet smell of Life for 'the strain of God', a smell of Death for those who have rejected the Vine.

When St. Paul revealed to the Thessalonians that the 'mystery of evil' is already at work, he gave his reason for its success amongst sinners: "because they did not possess <u>the love of truth</u> that could have saved them". (2 Thess. 2:10) Love of Truth - how simple really is the solution. We are not even required to be in possession of all the Truth, as long as we welcome it whenever it reveals itself to us. All that is asked of a sinner is that he truthfully acknowledges the true spiritual state of his wretchedness and his need for forgiveness. Then, accepting this truth, act upon it in the only effective manner: "I will rise and go to my Father'.

Readers of the Gospel story of 'the prodigal son' will note that initially there was not even a true repentance of the life of debauchery he had lived: all that there was in the beginning was the acceptance of the truth that he had managed to get himself into a state of physical discomfort. But when such a simple truth is welcomed, or as St. Paul puts it, loved, the rest will follow from there. Even, as the Gospel tells us, a transition from sorrow over a natural state of discomfort to the truly supernatural sorrow and repentance of having offended God with our sins. That this 'love of Truth' is not as easy as it may sound is learned form the fact that, of the whole human race before the Flood, only eight people have been revealed to possess it.

And so an Old World vanished 'because it did not love the Truth'! But Satan was frustrated once again, because the corruption did not go far enough: an Ark, a simple wooden ship, carried the Promise of God's Deliverer within its fragile hold; a Promise which, if fulfilled, would even reach out to some of the wretches who had just perished in the waters outside the walls of this amazing structure, and would snatch them away from the Second Death, to which he and his angels had been irrevocably condemned forever.

Faith in God's Promise, and faith in an Ark: it all came down to one and the same thing ...

One day, he was sure, the function of this Ark would be taken over by the 'Woman' who would carry within Herself the fulfilment of God's Promise: the Seed that would crush his head and vanquish his kingdom. Faith in God's Promise then, and Love for His Truth, would then also find themselves a simple translation in love for this Woman, a new Ark, which would carry God's faithful children over the Second Deluge of corruption away from the Second Death.

Yes, viewed thus, Satan could clearly perceive that God had spoken the truth when He declared that the Perpetual Enmity would be between him and the Woman. Her Faith and Her action would finally result in the overthrow of his empire and the release of his prisoners. If Her activities would allow Her Seed to reach as far as the world that lay now perished at his feet, then, in Truth, "all generations would call Her Blessed ..."

Only 'The Vine' makes sense

The greatest significance for our times of antediluvian human history is, that only when the Vine was safely aboard the Ark, its unique nature stood out in all its glory! Only when the Vine was the one thing left, was it possible to see all of it. Only at the very moment that there was nothing else, did the Vine come into its own and became Everything. Only when there was nothing else left to compare it with, has it become the measure against which all history must now be compared: past, present and future. Only when nothing else made sense, was the Vine the only thing that did!

All that was with the Vine inside the Ark made sense; the utter confusion and ruin outside the Ark did not. But if all that was lost outside the Ark perished because it was cut off from the Vine inside the Ark, then this must bring home in a most awesome way, that the centuries leading up to this destruction do not make sense either. And we know from Sacred Scripture what it was that led up to it. Those who had treasured and faithfully guarded the Vine, were all inside the Ark; those who had not bothered were perishing outside in the most gruesome way. But if perishing in the universal Flood away from the Vine refused to make sense in Noah's days, it will not make sense at any time. And then any 'hundreds of years' spent cut off from the Vine at any time in history will make no sense at all, no matter how brilliant its 'civilization', since separation from the Vine will always lead to the same terrible doom.

What perished in Noah's days would perish now; and what does not make sense now, would have been cut off from the Vine at the time of the Flood, would have been outside the Ark, and thus will perish now as sure as it would have vanished then. If now Governments, education systems, social behaviour, economics and finance, the media and the courts of law 'have all ceased to make sense', then we know why that is, and what will be the result.

Chapter Two

The Hedge

Error cannot force Truth to walk a certain path, for Truth is there before error to identify it. Evil cannot make Good follow a certain road for Good is needed to point out the evil and everywhere surpasses it. Neither can Satan force the hand of God, for God is still there where the devil has no longer access. So, when God destroyed humanity in the Great Flood, it may take on the appearance of a victory for Satan, as if God had been forced to resort to this deed in response to Satan's triumph in the corruption of all flesh. But when Satan witnessed the arrival of the Ark at its destination and saw the descent of the new human family from it, he knew too late not only that the foreshadowed enmity between the Woman and himself, and between Her Seed and his had not been terminated with the universal destruction, but also that, for that very reason, the Promised Deliverer would still have undiminished dominion over all human life, even over life that had just perished. Truth and Goodness had once again circumvented his most ambitious program yet because they were there ahead of him and before him. They could read him like an open book and so were able to carry out their own designs in complete independence of him, frustrating once again his every advantage.

With the death of Abel he had hoped to achieve the direct destruction of the seed of the woman itself. With the universal corruption of Adamic womanhood before the Flood, he had meant to make the arrival of the Deliverer impossible. But these hopes and calculations too perished in the swirling waters of the Great Flood, as these revealed to him conclusively that once again he had hoped in vain. It was the awful totality of the destruction which forced him to admit that, in God's eyes, the time had not yet come and that his own attempts, however thorough they may have been, had been premature and proven to be altogether out of touch with a Divine Masterplan to which he had no access. With the descent of eight people from the Ark, he saw that a new order of things was being initiated by the survivors under Divine direction. He had, it is true, allowed himself to become convinced that the overall success of his plans for 'self-defence' demanded a universal and absolute corruption of humanity. However, the sight of the Ark had shown him conclusively, that such an absolute corruption was as impossible to get as it was necessary. The Vine, carrying the 'strain of God' and the Hope of the Promise, had been allotted a protection far beyond his calculations. If a New Order had been conceived within the four walls of this astonishing craft to which he had not been privy, then an altogether new order would be initiated by him as well.

The New Strategy From Hell

There is every indication that around this time Satan decided to abandon wasting his efforts at thwarting the arrival of the Promised Deliverer. Without altogether ignoring the Vine and its divine strain, he would concentrate instead on building his own empire, and indoctrinating his parallel 'strain', in preparation for the arri-

Chapter Two: The Hedge

val on earth of his own most terrifying 'seed': Anti-Deliverer, to become known as Antichrist.

As far as it was conceived on the basic understanding that it would make him independent of God's timetable, it was the only move left over to him. If the Flood had taught him that total corruption was out of his reach and that he had to be satisfied with less, the enormous success of the antediluvian depravity gave him confidence that he could count again on the moral collapse of the greater part of humanity. If he could not prevent the arrival of God's Deliverer into this world, then at least he could try everything to be prepared for His coming; to check-mate and isolate Him and so contain His Kingdom by sheer weight of numbers. In fact, the longer God took in sending the Promised Seed of the Woman, the more difficult Satan would have matters at His Epiphany. If it was the divine purpose to gather together all Creation under one Head, the 'Seed of the Woman', then it became mandatory for Satan to gather all that constitutes his domain also under one head: his own future seed, Antichrist. Therefore, what was required from now on, was not a repetition of the things that had been tried before and found wanting, a more universal yet undirected corruption, but a highly organised resistance, a universal <u>unification</u> under evil, a 'Handbook of Revolution' with a clear and purposeful approach, and an intelligent and unified response.

If <u>The</u> Vine was beyond reach, and could not be touched and destroyed, then at least its shoots and branches, the Faith by which the strain was carried in individual human beings could be cut and poisoned again, as had been done so successfully in the Sethites before the Flood. But it would be better still if this faith could be 'bent' to suit his own kingdom, and redirected towards the arrival on earth of a deliverer of his own design. The fundamental concept of 'parallel system': the root and foundation of every heresy, was born.

Thee obvious advantage of this was, that Satan from then on could depend on the loyalties of his own seed, who within the twisted faith of their distorted brains had been implanted with a purpose and a goal beyond the restrictions of their limited comprehension.

The obvious weakness was that even such a bold and worldwide 'unification under evil' had no substance. That once again he had 'forgotten' the Curse that it was not God but a creature, 'the Woman', who had been made his Adversary, and that he and his seed had been condemned forever 'to collect, eat and produce dust'.

The Deep Significance for us of the 'Tower of Babel' Incident

That (i) Satan and (ii) his <u>new</u> approach of a unifying movement were behind the 'Tower of Babel' incident is made clear in Sacred Scripture.

1. First, there is the revealed fact of direct Divine intervention, showing that the use to which, whatever was being developed there, was being put, displeased the Blessed Trinity sufficiently to effectively hamper its progress for thousands of years.

2. That <u>some</u> power of control was there is evidenced by the people's unity of thought, action and, as Scripture says, purpose, the best translation here of the Hebrew word "d'vharim". (See Neh. 8: 4). That it was <u>Satan's</u> power-to-control that was present is evidenced again by the Divine displeasure with regard to its future development and use.
3. But there is more to it than this: Satan's creature was there as well in the person of Nimrod.

It is said of Nimrod 'that he was a mighty hunter before the Lord'. This however must not be taken as some kind of praise, for if the mention of being a mighty hunter before the Lord was indicative of some great and meritorious feat, then surely Nimrod's name would have been included in the several lists in which biblical authors have preserved for us the names of those who showed great Wisdom or Faith, as well as the deeds in which this Wisdom shone or to which this Faith was put to good use. On the contrary: in the only passage outside Genesis where the name of this Nimrod occurs, in Mi. 5: 6, it is made clear that the coming Messiah will use force "against the dominion of Nimrod".

In the Genesis text, the statement preceding the mention of his hunting prowess runs as follows: 'he began to be a mighty one on the earth'. And the one following it informs us that 'the beginning of his kingdom was Babel'. One must concede that 'hunting animals' does not found kingdoms. The context shows clearly that Nimrod was 'a hunter of man'. The remark that the beginning of his kingdom was that mysterious city, the building of which God had stopped, confirms the foregone conclusion that Nimrod was the dominating spirit of the evil-begotten movement described in the opening verses of Genesis 11. The use of an intermediary as an instrument strongly suggests that the evil purpose to which the whole thing was set up by Satan was the preparation for the arrival on earth of his most dreaded seed, Antichrist, of which the ancient empire builder Nimrod was only a pale reflection, the first in a long line.

4. For final confirmation of the accuracy of the above made observations and deductions, we quote Sacred Scripture about the pride that motivated these people: "Let us make <u>our</u> (not Yahweh's) name famous ...", and about the precautions these people took to preserve their own vain glory and dominant influence over the slowly drifting sections of humanity: "... before we be scattered abroad". (Gen. 11:4)

That the preservation of the glory and service of God was not the concern of these people when they took steps to maintain their own leadership over the naturally occurring dispersion of mankind over the face of the earth, has been highlighted once and for all by the Divine Undertaking 'to confuse their speech'. (Gen. 11: 7) This would have never been necessary if the glory and the service of the one true God had accompanied the natural dispersion and had been the concern of the leaders of the day. But not only did the Divine Majesty confuse their language, He also accelerated the slow process of natural dispersion.

Confounding: the most significant aftermath of 'Babel'

Confounding is the common punishment for lying and misdirected 'science' in the use of 'mind control'. We have this on the best authority, from the famous text in St. Paul's Letter to the Romans, which, as Ben Adam so clearly analyses in his book *The Beginning of Heathendom*, is not a hazy description of what is commonly called 'the heathen world', but the Divinely inspired analysis of the beginning of it somewhere in time. Mankind did not begin 'heathen', and then improve itself through 'education'. On the contrary: mankind, as we know, started off on the highest level possible, with a true knowledge of God both as Elohim, the Mighty Creator; and as Yahweh, the Lord, with Whom it was in Covenant.

The awesome state so graphically described by St. Paul in Romans 1: 18-28 is the state into which mankind lapsed because of deliberate Sin 'not having the Love of Truth which could have saved them', (2. Thess. 2: 10) and from which <u>no civilization however high</u> has ever rescued man, not even our own! Here then is that passage of St. Paul in that solemn, old English tongue which adds to its dignity.

> "For the wrath of God is revealed from heaven against all ungodliness and unrighteousness of men, who hold the truth in unrighteousness;
>
> Because that which may be known of God is manifest in them; for God hath shewed it unto them.
>
> For the invisible things of him from the creation of the world are clearly seen, being understood by the things that are

made, even his eternal power and Godhead; so that they are without excuse:

Because that, when they knew God, they glorified him not as God, neither were thankful; but became vain in their imaginations, and their foolish heart was darkened.

Professing themselves to be wise, they became fools,

And changed the glory of the uncorruptible God into an image made like to corruptible man, and to birds, and fourfooted beasts, and creeping things.

Wherefore God also gave them up to uncleanness through the lusts of their own hearts, to dishonour their own bodies between themselves:

Who changed the truth of God into a lie, and worshipped and served the creature more than the Creator, who is blessed for ever. Amen.

For this cause God gave them up unto vile affections: for even their women did change the natural use into that which is against nature:

And likewise also the men, leaving the natural use of the woman, burned in their lust one toward another; men with men working that which is unseemly, and receiving in themselves that recompense of their error which was meet.

And even as they did not like to retain God in their knowledge, God gave them over to a reprobate mind, to do those things which are not convenient; being filled with all unrighteousness ..."

Chapter Two: The Hedge

This is not the description of 'primitive man' working himself up to the light 'by his religious instinct' but of a highly articulate person deliberately excluding God from his life 'in the conceit of his heart' and so sinking below the animals in the field. For it has become impossible to avert the certainty that St. Paul had also our times in mind when he composed this inspired description of an ignoble past! And since he is right in assigning here effects to very clearly defined causes, then these effects and causes will always remain in this strong relationship no matter what time in human history they come into play.

The Essentials of Confounding

In the light of these revelations by the Holy Spirit in the Old and New Testaments, it may be fruitful to look a bit deeper into the last aspect of the Babel incident: the <u>confounding</u> of minds and speech. The dictionary gives several meanings to the verb 'to confound':

- ❖ To mingle so that the elements can no longer be distinguished or separated.
- ❖ To treat or regard erroneously as identical.
- ❖ To mix or associate by mistake.
- ❖ To throw into confusion or disorder.
- ❖ To <u>perplex</u> as with sudden disturbance or surprise.
- ❖ To refute in argument; contradict.

Since, as Sacred Scripture reveals, God also confounds the Devil, it will help to have a clear understanding of the verb 'to perplex'. Its first meaning is: "To cause puzzlement over what is not understood or certain". This will do since it pinpoints accurately for us that 'Satan does not comprehend God' and only has an incomplete understanding of that which has been revealed.

So far, and only speaking globally, God had confounded up to three times the Devil's ambitious plans of (a) preventing the arrival of the Woman's Seed; (b) of forestalling the arrival; and (c) of arming his own seed with superior knowledge in preparation of the arrival of his final seed: Antichrist. Since in our own days a great number of people show a distinct delight in Satan's empty promises of 'secret knowledge' because of the 'power' it is supposed to give, we may confidently assume that this was inherited from times immemorial, and that at the time of the 'Tower of Babel', when Nimrod was hunting for souls, to lay the foundation of Satan's kingdom, a great number of 'empire-builders' were attracted to astrology, or were fascinated by a misdirected 'promise of power' from astronomy.

To thwart the latest satanic attempt, the one of making humanity look forward not to the Woman's Seed but to Satan's, God confounded in humanity as a whole both the understanding of, and also the delight in, Satan's scheme: the twisting of the Promise of Redemption into preparation for his own seed, Antichrist. The thorough confusion of languages, accompanied by an accelerated scattering of people over the earth, had as its immediate result, that no one person or race held the complete understanding of the original satanic blueprint.

Chapter Two: The Hedge

That is, after the dispersion, neither humanity as a whole nor any individual nation or person understood how to unlock from the study of the heavens, Astronomy, the vital link with Physics on earth, a transfer needed to lead to the most advanced 'independence from God', SCIENCE, for the basic 'unification of humanity in evil', itself a necessary prerequisite for the final unification of humanity in Satan's kingdom under Antichrist.

All this would only become possible, with Divine Permission, centuries later, when Mathematics and Physics had again restored the 'universal language' and the necessary 'understanding', but, and this is of decisive significance, after Redemption had provided the necessary antidote.

What I am saying is that there is every reason to believe that after the Flood Satan made 'his seed' look up to the stars, to unlock from the movements of the inner and outer planets what Kepler and Newton did: the necessary understanding of the foundations of Physics on earth, leading within the span of a mere four hundred years all the way to the atomic bomb and Antichrist!

What the Blessed Trinity said at the inspection of the Tower of Babel: "This is what they begin to do and now nothing will be restrained from them what they have imagined to do", (Gen. 11: 6) may be applied directly to the unleashing of our own 'scientific revolution' in the wake of the Protestant Revolt.

This makes us conclude that the drastic confounding God applied was a necessary brake to prevent our so-called 'advancement in science' with its all too obvious 'unification in evil' to appear on earth before the Redemption. Kepler's 'Three Laws of Planetary

Motion' are really 'Three Laws of <u>Forces</u>', and that was all Newton needed to put the <u>whole</u> of modern Physics on its present footing.

The <u>type of confounding</u>, emanating as it does from Divine Wisdom, reveals to us the <u>type of satanic thinking</u> that is to be confused. Since the latest confounding is basically only a retarding, a set-back, its perplexing quality is essentially geared to the Devil's intelligence, not ours. It is not humanity that is required to 'put its act together' but Satan. If he so desires, he will have to find his own ways and means of breaking the language barriers, for they were created in the first place for the protection of humanity against his latest and most dangerous attempts at corruption. God the Holy Spirit has His own ways of overcoming barriers.

This brings us at last to the heart of this whole matter of:

The Hedge

Satan, having irrevocably fallen from Grace, has achieved that his 'mind-set' is forever in conflict with Truth: St. Paul's Letter to the Romans. Not only is he forever barred from access to the Supernatural; not only can he work only on the level of created intelligence: as a result of being in conflict with Truth ('the father of lies'), his 'mind' can always be grasped on the human level as being twisted; and so can always be perfectly understood 'as not making sense' by an human intelligence in the possession of the Truth.

When, at the Third Temptation of Christ, Satan offered Our Lord "all the kingdoms of the world, and the glory of them" (including ours), he offered (to the One sent to redeem those kingdoms from this 'glory') DUST in return for a LIE as he had been cursed to do. He did not know that here he was talking to the One Who, at the Tower of Babel, had thwarted the ultimate in this 'glory', the arrival of Antichrist, until long after He had come down 'to testify to the Truth': that there is only One Truth, and that He is it!

Indeed there is only one Truth and Truth is only one. Everything that is true, is true by the same Truth, which emanates from the Divine Essence. There is only Truth, and the distortion of it. The distortion of the Truth can never be Truth: the chasm between Truth and its distortion is absolute and easily recognised.

Truth is the same for any mind: for the uncreated Mind of God as it is for the created mind of anyone 'coming into this world'. There are no different 'truths' for different people. There is only one Truth for everybody. There may be more ways to come to the One Truth, all leading to the same Truth, but there is neither <u>one</u> way nor many ways to come to two different 'truths', as the Modernists and Teilhardians relentlessly try to impress upon the Church. There is not One Road (Christ) at the end of which one can be both a true and genuine Catholic <u>and</u> a Teilhardian one; a true Nun and a Teilhardian one; a true Priest and a Modernist one. We cannot arrive at a True Catholic Church and the Modernist 'anti-church of darkness' from the same infallible teaching.

If Catholic Faith is two thousand years old, and has always been the same during that time, then it cannot be used to accept the twisted 'truths' of Modernism, which truly are the distortion of Catholicism and so its contradiction. Nor can Modernism and Evolution be held up as being the same 'truth' as the real Catholicism.

"Contrary 'truths' cannot exist", is the inerrant teaching of Pope John XXIII in his first encyclical *Ad Petri Cathedram*, 1959.

Truth and its contrary cannot be both true. The contrary of the truth is its distortion, the lie …

The distortion of the Truth is by necessity always recognised for what it truly is: a distortion, and will remain the <u>same</u> for <u>any</u> mind: the Divine Mind, the angelic mind, the human mind. The One Truth will always hold up the distortion anywhere and forever for what it is: the distortion of the One Truth.

Here then, we have a clear view of 'The Hedge of the Vine'. The Vine, a magnificent Supernatural Gift from God, is adequately protected by Truth, natural as well as Revealed, because there is only one Truth. Whoever speaks the Truth out of love for the Truth is allowed access to the Vine through the gate, because Christ is the Gate, and Christ is the Truth. But any distortion of the Truth is immediately picked up by Truth as a distortion, and will be repelled as by a hedge around the Vine until the hedge is forced. This is thus the way meant by the Creator, by which Catholic Faith in any human mind is protected from contamination by distortion and lies, because even contradictions of Supernatural and Revealed Truths are immediately picked up as contradictions of Truth itself by the light of the ordinary human mind.

Thus it came about that Thomistic Philosophy, being the only everlasting and thorough training of the human mind in its proper object, Truth, was identified by Pope Leo XIII as truly "the hedge and fence of the Faith". Why? Because "his teachings are such that those who hold to it are never found swerving from the path of truth, and those who dare assail it will always be suspected of error". (Leo XIII, *Aeterni Patris*, 1879)

And because this Philosophy is the only all-time high in existence, a subsequent Pope had no trouble in giving the reason for this unique function of 'the hedge of the Faith', when he wrote with the authority of Christ:

"One thing is clearly established by the long experience of the ages: his teaching appears to chime in, by a kind of pre-established harmony, with Divine Revelation. No surer way to safeguard the First Principles of the Faith." (Pope Pius XII, *Humani Generis*, 1950)

To any intelligent person it must be obvious that this 'Defence of Catholic Faith' does exist, that it is the most important thing on earth, and that the neglect and destruction of this ultimate in value must have the most devastating and far-reaching consequences. This brings us to the subject matter of the next chapter.

Chapter Three

The Snake in the Hedge

"If Catholic doctrine is once deprived of this strong bulwark, it is useless to seek the slightest assistance for its defence in a philosophy whose principles are either common to the errors of materialism, monism, pantheism, socialism and modernism, or certainly not opposed to such systems. The reason is that the capital theses in the philosophy of St. Thomas are not to be placed in the category of opinions capable of being debated one way or another, but are to be considered as the foundations upon which the whole science of natural and divine things is based. If such principles are once removed or in any way impaired, it must necessarily follow that students of the sacred sciences will ultimately fail to perceive so much as the meaning of the words in which the dogmas of divine revelation are proposed by the Magisterium of the Church." (St. Pius X. *Doctoris Angelici*. 1914)

The 'darkening of the Catholic mind', failing to perceive so much as the simple meaning of words once the 'hedge of the Faith' has been dismantled, resulting in unbelief: the loss of the priceless Vine.

Anyone who would like to study in all seriousness the meaning of the Divinely inspired saying, unmistakenly referred to hear by a Pope and Saint, that "he who dismantles a hedge, a snake will bite him", (Eccl. 10: 8) let him or her go to the Garden of Eden, and see how Eve 'uprooted the hedge around her Vine', and 'by what serpent she got bitten'! And then see if, after the darkening of that mind and the loss of that Faith, he or she is prepared to put up 'opinions, capable of being debated one way or the other' against 'devastating and far-reaching consequences'.

The story of Man's creation is full of Divine Wisdom; and over the centuries great scholars and spiritual writers have succeeded in painstakingly piecing together for us Invisible Realities which were in the Divine Mind, when the story of the visible details of our First Parent's Creation and Fall was made by the Creator the foundation of all human knowledge and understanding. The lore is so immensely rich, every detail so carefully chosen, with ramifications in so many directions, following one another in never ending successions, that the sheer impossibility of exhausting the undiminished flow of human insights and applications shows how truly Divine the inspiration to the original story is. Against the towering immobility of the Divine Will, rising majestically above the murky waters of Modernism and Teilhardism lapping at its base, the pompous pretence at dismissal of Genesis reduces Modernism shamefully to the everlasting impotence of its own infinitesimal minuteness.

That God had the Second Adam in Mind when He created the first, and the Church when He created Eve, is but one of those rich lodes, where the gold of true insight becomes the reward of prayer and humble, but earnest study. And the delicate requirement "that the Church needed a model in another Eve, a New Eve", once Her likeness to the first Eve, spotless in her creation, ceased altogether with the old Eve's Fall, was handled by God as can only be expected from a Divine Intelligence which takes everything into consideration.

Chapter Three: The Snake in the Hedge

As we already know, it was written of someone: "I was formed from Eternity and of old, before the earth was made". (Proverbs 8: 23). The New Eve was conceived where the New Adam already lived as the Son of God: in Eternity. Present then in the Mind of God, She was invisibly present in the story of the Creation and Fall. For the difficulty is that there are 'Three Eves' in the story: Eve the sinner, the old one; Mary, the New Eve; and also the Church, the spotless Bride of the Lamb of God – composed of sinners like the Old Eve, but Herself "without spot or wrinkle" like the New Eve. (Eph. 5: 27)

It was sin, the new element introduced by the Fall, which demands these distinctions, as it makes the New Eve, Our Lady, as much the counterpart of Eve as Christ became the complete opposite of Adam, which leaves room for a 'third Eve': the Church, Daughter and Spouse. The behaviour displayed by Eve immediately before, during and after the Fall, is by contrast a most powerful revelation of how Mary, the New Eve, would have acted in her place, and would act in the future. Which in turn then becomes a most powerful revelation of the Marian ideal of the Church, the Eve in the middle, also conceived and formed in the Divine Mind from Eternity and also, as Virgo, given an expression of in the stars.

For the purpose of this narrative then, it is sufficient to begin with the recorded 'dialogue', which Eve had with Satan in the Garden. It is as much a revelation of what Satan had uncovered after careful study, as it provides us with the key to the future qualities of the 'Woman of Genesis', which can be unlocked to us by an equally careful study of the contrast to the behaviour displayed here by Eve under temptation.

G.H. Pember, M.A., in the book quoted from earlier: *Earth's Earliest Ages*, first published in 1876, has this to say on some of the circumstances surrounding the temptation of Eve.

"Our first parents too [as were some of the Angels] were about to be overcome by evil. They were soon to experience the meaning of that awful word, death, which the lips of the Creator had uttered; to feel the terror of His wrath, the desolation of ruin, the horrors of corruption. For the all-wise God well knew the great obstacle to perfection in the creature, and that, until it could be removed, He was unable to show forth His love and pour out His bounty to the full. He could not endow men with great power and wisdom; He could not make them excellent in majesty, glorious in might, swift as the winds or the lightning, to do His will, until after they had passed the danger of abusing His gifts and falling, as the sinful angels had done before them. Man should therefore not be all-perfect from the day of his creation."

Here we have come into the presence of a mystery which St. Paul has named "the mystery of evil". (2. Thess. 2: 7) God's first creatures, the Angels and our First Parents, were created in the image and likeness of God. They were perfect when they came forth from the hands of the Creator, but they were not yet all-perfect. Somehow it was possible to drive a wedge between these two states. Somehow it appeared possible to separate the creature from his state of near perfection, and reduce him to a state of near ruin. And only then, when, by a painful and yet most salutary experience, men had learned their own creature weakness, when they had been imprisoned "in bodies of humiliation" (Phil. 3: 21), when they had been left to try how far their own strength would go in saving themselves by their own arm amid the hostile powers of darkness: only then could an all-merciful God lavish His love freely on creatures who would turn to Him in their affliction.

The 'Key' to this profound knowledge: that fallen man must die but not immediately; that disobedient man is punished, but not consigned to the doom of the obstinately rebellious, as the fallen angels had been, this 'Key', God had guarded very carefully: not even Satan with all his cunning had any inkling, as we shall see, of this totally unexpected turn of events. For this Key unlocks the door to that other even more inscrutable Mystery: that fallen men were to be saved by a power not of their own. That, overtaken by darkness, helpless, distraught, not knowing where to turn, they would be led by the hand of Another. That their sin, which they would be utterly unable to expiate, was to be punished in the Person of a Substitute. And what is more, that it was already preordained that this Lamb of God, the only-begotten Son of their loving Creator, Who had been found willing to undergo a cruel death in their stead, had in turn found Himself a Helpmate who also had learnt obedience without a previous transgression and, though sinless, was found utterly willing to suffer and to die with Him, in order that their children might live.

We must now return to Eve, the object of intense scrutiny by Satan, in order that we may learn by contrast what God is going to reveal about the nature of His future Helpmate, an as yet Mystery Woman, 'the Woman of Genesis'. G.H. Pember again:

"We must now return to Adam and Eve whom we left enjoying in innocence the pleasures which God had provided for them. But short indeed was their time of happiness, for the powers of evil were already setting the fatal snare, instigated no doubt at this stage to their foul purpose by pure malignity: to oppose God at every turn.

The course of action adopted by Satan shows that God had not deprived him of his powerful intellect, although it had been changed by his own fall from the noble power of a prince of the Most High to a base cunning of a deceitful intriguer. He would not make his assault with power and terror, for that would drive the assailed into the arms of their Protector instead of alluring them away from Him. He would present himself in the form of an inferior and subject animal, from which they would never suspect harm. For, like all his seed of this world, Satan, though proud even to destruction can yet degrade himself to the very dust in order to carry out his deadly purpose.

Neither would he consider approaching the man and the woman together, for combined, they might uphold one another in their duty of obedience and love of God. And he well knew that, once he was detected, a second attempt would be met with far greater resistance.

And finally, several reasons seem to have deterred him from tempting Adam alone. For one, had he begun by overcoming the man, and then through him worked the fall of the woman, her ruin would have been incomplete. She would not have been wholly without excuse before God since she would have acted on the orders or under the influence of the one *whom He had set over her as her head.* But a deeper, more subtle, and so a more cogent reason would have been that his study of the male and female natures and psychologies revealed to Satan the important differences in qualities and temperament with which a wise Creator had endowed each *to complement the other.* Having accurately grasped that in both natures the strongest qualities become the weak point when isolated, that is, when they are *not used for the perfection of the partner* but for the gratification of self, he must have come to the conclusion that, for the purpose of his devious scheme, the misdirection of the female qualities and endowments would meet with the greater chance of success."

Here we point to the complete and savage disregard for the beautiful balance between the male and female qualities displayed by the 'feminists' of our days. For the destruction of this balance is pursued exclusively 'for the gratification of self', which is destroying the femininity in their followers. This degradation of both sexes is by now being finalised into law in many 'civilised' countries, as a weapon in the final onslaught on the only Church created in the image and likeness of a Virgin!

Influenced, then, by considerations such as these, we find Eve by herself in the vicinity of the 'tree of good and evil'. God's command had been clear, and was fully open for prayerful reflection and meditation, leading to a deeper understanding of God, and love for Him. It was also fully open to female curiosity and speculation! The first road would be taken by Eve's complete counterpart many centuries later: "But Mary kept all these words, pondering them in her heart" (Lk. 2:19, 51). In this She was acting in accordance with what Her holy forefather Jacob had done: "His brothers therefore envied him (Joseph), but the father considered this matter with himself", (Gen. 37: 11). Maybe the beautiful addition found in St. Luke: "in her heart", was missing in Eve. Maybe she did not love God's command sufficiently yet; and so her speculations remained idle curiosity in her mind, without being allowed entry into her heart as a basis for prayer.

From the recorded conversation with the devil which now follows in Scripture, we may conclude that she was musing on the strangeness of God's prohibition near the fatal tree: Wherefore had He planted the tree in their garden if they were not to enjoy it? What so great difference could there be between it and the other trees, of which they could eat freely? Maybe even a more strongly felt curiosity may have moved her to examine the forbidden object more closely in order to see if she could detect its peculiarity.

That Eve was here on a crossroad is obvious. Had she allowed these legitimate questions to enter into her heart where she could ponder them prayerfully with God, as was her duty and privilege as creature, she would have found all the correct answers.

As it was, when Eve was standing near the tree, her guard dangerously low, 'a serpent approached and addressed her'. That she was not at all startled by such an occurrence seems to point to the existence of an intelligent communication between man and the inferior creatures before the Fall. But we must not of course think of the serpent as the repulsive and venomous reptile to which we feel now an instinctive antipathy. For it had not been cursed, but held itself upright, one of the most intelligent, and probably the most beautiful, of all the beasts of the field. The creature was thus still free from (physical) venom, and not improbably winged, while

Chapter Three: The Snake in the Hedge

its scales glittered in the sun's rays like deep-burnished gold. It must have been a most arresting sight. Little did Eve suspect that beneath that beautiful and apparently innocent form lurked a most powerful (and for her spiritual well being a most venomous) enemy.

"Can it be true that God has forbidden you to eat of any tree in the garden?"

So began Satan the opening up one of the most far-reaching conversations ever recorded in human history. Simple as this crafty question may seem at first appearance, it was full of dangerous guile, so marvellously adapted to the purpose of disturbing still further the moral fibre of the woman whose disquiet had begun with musings of the mind only, without being allowed entry into her heart for prayerful consideration with her God. In preparing the way for one's complete subversion, the skilled tempter invariably uses openings afforded by the thoughts of those approached. Here we hear Eve's musings spoken out aloud by Satan, and we see him drive a wedge between the near perfection of Eve, as she had come forth from the hands of the Creator, and His all perfect creature she is yet to become. The tempter puts to her the sly suggestion that she abstains, because God has harshly forbidden her and her husband to touch any of all that delicious fruit around them. And so by this brief but most skilful question, Satan begins an interrogation which envelops his unsuspecting victim in the fog of potentially grave error, strongly insinuated to her from at least five suggestions.

1. First, he throws her off guard by his assumed ignorance.

2. Then, he stirs up vanity from the depth of her self-consciousness by giving her an opportunity to correct him and so remain 'in dialogue' with him.
3. Thirdly, he uses the term 'Elohim' for God and not the covenant name 'Yahweh', to present the Creator as remote and as having little concern with His creatures.
4. After that he puts a doubt in her mind as to whether God had really uttered the prohibition, thereby strongly suggesting the possibility of a mistake.
5. Lastly, he insinuates to her the blasphemous thought that harshness and caprice on God's part are not inconceivable but indeed may sometimes be expected.

Here we may interrupt Mr. Pember's account of the lead-up to Eve's fall for two considerations.

In the first one of these I wish to draw the attention of the reader to the compelling accuracy and timelessness of God's Revelation in Sacred Scripture. How could the thoughts of those reading the above be prevented from straying away from the setting in the Garden of Eden to the uncanny similarity of our modern 'Eves', faced with the equally forbidden fruit of the 'contraceptive pill'? What harshness the sure command does assume, if it is only considered *in the mind*, without being allowed prayerful consideration with God *in the heart*. How remote and unconcerned God could become, if He is not seen as the Father who with His command is closer to us and our real happiness than we are to ourselves?

And what are we to make of all those bishops and priests who, like the serpent in the Garden, diminish the Divine command with

Chapter Three: The Snake in the Hedge

disturbing appeals to loopholes or individual consciences? Are the innuendos of 'harshness' and even 'caprice' on the part of God all that far removed from the minds of such bishops and priests, and so-called theologians and catechists? Do we not detect here again as we did before, the terrible vengeance of God on all those who interfere with His Holy Tradition in the mistaken belief that Genesis chapters 1 - 11 are nothing but a collection of myths? Stories with no bearing on the 'Real reality' as it is known to 'modern man', that pathetic end-product of a faked evolution? Is not this whole affair covered by Divine Inerrancy affirming the reality of the devil's first question? Meant as an instruction for every woman after Eve, including all the modern women-on-the-pill? And as a dire warning for all those, who would like to assume the role of Satan in these matters, bringing doubt to Catholic minds?

The other matter I would like to draw attention to at this stage of the narrative is Pember's astute observation of the distinction between the two names for God in the Hebrew Bible: 'Elohim' and 'Yahweh'. One of the crumbling pillars of salt on which the tattered remains of the *Documentary Hypothesis* claims its so-called 'researches' to rest, is the totally unwarranted and equally unfounded fable that these different names for God must point to two different 'sources' for the writing of Genesis: one the so-called 'Elohist' document, the other 'Yahwist'. This was then accepted as 'proof' that Genesis was composed at a much later date, from which then the inevitable conclusion must be drawn that, unfortunately, Moses can no longer be considered to be the author of Genesis. For, so the argument goes, if he was, he would not have jumped from the use of one Name of God to the other.

Earlier in his book Pember has drawn attention to this reasoning. This means that already by 1876, when the rationalist onslaught on Holy Scripture in the form of the 'Higher Critique' (of which the *Documentary Hypothesis* of our days is the poisonous fruit) was in full swing, reasoned argument against it was well known.

Pember started off with the observation that there is no mention of a covenant of God with Adam in the first chapter of Genesis, for there we have primarily a record of creation, and the injunction to the man to dress and watch over the Garden. At that stage he needed nothing more, for knowing well the single prohibition of his God, he could at once detect a foe in any being tempting him to disobey it. Immediately after this, we have the detailed account, in the so-called 'Second Creation Story' of how God-Yahweh came into covenant with man. In this supplementary account we are concerned with the moral responsibility of man. And immediately we are met with a change in the appellation of God. When looked upon only as Creator and Ruler, He is referred to as Elohim: God, the Mighty One. But as soon as He appears in covenant relation with man, He takes the title of Yahweh: God, the Lord. At its very first introduction the Name Yahweh is joined with Elohim to obviate any doubt as to the identity of the One Being, designated by both names, even when used separately.

"Now it is evident" continues Pember "that while either of these names is likely to suit some passages, there must nevertheless be many cases in which the one would be more appropriate than the other. Of this the sacred writers are always mindful and we will presently meet with other instances of their careful discrimination.

Chapter Three: The Snake in the Hedge

It thus appears that the occurrence of the two Names of God, adduced by the Rationalists as a proof that the Scriptures are a clumsy compilation of diverse and incongruous documents to which they give the names 'Elohistic' and 'Yahwistic' as to two imaginary 'sources', that this occurrence far from demonstrating the validity of their argument, shows the very opposite and beautifully exhibits the unity and consistency of the whole volume".

With our friend Pember and all the other scholars who have no use for the 'Documentary Hypothesis' we may attach great significance to the fact that Adam carefully records, that Satan used the word *Elohim* as God's Name when addressing a woman he knew to be in holy covenant with God and so knew Him much more intimately as her Lord *Yahweh*. The significance of this digression will come to light immediately.

Returning now to the analysis of the temptation of Eve in the garden, we see from her answer the blinding effect this first question of the devil had on her.

She states that they could eat of the other trees in the garden, and had only been warned away from the one in the centre. Of this one alone "God had commanded us that we should not eat of it, and that we should not touch it, lest perhaps we die" (Douay translation). But God had not prohibited them to touch it! Thus we may read in the exaggeration of this added clause a secret discontent as well as an inclination to set the command of the Almighty, 'God-Elohim', in as harsh a light as possible.

Nor is this all; not only does Eve increase the stringency of the law, she also weakens the penalty. God had declared: "Thou shalt surely die", which she alters to "lest perhaps we die" (Gen. 3:3, Douay version).

Doubt is already doing its work in her mind; she is now prepared to hear the Truth of God openly denied. It is clear from her inexcusable exaggeration of the Divine Imposition, that she had taken up Satan's lead into the dark, and speaks of her Creator and Benefactor as *Elohim*, the 'Power', mighty indeed, but to men vague, distant, and almost unknown. For the success of his advances, Satan had recognised the necessity to banish from her heart all thought of a near and closely connected God, and she accepts his suggestion and cooperates with him. For the image of *Yahweh* and His Sacred Covenant are rapidly fading from her mind and instead, self and sin are beginning to take its place.

Solemn indeed is the warning to her descendants when Eve's thoughts are analysed as revealed by her words, a warning to an offspring, by whose feet her own sad path is ceaselessly trodden. How often, when we are perfectly aware of some direct command of God which we do not wish to obey, are we seduced into an exaggeration of its magnitude until at length, by the continual play of evil imaginings, we almost arrive at its impossibility. At the same time, is there not an equal determination afoot today to diminish the importance of the Divine Commandments <u>and also of the penalty</u>, <u>hell</u>, bound to our transgressions not only by an Almighty and faraway God-Elohim, living beyond our earthly sphere "in inaccessible Light" (1 Tim. 6:16), but by a loving Father who cares for us more than we can ever love ourselves?

Satan quickly perceived the state of Eve's mind. His plan of attack was succeeding: she had begun to doubt! He instantly pressed his advantage by a bold lie "Ye shall not surely die"! Thus "the liar from the beginning" (Jo. 8:44) dared to place his own assertion in direct opposition to that of the Almighty. And Eve believed him, believed this beast of the field rather than God, as millions of Catholics now prefer to believe the innumerable contradictions and distortions of Catholic Dogma, disseminated by the Modernists on the say-so of a Teilhard de Chardin and his horde of Modernist 'theologians'.

"For God knows" pursued the tempter, "that in the day ye eat thereof; your eyes shall be opened and ye shall be as God, knowing good and evil".

On hearing this distortion of the Truth, Eve immediately knew two things:

(i) She did not know 'evil', and she was fully aware that she did not know it,
(ii) She <u>did</u> know that, whatever 'evil' was, she would never know it "as God knows".

At this desperately late hour it should have occurred to Eve that God also knew more: that this "opening of their eyes" would be no addition to their happiness but instead harmful and destructive. Otherwise, she could have reasoned, He would surely have given to them this 'higher knowledge' if it had been necessary for their happiness. Could she not by a moment's reflection perceive the fearful responsibility which the knowledge of this mysterious, unknown thing would necessarily involve, and bless the Lord God, Who had spared her from its perils? Or could she not at least trust the Love of Him Who had called her into being, and turn with horror and disgust from the blasphemous impiety which suggested to her the real possibility of in any way raising herself to His height? She could not for she was deceived, as St. Paul so clearly teaches in 1 Tim. 2:14: "Adam was not deceived, but the woman was deceived, and so became a transgressor". Her reason had become perverted by desire, a vision of self exaltation had intoxicated her. There had been no error in Satan's judgment: he had detected the weakest point when he appealed to her vanity and suggested to her the source of his own downfall: *the idea of becoming as God....*

Slowly an outline of the other 'Woman of Genesis' is emerging. We may now be in a better position to appreciate why St. Louis de Montfort wrote in the 'Introduction to the True Devotion': why Our Blessed Lady had no inclination on earth more powerful or more constant of hiding Herself from Herself as well as from every other creature (including the devil!) so as to be known only to God. Her meditations on Sacred Scripture must have given Her that horror and disgust for Sin which Eve should have felt in the presence of God. In the Light of the Holy Spirit She must have been contemplating in a most perfect way what we are trying to do here: to retrace the steps leading to the Fall, so as to be able to give the greatest possible glory to God in obedience and humility, in Faith and Love. And to undo as much of the damage in Her lifetime and in Her surroundings as God would allow Her. Little did the humble Virgin of Nazareth suspect how God was going to answer Her prayer 'to alleviate the misery of Sin' in Her fellow men. Only after the Annunciation was it clear to Her that God had chosen Her to be 'the Woman of the Promise in Eden'. But on what rocklike foundations of utter humility was this exaltation resting.

And so Eve sinned ....

"The woman was deceived" said St. Paul "and so became a transgressor". Her deception and her terrible Sin were only in her mind! There were as yet no inordinate and rebellious passions in her. She did not fall through weakness, as we so often do. The direction which her thoughts took could, at any stage of the Temptation, have been scrutinised by her clear and objective mind and its mighty reasoning powers. But her uneasiness lay with the Divine Prohibition, which became unchecked when she deliberately withheld from it the power of prayer and the incisiveness of her as yet uncorrupted mind, and on which the devil seized to enlarge it to resentment, caused her to lapse into one of the worst possible states into which a soul can sink in the sight of God: unchecked and paralysing <u>doubt</u>! I say paralysing advisedly because it prevented her from taking refuge in prayer, when she deliberately refused to check with her Creator with whom she was in covenant, the devil's preposterous logic and claims.

Does the unprecedented paralysis of many bishops in the face of the preposterous 'logic' and claims of the Modernists and Teilhardians with regard to Catholic Truth show us that in our days too a grave doubt is present in episcopal minds; a doubt to which once again ready access to the powerful light of objective reasoning and scrutiny is being refused? Will prayer prove a substitute for this unwillingness if prayer <u>demands</u> an honest reappraisal and about-face? Could that be the reason why public devotion to the Mother of God is at an all-time low because 'the Woman of Genesis' is such a stark antithesis of this universal re-enactment of Eve's Sin?

After Eve's Sin, Adam's hands were tied: 'the knot of Eve'.

What was he to do? Again we notice the refusal to turn to God for advice and help in prayer. According to St. Paul, Adam was not deceived. His refusal to pray shows he had made up his mind to accommodate the creature, his wife, in preference to God. His was a deliberate choice, a Sin of unprecedented malice in the human race: the Original Sin. For he knew that giving in to her was not the way to come to his wife's aid and help her out of her disgrace.

Thus the prince of this world finally prevailed. The new creation had been seduced to rebellion and condemned to death. There was no longer any bar to the expansion of his dominion. Up from the ground he rose, silently and invisibly, expanding his shadowy wings over his newly acquired territory, impeding the pure rays of God's sun, and dropping thick the poisonous mist of sin, under which earth's flowers faded, her fruits withered, her plenty was reduced and she brought forth evil as well as good.

But one clear command of God Most High called him back, bringing him once again sharply to heel.

And so we could go on, exploring the never-ending riches of every sentence, every word, every meaning of this Divine account of our own beginning. How the eyes of our first parents were indeed opened, but only to perceive clearly their unfitness to be seen. How shame was their redeeming feature in this whole shabby affair, for it set the pair apart from the unrepentant tempter. But since the dismantling of Eve's natural defences against access to the Vine in her supernatural self was the main ground for this study, we must conclude here, but we could not finish it on a better note than to glean from the condemnation of the devil to 'whom' and to 'what' she had freely consented to 'uproot her hedge'.

Patiently the Lord God had listened to what the two culprits had to say in their defence and had given them every opportunity of explaining themselves. But when He turns to the serpent His whole manner changes. He asks the tempter no questions, gives him no chance of defence; but treating him as already condemned, immediately pronounces sentence. What deep thoughts are suggested by this change of procedure!

"Because thou hast done this ..."

There is no mistake as to the reason for the curse. It is no accident, not just a merely natural misfortune, but the deeply-burnt brand which testifies to God's abhorrence of him who brought sin into Creation. The first part of the sentence has immediate and literal reference to the serpent, carrying in its future appearance a physical and all-time manifestation of the terrible degradation of Lucifer himself. For in undergoing the visible transformation, the vile serpent is a type of Satan whose condition is hopeless. But in what follows next, the serpent as a type is receding from view, and the great adversary himself who had been concealed in its form is dragged forth to judgement. He hears of the frustration of all his hopes of having the Almighty as his adversary; of the brevity of his triumph, and of his terrible and inevitable doom.

Satan had deluded Eve into an alliance with himself against the Creator; but God would break up the confederation; the covenant with Death should be disannulled; the agreement with Hell should not stand forever:

"I will put enmity between thee and the Woman", said God, revealing an inscrutable mystery - defying understanding until God provides the Key. In these words lie concealed the secrets of a new Covenant of God with man. They contain the mystery of how God is going to break up the confederation, will disannul the covenant with Death, and intends to make void the agreement with Hell. Its central concept is a 'Woman and Her Seed'.

These words made several things clear to Satan: that Adam and Eve would not die immediately, not until children were born to them; that the fight would be contained on the human level; that the final victory would not be his, but would go to someone in the future; that his most dangerous, yes even his deadly foe would not be directly the Almighty Himself, which in his blind pride he had come to expect as a foregone conclusion; but that he was forced to fight a losing battle with a mystery Woman: 'a Woman and Her Offspring', a Woman fighting on the side of God who in the end would "crush his head" at the behest of Her Seed.

No wonder God had called him back from his triumphant flight from the Garden to be acquainted with his punishment in the presence of his victims! Who would ever match him in seeing his triumph so short-lived and even vanish altogether, and to hear that his whole life's work is going to be in vain?

Yet in the eyes of God it was of the utmost importance that the fallen pair should start to fathom the mercy shown to them against the starkest contrast and the blackest background possible: the utter hopelessness of Satan. Here we can only pause in amazement and render thanks to God for the mercy vouchsafed to our first parents.

Chapter Three: The Snake in the Hedge

God could not indeed give Adam a direct promise at a time when the man was waiting as a condemned criminal to receive sentence. Therefore His Love devised the plan of first pronouncing judgement on the serpent, therein implying that the fallen pair had no need to sink hopelessly to the condition of their deceiver, but be set in sharp opposition to him. Until, after a painful struggle, the Woman and Her conquering Seed would crush him under their feet, and make the Death from which they both shrank, but must now undergo, and the bond of Sin to be gone forever. That way a bright ray of hope broke through their own despair and they were greatly strengthened to hear the sentence which the Divine Judge was now going to pronounce on them.

Thus was sentence passed. Upon the serpent the judgement was eternal, while the man and his wife were doomed to anguish and degradation, but not forever. As a sign of that new trust in the Lord God, Adam called his wife 'the mother of all the <u>living</u>'.

That is the story of how Eve got bitten by a snake while dismantling her hedge; and in her we all were bitten. And going by the ominous words of a Pope and Saint: 'the great movement of apostasy, organised in every country for the establishment of a One-World Church', millions of Catholics wanted to be bitten again and again. They cheerfully dismantle their own hedges, allow the Vine inside them thus exposed to be trampled underfoot, and walk away as psycho-babbling zombies in the night clutching their snakes.

Analysing the devil's words spoken to Eve, we can clearly see (i) what they <u>were</u>, and (ii) what they <u>intended</u> to do. They <u>were</u> 'twistings of the Truth', ending up as direct contradictions of Revealed Truth, accompanied by an appeal to make herself equal to God: the final attack on the Vine.

Satan has been cursed by God to always speak like this, and his words can always be recognised as such. Secondly, his words <u>intended</u> to put belief in his lies and cunning in the woman's mind. Yet, at that time still from <u>outside</u> of the Hedge: Eve's clear understanding of the demand being made on her: to believe a contradiction of the truth as true! Outside this hedge of clear understanding stood a deceiver, a being fallen from Grace, condemned to Hell, intending to make her as damned as he was. On the inside of the hedge, her glorious intellect, was the incomparable gift of the Vine: the Divine gifts of her infused Faith, and Hope in God, her love for Him, together with the indwelling of the Blessed Trinity in Sanctifying Grace. And to accommodate the deceiver she dismantled the hedge. She accepted a lie as true, and through the bite of the snake the Vine inside her died.

And that is the way Catholic Faith will suffer injury and die in the end. When the mind of man starts to believe untruth as true, it ceases to be 'the hedge of the Faith', but in the bite of the serpent that follows, not only is Faith mortally effected, but also the mind itself! As remarked before: 'God had not deprived Satan of his powerful intellect although it had been <u>changed</u> by his own fall from grace from the noble power of a prince of the Most High to a base cunning of a deceitful intriguer'.

A mind condemned to produce nothing but dust and deception, like Modernism, Evolution and Teilhardism, 'Melbourne Guidelines', RENEW, 'Parish 2000' and their never ending CROPP of dirty follow-up programs. Psycho-babbling trivia of the Cainite 'strain', held up and paraded before 'the strain of God by the insanity of destroyed Catholic minds as the proper replacement of the Everlasting Vine...

Yes, St. Pius X was more than humanly right when he wrote:

"If such principles are once removed or in any way impaired, it must necessarily follow that students of the sacred sciences will ultimately fail to perceive so much as the meaning of the words in which the dogmas of divine revelation are proposed by the Magisterium of the Church."

Chapter Four

I Will Take Away its Hedge

When the collective minds of "the inhabitants of Jerusalem and the men of Judah" had gone beyond the point of no return in their worship of Baal, with the unchecked licentiousness and immorality commonly associated with idolatry, God made the prophet Isaiah say that "the vineyard of Yahweh Saboath, the house of Israel, would be laid waste". And how?

"I will take away its hedge for it to be grazed on, and knock down its wall for it to be trampled upon." (Is. 5: 1-7)

When that which had been given for the protection of the Vine no longer rejoices in fulfilling its role, it will not be allowed to find its delight in any 'substitute'. As a consequence, even Jerusalem had to endure for seventy years the 'senselessness' of the Babylonian captivity.

"See what days are coming,
- it is the Lord Yahweh who speaks -
days when I will bring famine on the country,
a famine not of bread, a drought not of water,
but of hearing the Word of Yahweh.
They will stagger from sea to sea,
wander from north to east,
seeking the Word of Yahweh,
and failing to find it." (Amos. 8: 11-12)

In many, many places of Holy Scripture it has been clearly stated that it is exclusively the Divine prerogative 'to punish evil'. God punishes evil. The proud and haughty may think for themselves that the Vine is not worth having, and that it is up to them to decide when the time has come 'to take down the hedge' so the Vine can be trampled underfoot. But this is because, in the conceit of their hearts, they are equally convinced, since that first action appeared to be solely left to their own will and decision, that the reversal is also up to them, and that, when they so feel like it, they can restore the hedge and plant the Vine anew at will. Such conceit was the sin of Pharaoh at the time of Moses.

"When Pharaoh saw that rain and hail and thunder had stopped, he sinned yet again. He became adamant, he and his courtiers. The heart of Pharaoh was stubborn and, as Yahweh had foretold through Moses, he did not let the sons of Israel go." (Ex. 9: 34-35)

Pharaoh was convinced that he himself was master over his own stubborn heart, and that he could turn it on and off at will. But Moses knew better and wrote instead:

"But Yahweh made Pharaoh's heart stubborn, and he did not let the sons of Israel go." (Ex. 10: 20, 27 etc.)

This too was the grave sin of Jesus' contemporaries. (Mt. 11: 21-24)

"Alas for you, Chorazin!

Alas for you Bethsaida! ...

And as for you Capernaum, did you want to be exalted as high as heaven? You shall be thrown down to hell."

Chapter Four: I Will Take Away its Hedge

And the result? It was only after all His previous teaching contained in the 'Evangelical or Apostolic Discourse', (Mt. 5-10 incl.) had not been accepted, and after a whole series of miracles had made no impression, and after the warning given to His contemporaries had fallen on deaf ears, that Our Blessed Lord changed His style of teaching. And the prophecy of Isaiah invoked at this point by Our Lord Himself and quoted by three Evangelists shows that it had to be taken as a necessary punishment! For, when asked by His disciples 'why He taught the crowds in parables', something He had not done before, He answered:

"The mysteries of the Kingdom of Heaven are revealed to you, but they are not revealed to them. For anyone who has, will be given more ... but from anyone who has not, even what he has <u>will be taken away</u>. The reason I talk to them in parables is that they look without seeing and listen without hearing or understanding. So in their case the prophecy of Isaiah is being fulfilled:

'You will listen and listen again, but not understand;
see and see again, but not perceive.
For the heart of this nation has grown coarse;
their ears are dull of hearing, and they have shut their eyes,
for fear that they should see with their eyes,
hear with their ears,
understand with their heart,
and be converted,
and be healed by Me'." (Mt. 13: 10-15)

"But from anyone who has not ...", who has no Faith, no love of 'the Vine', no love of Truth,

"even what he has", the Hedge: the use of his God-given intellect for the protection of 'this Vine of Immortal Faith',

"<u>will be taken away</u> ...!"

What use of the intellect will then be left over for a Modernist?

"Alas for you Scribes and Pharisees, you hypocrites!

You who travel over sea and land to make a single proselyte, and when you have him you make him twice as fit for hell as you are." (Mt. 23: 15)

The roaming of present-day Modernists to bring back from overseas a never-ending stream of dirty programs and their 'experts'.

From all the foregoing the conclusion is inescapable that contempt for the Vine of Catholic Faith with the subsequent loss of it, is not some kind of liberation of the human intellect but its <u>confounding</u>! Just as the fall from Grace did not ennoble the satanic mind, but forever condemned it to be satisfied with <u>dust</u>, useless projects which cannot hold out against the Flood of God's anger, but are swept away thereby. And this confounding is God-willed.

And so we have returned to where we started from, psycho-babbling. In the Foreword it was called a punishment; it may now be appreciated why. Just as a strange tongue, suddenly heard at the time of the confounding at Babel, did not make sense to anyone except to those of the same 'mind-set', so psycho-babbling by a Modernist is incomprehensible to a child of Mary, and only makes 'sense' to a proselyte of Modernism, made twice as fit for hell than his gurus.

Chapter Four: I Will Take Away its Hedge

And just as the confusion of tongues at Babel was for the protection of the human race against the latest satanic plot, so now psycho-babbling must be seen as the Divine protection of the 'strain of God' against the seduction of becoming part of the satanic plot: the unification of the world under evil in preparation for Antichrist.

For the 'success' of this ultimate in evil, the shoots of the 'Ancient Vine' had to be rooted up in individual souls, then as now, and the residual 'faith' had to be bent to secure uniform cooperation towards the appearance of Satan's most gruesome seed, 'the beast' of the Apocalypse. Which makes it crystal clear why Modernism, as 'the second beast', is equally of satanic origin: because it is being used to bend residual 'catholic' faith to help the 'religion' of the WCC in the preparation for Antichrist! 'For the second beast will do everything in its power to subjugate the whole world to the tyranny of the first beast'. Once a Catholic gives in to this, he receives as punishment a 'mind-set' that is only 'attuned' to psycho-babbling, to be put to good use in Satan's concentration camp for the welcoming of his own 'deliverer', the ruler of the world.

- Since _everything_ on earth except 'the Vine' has now been geared to this: Governments, the economy, education, 'religion', the media, art and science, finance, social behaviour, medicine, sport,
- it will _all_ suffer from the triple curse attached to this perversion of human integrity.

I. It will not make sense, except as seen by the 'strain of God' for what it is: perversion to prepare for the ultimate in evil.

II. It will carry 'the mark of the Beast'. And being on the wrong side of the 'Everlasting Enmity', it is

III.

- ❖ cut off from the Vine
- ❖ outside the Ark, and so
- ❖ condemned to perish in the overthrow of Antichrist: "the crushing of Satan's head".

We have weighty confirmation of the foregoing from official Catholic teaching.

When Pope Pius XII in line with his predecessors warned Catholic against tampering with Dogma and the Church's very foundations to make a breach for 'unity', he wrote:

"But the hot-headed supporters of appeasement are not content with that (merely changes in Church discipline). They see obstacles to the restoration of brotherly unity everywhere, even in claims that are founded upon the very laws and principles which Christ gave us, even in the Institutions He Himself founded. Yet what are these but <u>the bulwarks which protect the Faith</u> in its entirety."

And then the Holy Father added these prophetic words, of which this little book may be considered an enlargement:

"Let these fall, and the world may indeed be united,

but only in a common ruin ..." (*Humani Generis*. 1950)

This teaching is astonishing in its utter simplicity. If 'The Vine', the Catholic Church as She was handed down to us from the Apostles, and the Catholic Faith within Her, are being uprooted to make room for a 'church of the false ecumenism', then the <u>world</u>: Governments, politics, economics, education, art, science, the media, medicine, sport, 'religion', social behaviour, the lot <u>will be united</u>, but only in a common <u>ruin</u>. And the Ark with all its inhabitants will once again be the only One to survive, the only Thing that makes sense.

By Divine teaching, stripping the Catholic Faith from its God-given protection 'does not make sense'; for it makes the perpetrators part of the 'common ruin'. But the very thing they want changed, the Church, survives intact! Yet how many priests and bishops are there now, who are either convinced that <u>now</u> 'a new church' has suddenly started to make a lot of sense, or else, if they are not part of the pulling up of the shoots of the Vine, turn a blind eye to it, for fear of otherwise being noticed as being out-of-step with their entire surroundings: Government departments, bishops, fellow clergy, Catholic women-on-the-pill, their RENEWED parish schools, the wave of immorality of the 'New Age', and the whole false ecumenism of the WCC. And in Catholics the curse of psycho-babbling starts when Catholic minds accept the dictates of an evil will, and try to justify their role in this totally immoral switch away from Divine Truth, whether they are part of it or simply condone it.

This concludes the main thesis of this book: the story of 'the Vine', a delicate plant with its astonishing capacity to survive, surrounded as it is by Truth which is not of human but of Divine origin. The story of this Vine is the story of 'the strain of God', which has the secret of its survival encoded in its spiritual chromosomes: to be always unerringly on the side of the 'Everlasting Enmity' where the 'Woman of Genesis' is: "our life, our sweetness and our hope".

Epilogue

Many 'Tridentiners' would believe me fair dinkum if only I was prepared to accuse the Novus Ordo of being part of this 'stripping of the Faith'. But the Novus Ordo is like the Humanity of Christ: it is vulnerable. Both are outward appearances of a Revealed Inner Reality. Both can be treated with veneration, or they can be abused. Both can be kissed, or scourged. The remarkable fact is that it was not the veneration of Christ's Human Body that became our salvation, but the scourging of it! That Infinite Love with which the mortal sins committed by His torturers against that Sacred Humanity were endured.

It is just as ludicrous to tell the Holy Church: "You should not have allowed the Holy Father to give us the Novus Ordo: see what they did to it!", as it would have been preposterous to tell Our Lady during the Sacred Passion of Her Son: "You should not have given Him a Human Body: see what they did to it!"

I am convinced that a prime reason why the Holy Spirit gave the Novus Ordo to the Church in the time of Her own Crucifixion was to lay bare before us what was known in Heaven: the inner dispositions of disobedience and revolt of the Modernists and Tridentiners. The former show it in abusing the new Mass format; the latter in rejecting it, making it impossible for the two camps to share in this Passion!

I am not talking here about Catholics who go to a Latin Mass for peace of mind and to avoid the glaring abuses to which the New Mass is being increasingly subjected by dyed-in-the-wool Modernists who know how to hurt! Here I am referring only to those equally dyed-in-the-wool Tridentiners who abuse the Church and the Holy Father (and blame the Freemasons) for replacing the old Mass format for the new one; and who are prepared to go much further.

But there is more, infinitely more, to this whole matter of accepting the Novus Ordo.

(ed. See the author's *In Defense of the Novus Ordo Missae of His Holiness Pope Paul VI*, in "The Selected Works of Frits Albers, Volume 2." En Route Books and Media. 2024.)

As this little book makes clear, <u>anything</u> or <u>anyone</u> that wishes to have access to the Faith of a Catholic, is first referred to the Gate in the Hedge. There in the presence of Christ, 'Who is the Truth', credentials are checked by the glorious human intellect against Truths already ascertained, or as Pope Pius XII put it:

"... so as not to light on something which contradicts truths already ascertained. The Christian will weigh the latest fancy carefully, making sure that he does not lose hold of truths already in his possession, or contaminate them in any way with great danger and perhaps great loss to the Faith itself." (*Humani Generis*)

And if anything is proposed that does contradict any truth, whether ordinary or Revealed, already in a Catholic's possession, it will be barred at the gate.

Now comes the crunch! In order to get that, which has been rejected at the gate, into that Catholic's mind, <u>violence</u> will have to be done to the intellect which by nature is attuned only to the truth. And that is how 'the hedge gets pulled up' by the owner, how the

Epilogue

Vine gets exposed, and how the owner's mind and Faith get bitten by a snake.

But there is One Exception.

There is one person on earth for whom, if he presents himself at the gate, even Our Lord steps back to let him in without the checking of credentials. There is one person on earth who has direct access to the Vine because he will never do violence to it. And if this man by the name of 'Peter the Rock' firmly declares 'that the use of artificial contraceptives is intrinsically evil', then he is allowed to come in and graft this information onto the Vine. And instead of him giving reasons to the intellect, the human intellect will accept the new information, will continue its role, and, as the Hedge of the Vine, will find reasons to defend the new graft on the Vine.

If this same man presents himself again, and declares 'that the Novus Ordo is the new format of the Holy Sacrifice of the Mass for our times', then we know he says that with the Authority of the Man at the Gate, Who let him through because the information carried by 'Peter the Rock' is completely in tune with the Truth the Man at the gate happens <u>to be</u> in Person.

If then afterwards <u>anyone</u> else presents him or herself at the gate, and now tries to convince the Gatekeeper that the information contained in *Humanae Vitae* is incorrect, or that the New Mass is the cause of all the troubles in the Church, then the Man at the Gate will not allow this 'misinformation' to pass through because it contradicts 'truths already in this Catholic's possession'. It would do violence to the Vine.

If now a Catholic is dissatisfied with this decision at the gate, and wants to possess 'in his or her mind' the cherished but contrary information 'as true', then again, as in Eve's case, the hedge will have to be dismantled for the lie to enter. And the poison of the bite of the snake in the hedge will harm the intellect as much as it will harm the Faith. From then on, any attempt at defending the indefensible: that untruth must be accepted side by side with truth, will sound shrill, hollow and unconvincing: the first signs of the terrible affliction of psycho-babbling.

There *is* only one Truth. One Truth by which a contradiction of any truth, be it a natural or supernatural one, can be recognised. We do not need the Supernatural Light of Faith to recognise a contradiction of the Truth. That is why the mind of man is the hedge of the Faith. It is superbly equipped for the job if it is 'in love with Truth'. No truth can harm the Vine. Truths are let in at the gate, untruths, contradictions, distortions and twistings are barred from entering. What is refused entry at the gate is repelled by the hedge. Violence must be done to the hedge, the human intellect, to make distortions of the truth enter as 'acceptable or compatible or alternative truths'. And in the process <u>both</u> the mind and the Vine, the precious gift of Faith, get injured 'from the poison of the bite of the snake in the hedge'.

Armed with this information we can now look with understanding at St. Thomas' doctrine of the "two levels of arguing".

There is only one Truth, but a Supernatural Truth can only be seen by someone who has the Supernatural Light of Faith. But because there *is* only one Truth, any contradiction of a Supernatural Truth must also contradict an ordinary truth ascertainable by the light of reason. It is the job of the skilled debater to find just that contradiction. It is also a requirement of love. If we love the truth and love the salvation of our opponent who may be an agnostic, we must find the natural truth that is contradicted by his contradiction of our Supernatural Truth, so that we can make him 'see reason'.

If for instance a non Catholic tries to argue that the use of the contraceptive pill is alright, we cannot hold up to him what we can 'see' in the Light of Faith, but he cannot see. We must let him talk and let him bring out reasons and facts for his belief, which are all on the level of the ordinary intellect. Now amongst those we will detect some reason or fact which is not true. He must be patiently convinced of that. If he has not given the matter much thought and just 'follows the crowd', it is up to us to look for 'issues' on which an argument can be based. It will soon show if he is sincere and 'in love with truth' or not. The foundations of thomistic philosophy are eminently suited to sort out an opponent's mind, but since Grace is hopefully at work in God's 'bridgehead' in his conscience, we can depend on the Holy Spirit to help us out in an act of brotherly love. Even if we are unfamiliar with these foundations, the Holy Spirit is not.

However, it is virtually impossible to argue with Catholics who lost or at least severely impaired and damaged their Catholic Faith by accepting lies as 'truths': Modernists, and extreme Tridentiners. The reason for this has been made clear in this book: their minds have been <u>confounded</u>! They cannot be made to 'see reason', not even at the ordinary level. But in love, maybe somewhere in those extreme cases a piece of common ground can be found. And if they can be made to love that one little truth we have in common, then as the 'prodigal son', or better still, the Father of the prodigal son showed us, all is not lost.

This leads us to a capital conclusion: true Science, true insights, 'love of Truth' are not readily found in <u>confounded</u> minds. Especially not in minds which are in dissent with, or in revolt against, what is now 'The Vine': Catholic Faith and the Holy Catholic Church that gives it. In minds which, as this book shows, have been bitten by a snake from hell, when they were determined to break down the hedge of the Vine in order to let dissent and revolt, untruth and error trample all over It.

The whole of modern astronomy is still locked up in its own private universe, because, as with the 'Tower of Babel' it sprang prematurely from a Satan-inspired dissent and revolt; the Protestant Reformation, an error which kept astronomy on the wrong side of the 'Everlasting Enmity' with regard to truths, even historical and scientific ones, Divinely revealed in Sacred Scripture. And modern Science too is still on the same war-footing with Truth, shackled to faulty assumptions it inherited from Renaissance – and subsequent 'Cainite' insights, confounded by the errors of the Protestant Revolt which saw in the Holy Catholic Church nothing more than a backward organisation bent on preventing 'true scientific progress'.

Herein too we see the solution of that elusive mystery: how the distortion of the whole of the scientific explosion of the Renaissance (and especially the distortion of history') is being used by Satan's seed 'in the great movement of apostasy' to bend 'residual Catholic Faith' <u>away</u> from Salvation and <u>towards</u> the gradual but inevitable acceptance of his 'deliverer from all shackles': Antichrist, the head of the One-World 'concentration camp'. "And the whole world will run after the Beast."

The solution to this mystery lies in this fundamental truth: "that there is only One Truth: Christ". This makes it impossible that the rejection of Revealed Truth does not darken and confound the created mind with respect to <u>all</u> truth. True Science and True Understanding are two precious Gifts of the Holy Spirit which cannot be infused into a confounded mind because of the indivisibility of Truth.

Non Catholics who love the Truth are open to Catholic Grace and will try to live blameless lives, as the Sethites did before the Flood, as if protected by an invisible hedge. Catholics who are in dissent with their Church will have confounded minds with respect to all Truth. They will not lead blameless lives – showing that the hedge around their Vine has been impaired. The inevitable bite of the snake has poisoned both their Faith and their God-given human mind, as was the case with the antediluvian Cainites. Thus they cannot 'see' that their residual Catholic Faith is being bent for the success of the very thing Satan has been patiently working for since he was forced by the Blessed Trinity to pull 'his seed' away from finishing the 'Tower of Babel'.

www.ingramcontent.com/pod-product-compliance
Lightning Source LLC
Chambersburg PA
CBHW050851160426
43194CB00011B/2116